Naval Aviation in the Korean War

This book is dedicated to all the naval aviators and crewmen that served in the Korean War. Also to my mother, Mary J. Thompson, who was born in 1911, the year that marked the birth of US naval aviation.

The USS *Valley Forge* (CV 45) steams toward the North Korean coast just days after the Korean War started. Its Air Group-5 flew the first strikes deep info enemy territory on 3 and 4 July. The Panthers shown on the deck were from VF-51 and VF-52. (*US Navy*)

Naval Aviation in the Korean War

Warren E. Thompson

Pen & Sword
AVIATION

First published in Great Britain in 2012 by
Pen & Sword Aviation
47 Church Street
Barnsley
South Yorkshire
S70 2AS

ISBN 978 1 84884 488 9

A CIP catalogue record for this book is
available from the British Library.

Typeset in 10pt Palatino by Mac Style, Beverley, East Yorkshire
Printed and bound by Replika Press Pvt. Ltd.

Pen & Sword Books Ltd incorporates the Imprints of Pen & Sword Aviation,
Pen & Sword Family History, Pen & Sword Maritime, Pen & Sword Military,
Pen & Sword Discovery, Wharncliffe Local History, Wharncliffe True Crime,
Wharncliffe Transport, Pen & Sword Select, Pen & Sword Military Classics,
Leo Cooper, The Praetorian Press, Remember When, Seaforth Publishing
and Frontline Publishing.

For a complete list of Pen & Sword titles please contact
PEN & SWORD BOOKS LIMITED
47 Church Street, Barnsley, South Yorkshire, S70 2AS, England
E-mail: enquiries@pen-and-sword.co.uk
Website: www.pen-and-sword.co.uk

Contents

Author's Note

This book is about US Navy aircraft in the Korean War. Although the US Marine Corps were considered part of this air arm, they also did such an outstanding job in Korea that they deserve a separate book, which will possibly come later. It would be next to impossible to go into details on every strike and operation that naval aircraft flew in Korea, so the author has tried to touch on as many as possible with the emphasis placed on personal comments and recollections from the pilots that flew the missions and their support personnel. Naval aviation contributed heavily to saving South Korea from communism, which allowed it to develop into the great country it is today.

Each aircraft carrier involved in combat operations off the coast of Korea had a detachment of the HO3S-1 helicopters, which were airborne when the air group launched aircraft and when they recovered them in case one of the pilots had to be pulled out of the water. This photograph was taken on the deck of the USS *Antietam* (CV 36) in 1952. (*National Archives*)

About the Author

Warren Thompson has been an avid military aviation historian for over forty years. He has written numerous books and magazine articles on subjects ranging from pre-World War II all the way to the present, including Operation *Iraqi Freedom* and the war in Afghanistan. Most of his efforts have been focused on the American night fighters in World War II and all aspects of the Korean War. He resides with his wife in Germantown, Tennessee.

The USS *Oriskany* (CVA 34) carried out one combat cruise that started in the autumn of 1952 and lasted until mid-May 1953. They had Detachment-G of VC-11 on board at that time. This specialized version of the Skyraider was known as the AD-3W. Only thirty-one of this model were built for the Navy. This one was part of Air Group-102. (*Dan Keough*)

Acknowledgements

The number of pilots, plane captains and carrier personnel that contributed to this project over a fourteen-year period are too numerous to list. However, some of them deserve special mentions because of their dedication to preserving naval aviation history for future generations: Doug Siegfried of The Tail Hook Association, Hill Goodspeed of The Naval Air Museum, Barrett Tillman, Frank Olynyk, Bill Burgess, Peter S. Swanson, George Smitman, Margie Brown, Dewey Ferrell, John Hotvedt, Thomas A. Smith, John Owen, E.M. 'Smokey' Tollgaard, Norman Edge, George Schnitzer, Edward V. Laney, Jettie Hill, Bob Balser, Bill Barron, Don Frazor, Tom Randall, Lee Boles, Hal Schwann, Donald McNaught, William 'Tex' Morgan, William C. Raposa, Ray Hosier, Clayton Fisher, Guy Lyons, Raymond Edinger, Robert Adkisson, Jack Hester, Benjamin Sutherlin, John M. Sherly, Neil Armstrong, Sam Catterlin, William M. Gortney, Ken Kramer, Ernie Beauchamp, Ken Brownell, Ted Landrum, Jack Sauter, Richard A. Cantrell, John Corrigan, Frank Jones, Ace Jewell, Henry Champion, Royce Williams, Wayne J. Spence, Len Plog, Richard Starinchak, Walter Spangenberg Jr., Wes Ralston, Jack Schlosser, Pete Colapietro, George McCallister, Leon Bryant, John White, William R. Clarke, John Moore, John DeGoede, W.D. Davidson, Robair F. Mohrhardt, Frank Glendinning, James Williams, Tom Cathcart, Dan Keough, Bill Wallace, James V. Rowney, John Ferebee, Ro Kellum, Jim Dodge, Gene Bazore, R.J. Kaps, Ed Mason, Bruce Bagwell, Norb Melsek, Jerry Stipanov, Allen 'Boot' Hill, Joe Jannotta and Gerald H. Barkalow.

A destroyer pulls along side the USS *Princeton* off the coast of North Korea in the summer of 1952. On many occasions, this was to return a rescued pilot to his carrier. This had to be some rare downtime for the *Princeton* or there would have been no sunbathing on the deck. The F9F-2s in the background are from VF-191. (*John M. Sherly*)

Introduction

A fter World War II, the US military became totally focused on building an all-jet force, which included the naval air groups. This was accomplished much quicker in the Air Force because all they had to do was extend the runways to accommodate the new F-80 Shooting Stars. It was a little more complicated in naval aviation because their strike force still had to deal with the size of the existing carrier fleet and the much heavier jets such as the Grumman F9F Panther and F2H Banshee.

The US Navy had more than its share of problems after World War II, not only with drastic downsizing (all branches faced the same dilemma), but the potential use of the atom bomb seemed to diminish the effectiveness of carrier aviation in future wars unless aircraft could be designed and built to deliver an atomic bomb from their decks. The Air Force stated that the future of the US military was with the long-range bomber that could carry a heavy load of nuclear bombs. At the same time, the US Navy was trying to get funding for more aircraft carriers and, due to the limited space on the deck, they could not launch big heavy bombers. From its peak in the spring of 1945 to June 1950, the number of carriers in the inventory had shrunk from 98 down to 15 and the number of naval combat aircraft had dwindled from over 29,000 down to about 9,500. But, the Navy was not going down without a fight! Any thoughts of reducing their fighting potential any further went away in the summer of 1950. The Korean War bought them the time they needed to develop a war machine that would be second to none for the next 60 years.

In June 1950, the US Navy had seven attack carriers and nine carrier air groups (CAGs). Two aircraft carriers (CVs) and three CAGs were in the Pacific with the remainder being in the Atlantic. Though two CAGs and additional aircraft carriers were reactivated, it was determined that they needed more air groups, but Congress had already limited the number at seven. At this time, the standard CAG consisted of four fighter squadrons and one attack squadron with the required number of small specialized detachments. The decision was made to streamline this set-up to three fighter squadrons and one attack squadron. The smaller carriers took a lot of pressure off the others and they usually housed one Marine fighter squadron (equipped with F4U Corsairs).

Without warning, this transition was suddenly thrown out of rhythm on 25 June 1950. The North Korean People's Army crossed the 38th Parallel and invaded South Korea. The Air Force was caught with a large number of new F-80s in the Far East but their range was limited and the airfields that were available in South Korea were inadequate, so they had to conduct long-range missions out of Itazuke AB in Japan and their loiter time over targets was extremely short. This is where the Navy's carrier proved to be the answer to striking targets deep into North Korea, and they did an outstanding job throughout the war, while limited to only two types of jets with the overwhelming emphasis placed on the F9F Panther force.

This sudden invasion was not as significant as the attack on Pearl Harbor on 7 December 1941 because it was not an attack on American military assets, but it was a wake-up call for the US that its military posture had been grossly depleted since the end of World War II. It was also the first major test for the United Nations against communist aggression. While many of the member nations contributed to the war effort in some form, it was the United States and the British that carried the brunt of the effort to defeat the North Koreans and Chinese armies. Throughout the war and especially in the first year, it was the US Navy carriers that made any target in North Korea easily available thanks to their aggressive and capable air groups. Once the quality and number of air bases in South Korea were brought up to jet-standards, the entire air arm of the United States military in the Far East was unleashed on North Korea.

The timing by the North Koreans could not have been better, not only because the American military was at a low point, but also the US Air Force, Navy and Marines were in a period of transition, entering the new jet age. The USAF still had at least another two years remaining before it could boast of an all-jet inventory in its front-line units. Fortunately for the US, it still had an impressive inventory of

Just days after the Korean War started, the USAF started rounding up F-51D Mustangs from various Air National Guard units. They loaded up 145 of them on the USS *Boxer* and rushed them to the Far East for combat duty. Most of the F-51s were tied down on the deck and were heavily coated to prevent corrosion from the salt air. This photograph was taken in July 1950 on the *Boxer*. (*Robert Fogg*)

the World War II workhorses: mainly the F4U Corsair and the F-51 Mustang. The Navy also had a large number of AD Skyraiders, which would carry the brunt of the heavy bomb loads during all naval carrier operations in the Korean War.

President Harry Truman deemed this a 'Police Action', but for the hundreds of thousands of military personnel that were involved, it was anything but that. It was a bloody war with a total of 33,686 Americans killed in combat during the 37-month war. In comparison, the Vietnam War lasted 101 months with a total of 58,209 killed in combat. The reason for this vast difference was that the Korean War pitted huge numbers of ground troops against each other in close proximity. Figures released several years ago state that the Chinese lost 115,000 killed in action and over 210,000 wounded. This figure could actually be much higher. At its peak, the Chinese ground forces numbered about 1,340,000 on North Korean soil. A significant number of the KIA (Killed in Action) on the North Korean and Chinese side could be attributed to the persistent attacks carried out by the Navy's CAGs.

Although the Marine Corps has always been connected in some form with the US Navy, this book will deal only with the Navy's aircraft during the Korean War. Marine aviation's contribution was immense and they effectively utilized the same major aircraft types that the Navy did: the F9F, AD and F4U. However, the author deems them worthy of a book on their own. Some of their F4U squadrons operated

Skyraiders and Corsairs from Air Group-11 are shown on the deck of the USS *Philippine Sea* (CV 47) in March 1952. The F4Us were assigned to VF-113 and VF-114 while the ADs were in VA-115. At the time this picture was taken, the carrier was anchored in Yokosuka Harbor, Japan, during its third combat cruise. (*Sam Wallace*).

periodically from the smaller aircraft carriers and those will be mentioned along with their chronological appearances in combat off the coast of Korea, because those ships were manned by Navy personnel.

It would have been easy for President Harry Truman to back away and write off South Korea, but he chose to stop the spread of communism, using Korea as an example of the potential power of the fledgling United Nations to preserve democracy in the world. The potential killing power of a mobile naval force was paramount in slowing down the North Koreans as they pushed their way deep into South Korea. Their main assignment was to help prevent the fall of a democratic Korea and the mobility of an impressive carrier fleet proved to be one of the key ingredients in pulling this off. The US Navy's first responders, in addition to the USS *Valley Forge*, were the heavy cruiser USS *Rochester*, eight destroyers and three submarines. For several weeks, just one carrier air group's efforts had a huge impact on the North Korean military leaders. As more carriers moved into theatre, the impact increased many fold.

There are several figures and statistics that have been thrown around for years concerning what carrier aviation did during that thirty-seven-month war. Although the totals vary somewhat, the one thing they have in common is the fact they are all impressive. These do not separate the Navy from the Marines, but give one figure. The most commonly used statistic shows that both branches combined flew a total of 190,000+ sorties that are inclusive of all Navy and Marine combat aircraft types. With an emphasis on low-altitude close air support, you could expect more losses. When the war ended, they had lost about one aircraft every day, which was a heavy price to pay in such a condensed geographical area compared with World War II action.

One of VF-195's AD-4s catches the wire after flying a bombing mission over North Korea. Air Group-19's main strike squadrons all used the 'B' on the vertical stabilizer when serving on the USS *Princeton* in 1952. (*John M. Sherly*)

CHAPTER ONE

Slowing the North Korean Juggernaut

Within forty-eight hours of the North Korean military crossing the 38th Parallel, it was doubtful if the American military would have enough strength in the Far East to prevent the Southern Peninsula from falling into communist hands. The momentum was definitely on the side of the North and the meagre American occupation forces based in Japan were not in shape (physically and equipment-wise) to halt a well-trained force of approximately 180,000 North Korean troops that had a sizeable force of Soviet-built T-34 tanks. It was a grim situation at 5th Air Force HQ in Japan. Even with limited intelligence on the North, it was discovered that the North Korean People's Air Force (NKPAF) had two fully equipped air regiments of Russian Il-10 fighter-bombers and at least two Air Regiments of Yak-9P fighters along with other miscellaneous types. There were no known North Korean units equipped with the MiG-15 at that time.

The key to rapid response was shared by both the USAF and the US Navy. The 'all-jet' force touted by the USAF experienced difficulties in the early days due to the 'short legs' of the F-80s based in Japan and the poor conditions of air bases in South Korea, so this put a tremendous burden on the aircraft carriers and Task Force 77, based at Luzon in the Philippines. They were caught at a bad time on 25 June 1950. In the summer of 1950, the Navy had two carriers to cover the Pacific: the *Essex*-class USS *Valley Forge* (CV 45) that was docked in Hong Kong and a second carrier, the USS *Boxer* on the west coast at San Diego. The *Valley Forge* was the first to respond because it was closest to the Korean peninsula. Two days into the war (27 June), it was decided to send the carriers in to strike targets of opportunity in North Korea, so the *Valley Forge*, which was steaming toward the Philippines, changed course and headed for Okinawa at full speed. Fortunately, the Royal Navy had one light carrier, the HMS *Triumph*, in the area with forty combat aircraft on board and it immediately attached to Task Force 77.

During the late 1940s, the US Navy's requests for more aircraft carriers was being questioned by the USAF who were arguing that future wars would be won by the big land-based bombers, using the examples of what the B-17 and B-24 did to Germany and what the B-29 had done to Japan. This argument did result in the US Navy being temporarily limited in the number of carriers in their inventory. Some records indicate that they were down to seven fleet aircraft carriers. The majority of the funds available was placed on the military presence in Europe because of the imminent threat of communism. This left the US Navy with only three big carriers in the Pacific. Many months into the Korean War, the value of the carriers would be evident and, for decades, the necessary appropriations were in place to build a significant force that could support numerous air groups.

What went on behind the scenes during those early days of the war is what had proved to be so fascinating. First of all, the military leaders in the US first believed that the North Korean attack against South Korea might just be the first of several around the world that were planned by Russia and China, so there had to be a strong defensive strategy put in place immediately in case Korea was only a test or diversion. That is why Vice Admiral C. Turner Joy ordered the 7th Fleet into Okinawa rather than Sasebo naval base in Japan because it was out of striking distance for Soviet or Chinese aircraft. Up until 25 June 1950, the 7th Fleet's peacetime mission had been to visit the major ports in the Far East to show the flag and let any potential threats see that the US Navy was still readily available if the need arose. During the last week in May 1950, the 7th Fleet had conducted large-scale exercise in the Pacific, located between the coast of China and the Philippines.

It was very fortunate that the USS *Valley Forge*, with its Air Group-5, was in the area when the war started. In early 1950, the USS *Valley Forge* was the only west coast carrier fully equipped with two F9F Panther squadrons in its air group. The other carrier, the USS *Boxer*, only had prop-type aircraft in its air group. Also, the carrier's main escort ships, the cruisers USS *Rochester* and *Juneau*, were also among the most combat ready in the fleet. According to two of the top historians on the Naval War in Korea, Malcolm Cagle and Frank Manson, the early days of the conflict can be divided into four principal efforts: the flights of the carrier aircraft of Task Forces 77 and 96 on close air support, armed reconnaissance and

The winters in Korea were always harsh, which hampered carrier operations. This scene shows the conditions on the flight deck of the USS *Valley Forge* (CV 45) in January 1952. The AD Skyraider in the foreground was assigned to VF-194 with ATG-1. At this time, the *Valley Forge* was on its third combat cruise in the war. (*Tom Cathcart*)

interdiction missions; the naval gunfire support and bombardment efforts of the cruisers and destroyers along the east coast of South Korea; the timely amphibious landing at Pohang and the amphibious evacuation of the Third Republic of Korea (ROK) division in July and August, respectively; and the timely arrival of the US Marines (all references to ROK indicate forces or units pertaining to South Korea). Collectively, not individually, they can be credited with saving South Korea during those very early days. If these naval events had not been able to take place, Korea would not have been able to be saved, at least during this time period. This gave the Army and USAF, along with multiple United Nations units, a chance to gather and implement their forces against the North Koreans.

It is interesting to get some background on what happened with the *Valley Forge* and Air Group-5 prior to 25 June 1950. One of the F9F Panther pilots who was on that cruise with VF-51 gives a detailed narrative about what happened. The pilot was Lt (jg) William M. Gortney.

VF-51 was the first Navy fighter squadron to get jets when they flew the FJ-1 Fury, but this was short-lived. They quickly transitioned to the newer F9F Panthers before the Korean War started. We were scheduled to transition into the Dash-2s which, unfortunately for that model, had many engine problems which put us into the F9F-3 instead. It was during the time that Louis Johnson was Secretary of Defense and we were going through some severe cutbacks. We were so short on money when we got the Panthers in VF-51 that they gave us four Corsairs to use to get all of our flight time in. It was about that time that we got Major Edward F. Connor on temporary duty from the Air Force. He probably had more jet time than our entire squadron had when we deployed and at that time, we probably had about 50 hours in the jet. We had had only one weapons deployment and that was air-to-air shooting over at El Centro, California.

We had never worked as an air group and we had never flown with any of the other squadrons in the group. When we went aboard ship, we found all kinds of aircraft handling problems as this was the first time that they had had two squadrons of jets on any aircraft carrier. It ended up that both squadrons (VF-51 and VF-52) were sort of combined and put in the one ready room and our fighters were placed under one maintenance officer to help the ship. We never knew if we were going to fly an aircraft from our squadron or the other one. We went through our ORI [Operational Readiness Inspection] with very little time flying the jets and no air-to-ground! We left Honolulu and proceeded to Guam and relieved the USS *Boxer* (CV 21) that was coming out of the Far East at that time. We went on to Southeast Asia and during that time, the French were still in control of Vietnam (French Indochina) and we did an air show (flyby) over Saigon. I believe that this was the first time that both of our squadrons were airborne together. Later, as we were coming out of Hong Kong, we got word that the war had started in Korea and we headed full steam in that direction. We stopped in Okinawa to take on ammunition and fuel oil because there was not a working oiler in the Pacific at that time, so we took on fuel from a Japanese tanker. From there, we headed right into the action!

The US Navy's fast carriers could steam from California to Japan in about one week. During the early weeks of the war, the USS *Boxer* saved the day for the USAF when it rushed 145 North American F-51D Mustangs and pilots from Air National Guard units over to Korea. This was probably one of the most significant events to take place during the early stages of the war, because the North Koreans quickly had compressed the UN forces into a pocket called the 'Pusan Perimeter' and close air support was critical. This gave the USAF sufficient air power to supplement the jets in their efforts to save the peninsula. The *Boxer* would provide an outstanding contribution to the war effort as it would end up with four combat cruises off the coast of North Korea.

On 29 June, the American military leaders in the Far East met in Tokyo. They included Vice Admiral Struble, Admiral Joy, General MacArthur and General Stratemeyer (USAF). It was at this time that General MacArthur received word from the Joint Chiefs of Staff at the Pentagon that he would have operational control over the 7th Fleet (but he did not have tactical control over it). They discussed several options on how best to slow the North Korean offensive down and the key subject was how best to utilize the striking power of Air Group-5 on the USS *Valley Forge*. After evaluating all of the intelligence, it was a unanimous decision that military targets in and around the capitol city of Pyongyang should be hit hard. The order of importance on targets in this area was: all airfields, then any enemy aircraft parked on these fields, followed by the Pyongyang rail complex and bridges over which the majority of the North Korean munitions and supplies were being funnelled south of the 38th Parallel.

With their marching orders now in place, the *Valley Forge* headed full speed for the west coast of North Korea on 1 July. As the Task Force steamed toward Korea, they received a series of messages from the Commander of Naval Forces/Far East. It stated:

> CINCFE authorizes you to continue strikes past the first day (July 3rd) in view of the rapidly deteriorating situation in South Korea. Highest priority should be given to rail facilities in the vicinity of Kumchon, Sariwon and Sinanju!

On 3 July 1950, the US and Royal Navy got into the battle. The HMS *Triumph* made a pre-dawn launch of twelve Fireflies and nine Seafires that were to attack the airfield at Pyongyang and several nearby installations. The Seafires were loaded with rockets that were used against rail traffic and all of the *Triumph*'s aircraft returned to the carrier with just minor damage from flak. The *Valley Forge* (CV 45) had Air Group-5 on board with two squadrons of F9F-2 Panthers (VF-51 and VF-52) two squadrons of F4U-4B Corsairs (VF-53 and VF-54) and one squadron of Skyraiders (VA-55). They were also armed with detachments of several specialty aircraft that gave them the maximum strike capability expected of any air group. Right after dawn on the 3rd, Air Group-5 also initiated a major strike against targets within the North Korean capital. Records show that there were twelve AD Skyraiders and sixteen Corsairs armed with rockets and bombs in the first wave. The prop types took off first as they were slowest and the jets went last and it was timed that the entire formation would reach the target area at about the same time. This would be a standard procedure for the remainder of the war.

Records from the HMS *Triumph* state that the Seafires flew a total of 360 combat sorties before their tour was up. They only lost two of these aircraft; one to friendly fire from a B-29 bomber that probably didn't recognize the aircraft and mistook it for an enemy fighter and the other loss was only due to a landing accident when its arrestor hook failed to extend. The Seafire had its problems when it suffered from wrinkling in the rear fuselage caused by the heavy impact of landings on the carrier deck. The Royal Navy Fireflies carried out anti-shipping patrols and close air support. They were equipped with four 20-mm cannons and could carry a large number of rockets or two 1,000-lb bombs. Some time in September 1950, the HMS *Triumph* was replaced by another Royal Navy carrier: the HMS *Theseus*.

What happened next that early morning was a first for the US Navy when the Grumman F9F-3 Panthers from VF-51 took off from the *Valley Forge* to become the first US Navy jets to fly combat sorties. They sent out a significant number of Panthers that were timed to arrive over Pyongyang just minutes before the main force to make sure there was no air opposition from the enemy. As had been experienced on 27 and 28 June, by the USAF, over Kimpo Air Base, there were Yak-9s that were evidently sitting on alert and ready to take on any comers. VF-51 shot down two Yaks within seconds of each other and who was the first to make a kill is still a grey area.

Lt (jg) Leonard H. Plog was one of those pilots and he recalls his monumental feat on that mission. He and Ensign E.W. Brown would be the first naval aviators to score kills in jets and they were the first recorded kills by the Navy in the fledgling war. Lt (jg) Plog recalls the action.

I was one of many Panthers from VF-51 that launched off the deck of the USS *Valley Forge* at 0600 hours on that morning. Our target was an airfield close to Pyongyang and our primary assignment was to keep any North Korean fighters away from our main strike force, which consisted of Corsairs and Skyraiders. We arrived right before the others got there and our first priority was to strafe any parked aircraft that were there. Just as we went into our dives, one of the pilots reported a Yak-9 taking off and evidently a couple of others had just gotten airborne.

'My wingman and I broke off of our strafing run to go after this one Yak. I lined up on the one that had just taken off and out of the corner of my eye, I saw another one coming straight at me and he evidently misjudged the speed of my aircraft because he missed. Ensign Brown saw a Yak coming in on another element of F9Fs, which consisted of the CAG and his wingman Lt Bill Gortney. He closed on it quickly and blew him apart with his 20-mm cannon. This allowed me to re-focus on my Yak. I lined him up and fired a burst and a split second later, I saw his right wing disintegrate. We had killed two Yaks in a short span of time while our bombers worked the field over real good. We returned to the carrier with no losses. That afternoon, we launched again to attack the same airfield, but there wasn't much left to bomb, so our effectiveness on the second mission was unobtainable. Anti-aircraft fire was minimal on both strikes.

The *Valley Forge* got by on 3 July with no losses, but the following day, they weren't that lucky. Korwald Aircraft Loss records show that the air group lost five aircraft

Ensign Eldon W. Brown is awarded the Air Medal for heroism during the first major raid on North Korean soil by Navy aircraft. He was credited with one of the first aerial kills, at altitude, by a Navy pilot in the war. It happened on the famous raid on 3 July 1950 against an airfield close to Pyongyang. Presenting the medal is Vice Admiral Arthur Struble, Commander of the 7th Fleet. Ensign Brown was flying an F9F Panther with VF-53 when he shot down a Yak-9. (*Margie Brown*)

on the 4th: one Corsair and three Skyraiders. One of these was in a specialized detachment (AD-3W) with VC-11 and one was an HO3S helicopter. The next loss for the *Valley Forge* didn't occur until 16 July when they lost their first F9F. Not all of these were dur to enemy fire as operational losses were figured in also.

The accounts that have been published on the air group's action on 3 and 4 July are slightly conflicting in some instances. Probably the most accurate is the press releases given to the media soon after the two days of strikes. It involved personal comments from Lt Commander Bill Sisley (the Executive Officer of VF-51), a Lt (jg) L.T. Zuehlke and a USAF exchange pilot, Major Edward Connor, flying Panthers with the squadron. The air strikes up in the Pyongyang area were coordinated between the British aircraft carrier RMS *Triumph*'s fighter-bombers and Air Group-5's aircraft. After the dust had settled on the 4th, seventeen enemy aircraft had been destroyed with most of these parked around the airfield.

The strike aircraft had also destroyed several buildings that lined the perimeter of the airfield, along with most of the defensive gun positions. Major Connor was quoted as stating:

> We swept in over the airfield and caught them by surprise. I led a division of F9Fs on three attacks on two different airfields in the vicinity. We fired on numerous aircraft that were partially hidden in revetments around the field. There were some Yak-9s that attempted to take off and I got hits on one that was just getting airborne, but I never had a chance to see if he went in or stayed

in the air. We did draw some ground fire, but it was light. When we went back on the 4th, we finished what we had started even though the weather was not perfect. By the evening of the 4th, the North Koreans knew we had come to fight!

Lt (jg) Plog comments further:

After our two days of strikes against the airfield, VF-51 settled into concentrating on road and rail interdiction. The Air Force had their hands full down south around Pusan and with the flexibility of a mobile carrier force we were able to inflict a lot of damage to the enemy's efforts to send supplies and equipment below the 38th Parallel. I remember in Korea, in contrast to World War II when I was flying dive bombers, small arms fire was a bigger problem than anti-aircraft fire. The North Koreans had a difficult time adjusting to the fast speeds of our Panthers and we routinely saw the AA bursting anywhere from 50 to 500 yards behind us. We also had a problem with the engines as they were slightly underpowered to carry any significant ordnance off the deck. Take-off in a fully loaded F9F-3 required a 30+ knot wind over the deck which, in turn, required the *Valley Forge* to steam at speeds that were less than efficient for fuel consumption. Eventually, all surviving Dash-3s were given the J-42 and redesignated Dash-2s.

The Executive Officer for VF-51 during their first cruise was Lt Commander William R. 'Bill' Sisley. He expands further on the difficulties with the early Panther engines. To better understand what the early carrier deployments were facing with the straight decks and the first jet squadrons, he gives his views.

Both of our F9F squadrons had the Dash-3 Panthers with the Allison J-33 engines which as I recall, had 4,500 pounds of thrust. In those days, they had not perfected the turbine blades in jet engines and it wasn't unusual to 'throw a blade' and set up a vibration that got your attention in a hurry, but you could usually make it back to the boat. Also, we did not have an angled deck carrier, If your hook did not engage a wire, you ploughed into the 'Davis Barrier', which was heavy nylon stretched across the deck about 3 feet high that would engage the nose wheel and lift the heavy 1.5-inch wire cable up into the main gear. If that failed, you ran into the nylon barricade, which was at least 12 feet high with vertical streamers that would engage the wings and keep you from going into all the aircraft that were parked forward.

Another slight drawback; there were no 'blast shields' behind the jet turning up to full power on the catapult for launch. That made life miserable for the aircraft that were aft of the aircraft that was on the cat and all the deck hands! We began our cruise on the *Valley Forge* in the spring of 1950 on a peacetime basis. We sailed through Hawaii, Guam and the Philippines on our way to Hong Kong. Just as we were leaving Hong Kong, we got the news that the North Koreans had invaded South Korea and we were urgently needed on scene. We steamed straight to Manila and loaded up on ammo, fuel and bombs and headed north. The first time that we encountered any enemy aircraft that were airborne was on that July 3rd strike against the airfield close to Pyongyang.

Several of Air Group-5's pilots have commented that at the time they entered the war, there was no doubt that the North Koreans were winning as they easily forced the UN forces into the tiny Pusan Perimeter. They stated that the F9F-3 was really not the right aircraft to fight that kind of war and it was the Douglas AD Skyraider that was the workhorse that carried the heavy loads that were more than the World War II-era Boeing B-17 Flying Fortress could carry. What they were trying to convey was the fact that that particular model of the F9F was underpowered when it came to carrying a sizeable load off those short deck carriers. However, as the tides of war changed in favour of the UN forces, the F9Fs did an outstanding job in the close air support and interdiction roles.

A little known fact surfaced after the war had ended that pertained to the early days of the Pusan Perimeter. In addition to the carriers, there was a sizeable force of US destroyers and cruisers that was moving up and down the coast line. it was the first line of defence against any North Korean efforts to operate anything that pertained to shipping. What little the North had in the way of ships were quickly located and destroyed by naval gunfire. There was one major effort attempted by the enemy to land 600 troops near the port of Pusan. This was when the situation there was in doubt and before the troops could reach their objective the ships carrying them were sunk by the American ships. If they had landed, they could have done tremendous damage to the port and taken away from the defensive efforts by the handful of ROK and US troops fighting to keep their foothold on the peninsula.

By mid-July, the *Valley Forge* had set up along the west coast of South Korea to concentrate on helping the beleaguered ground troops that were being boxed in down around the Pusan area. On 18 July, the air group supported the landing of the First Cavalry Division at Pohang. This was done smoothly with no interference from the enemy. The naval air cover for this operation were loaded with bombs, but had to jettison them into the ocean as they had no targets that far south. However, the following day, several divisions of Skyraiders and Corsairs were launched to hit targets in the Wonsan area while the carrier was keeping a close watch on a Typhoon that was trying to move in their direction. At dawn on 22 July, both VF-51 and VF-52 took off to hit targets north of Seoul where North Korean equipment was jamming the roads leading to the south. The Typhoon was stirring up weather conditions far to the east, so Navy flight ops remained about 100 miles off the west coast.

Records from the *Valley Forge* for the July 1950 period reveal the details of their operations. During the early part of their combat ops, strikes were conducted by launching a thirty-eight-prop plane strike first (ADs and F4Us), followed by a twelve-plane jet sweep, followed by another twelve-plane jet launch. When preparing for this type of sequence, after the prop types took off, two F9Fs were spotted on the catapults with two more ready to taxi up and take their place followed by two more staggered off the centre line directly behind. The remaining six Panthers of the strike force were spotted at a forty-five-degree angle along the port side aft of the No. 2 elevator. The spares were spotted on the starboard side aft of the island structure. This method of spotting enabled the jets to turn up for pre-flight check prior to spotting on the catapults.

When taxiing out the six Panthers on the port side, the aft plane was taxied out first in order to reduce the blast effect on personnel. The second jet sweep was brought up to the catapult in the same manner. During the latter part of that cruise, strikes consisted of a twelve to sixteen-prop plane strike, then an eight-plane jet sweep one and a half hours later. This was followed by a twelve to sixteen-prop plane strike three hours after the first prop launch. The first jet sweep and the first prop strike force were recovered after the second wave was launched. Then one and a half hours later, the F9F Panthers took off. This was a routine repeated many times on most of the *Essex*-class carriers operating off the west and east coast of Korea.

The US Navy jets had some standard operating procedures that were followed throughout the war. For instance, when the F9Fs or F2H-2s were returning from strikes in North Korea, they normally flew at 20,000 feet, conserving fuel to be able to meet the requirement of having at least 1,200 pounds (200 gallons) at recovery time. The detection of incoming jets by the task force became more difficult as the altitude increased. It is also important to note that a jet fighter pointed directly at the radar station offers a very small cross-sectional target. The thinner wing and oval-shaped fuselage combined to give a poor radar image. If the jet is crossing at ninety degrees to the radar beam it will, however, have a larger return because the side profile offers a much larger return.

The following is from a report from the USS *Boxer*, dated 26 July 1951:

Jet aircraft not using IFF (Identification Friend or Foe) continue to present a very serious problem, particularly at altitudes in excess of 15,000 feet. While generally detected at an optimum range of 40 miles, it is not unusual for a

The specialized detachments that were on board every carrier deployment in the Korean War performed critical missions that included night interdiction and anti-submarine patrols to protect Task Force 77. This AD-4W was flown by Detachment-F of VC-11 on the USS *Boxer* in 1951. They were part of Air Group-101. (*Bill Wallace*).

section of jets (two aircraft) to call in overhead without having been detected or reported once. The seriousness of the inability to detect jet aircraft at altitude can be more readily appreciated when one considers that these conditions prevail while the task force has been searching with an average of 12-15 SPS-6B [the main air search radar that had the largest antenna on the mast] and at least 2 SX Radar.

If this information had fallen into the enemy's hands, it would have been easy for a two-ship or four-ship formation of MiG-15s to have pulled off a surprise strafing attack against one of the carriers that were operating far up the west coast of North Korea and well within their striking range.

Any F9Fs that were sitting alert on the catapult would not have had the chance to get airborne and defend the ship. Of course, the MiGs were not a threat until late December 1950 when they began flying south of the Yalu. One of the Panther pilots that flew combat during the mid-1951 period stated:

While the range of detection appears to be enough to alert the CAP aircraft to the presence of hostile aircraft, it should be pointed out that a jet flying at a ground speed of 450 knots or 522 mph, will cover the distance of 35 miles in about four minutes. That means an attacking jet such as a MiG-15 would be within firing range of the ships in the task force in a very short time. Furthermore, the jet

Words cannot describe the bitter cold winters in Korea. These F9F Panther pilots from VF-112 gather on a frozen deck after a snow storm with temperatures well below freezing. This photograph was taken on the USS *Philippine Sea* during the winter of 1950–51 off the North Korean east coast. (*Allen 'Boot' Hill*)

CAP [Combat Air Patrol] had to close and overtake a diving jet to engage it. In almost any scenario, it would not be possible!

Defending the carriers that were operating within range of the enemy had top priority over just about anything and, fortunately, no attempts were made. If any were detected out at maximum radar range, they broke off and turned around long before one of the CAP aircraft could get close enough to identify the intruder.

With the situation in South Korea deteriorating daily, the US Navy had three *Essex*-class aircraft carriers that were available for combat in Korea. With the *Valley Forge* already conducting operations in theatre, the USS *Philippine Sea* (CV 47) had just become part of the Navy's Pacific Fleet and it sailed on 5 July 1950 with Air Group-11 on board to join Task Force 77. They began flying combat strikes on 5 August. The *Philippine Sea*, along with escort carriers, the USS *Badoeng Strait* (CVE-116) and USS *Sicily* (CVE-118), became the first carrier reinforcements to help the *Valley Forge*. The smaller carriers would house Marine Corsair fighter-bombers during the war. Air Group-11 was equipped with two squadrons of F9F-2s (VF-111 and VF-112) and two squadrons of F4U-4B Corsairs (VF-113 and VF-114), along with one squadron of AD-4s (VA-115). All major carrier deployments would carry the usual specialized detachments of night-flying Corsairs, Skyraiders and photo-recce aircraft. This would be the first of four combat cruises for the *Philippine Sea*.

Ensign Allen 'Boot' Hill was one of the pilots in VF-112 on the *Philippine Sea*. During their first cruise, they were flying in the F9F-2. By late August, when the situation was looking more dismal by the day, the pressure was on the air groups flying from the *Valley Forge* and *Philippine Sea* to help hold the Pusan Perimeter. The name of the game at that time was close air support! Ensign Hill recalls a critical mission he flew during this period on 26 August 1950:

At the beginning of a routine road and railway hop just above the front lines, a Marine forward air controller saw our planes in the distance and made radio contact with us. He stated that a Marine Company was physically engaged with a numerically superior North Korean force and was being overrun. The enemy force was halfway up a ridgeline and clearly visible. Our Panthers were loaded with 5-inch HVARs [High Velocity Aerial Rockets]and 20-mm HEIs [High Explosive Incendiaries] and armour piercing (APs) rounds. After two dry runs, the concentrated group of enemy troops separated sufficiently to allow the Marines to put down coloured panels. We used two guns or one rocket at a time with the intent being to make as many runs as possible, keeping the enemy down in their holes until Marine reinforcements arrived. On every pass, we could see at least a hundred North Koreans out in the open, standing up and shooting at us with rifles.

We finally departed way below bingo fuel after a major convoy of Marines arrived on the scene at the base of the ridge. We ended up making 16 runs each and all four aircraft had numerous hits from small arms fire. The forward air controller thanked us until we were out of range. Upon our return, the Skipper had to report to both Bridges and explain why we were 10 minutes late and had only 600 pounds of fuel remaining. Within hours however, messages confirmed the FAC's statement that we had saved the company and accounted for over 200 enemy troops killed. At the time, I was 21 years old and had been an ensign for only three months. I remember thinking that if this is what being a carrier pilot was all about, I want to do it for ever!

Ship records state that the initial focus was on North Korean rail and communications centres that stretched from Seoul in the south to Wonsan (at that time, the North Koreans occupied all of this area). There were numerous days when the air group launched at least 140 sorties a day. CV 47 would spend the next three years in hostile waters off the coast of North Korea. The war took on a different face on 15 September 1950 when the Marines hit the enemy where they least expected it: Inchon. The amphibious assault was carried out to perfection and they quickly captured Kimpo airfield and Seoul, cutting off the majority of enemy forces that were totally engrossed around the Pusan Perimeter.

The Navy's Task Force comprised an armada of 230 amphibious and other ships involved in the landings, which was known as Operation *Chromite*. The *Philippine Sea*'s air group was a major factor in supporting the landings and the thrust toward Seoul. Their mission was to cut off any efforts to send reinforcements to the battered remnants of the North Korean forces in and around Seoul. Air Group-11 worked closely with the Marines and USAF in destroying anything that moved from the south and north, which led to mass panic among the enemy troops trapped in the southern tip of the peninsula.

The USS *Boxer* (CV 21) was delayed in entering into the war because it was tasked with carrying a large number of F-51 Mustangs from the US over to Japan. This tied them up from 14 July until the 22nd. They made the Pacific crossing in a record 8.5 days. One more of these fast treks cut that record down to 7 days and 10 hours. The *Boxer* was long overdue for a major overhaul, but the desperate need for carriers in Korea put that on hold indefinitely. Only ten days were spent in the Navy yard at Hunter's Point where just enough work was done to get her ready for combat. Air Group-2 was alerted on the East Coast and immediately moved over to Alameda to join the *Boxer* as its main strike force.

She finally left with her Air Group-2 intact for the Far East on 24 August with the first stop at Pearl Harbor. Unfortunately, a major typhoon between Hawaii and Japan forced another delay in joining Task Force 77's combat operations. Carrier records state that they departed the naval base at Sasebo on 14 September, accompanied by two destroyers and a cruiser. They arrived on station just in time to support the Inchon Landings in mid-September. Once the Marines had secured Seoul and cut off the retreating North Korean People's Army (NKPA), the *Boxer*'s air arm shifted its focus to attacking all targets in and around Pyongyang. When this assignment was completed, the carrier moved over to the east coast of North Korea in support of the advancing UN ground forces. Its air group levelled anything that was in the advancing troop's way as far north as Wonsan.

In desperate need for a major overhaul, the *Boxer*'s combat cruise was cut short as she departed the combat zone for the US on 11 November. It marked the end of the first of four combat stints in the war. Navy records state that while the *Boxer* was involved in its first cruise, however brief, that its air group had averaged 100 combat sorties per day. Once back in the States, it would take three months to get her ready for a second cruise. She would join Task Force 77 again and this time she would have Air Group-101 on board. It was an all-reserve group composed of 'week-end personnel from Naval Air Stations located at Dallas, Texas, Memphis, Tennessee, Olathe, Kansas and Glenview, Illinois'. They would achieve a remarkable record in combat. This would not happen until early March 1951 though.

Once up to full strength, Task Force 77 comprised three *Essex*-class carriers, two cruisers and three divisions of destroyers. This set-up would remain constant for most of the war. Their orders, in mid-September, were to maintain air supremacy with their F9Fs, isolate the objective area and provide constant air cover and support operations for the attack force in its initial assault on Inchon, the capture of Kimpo Airport and the push inland to Seoul. The carriers supporting this operation maintained a distance of sixty miles off the coast, which also gave them a safe distance for unmolested replenishment. With three carriers conducting air ops, the standard procedure for this was to have two carriers maintaining pressure on the enemy with their air groups, while the third was involved in taking on ordnance and supplies.

One of the first major contributions by the Navy to maintaining a toe hold on South Korea occurred on 17 July, when the First Cavalry Division was transported from Japan to Pohang with no opposition from the enemy. There was the chance that Pohang would fall before the reinforcements could get there, but it had held and by midnight, over 10,000 troops, 2,000 vehicles and supporting equipment had unloaded and their efforts over the next few days ensured that the area would hold and the North Korean advance would bog down in that area. It should be noted here that the First Cavalry stopped the enemy advance down the Taegu-Pusan highway. Aircraft from Itazuke AB Japan (USAF) and the *Valley Forge* contributed heavily to this effort.

After the reinforcements had been unloaded at Pohang, the *Valley Forge*'s air group switched its focus to sending aircraft up the coast to search out and destroy any targets that they deemed important. Once in position, the carrier launched seven F9Fs on a sweep up the north-east coast right above Wonsan Harbour. Located on the south side of Wonsan close to the shore was an untouched oil refinery that had, up to that time, only been struck and missed in some smaller strikes. This information was relayed back to the carrier and a strike force was hastily assembled. At 1700 hours on 17 July 1950 twenty-one Corsairs and ADs took off with full bomb loads. The eleven Skyraiders were loaded with 1,000-lb and 500-lb bombs and the ten Corsairs from VF-53 had rockets and 20-mm ammo. The F4Us went in first, firing their rockets in pairs from 4,000 feet out. Immediately following the Corsairs, in trail, were the heavily loaded Skyraiders. By the time the attack was completed, it was difficult to even see the refinery as dense smoke covered the area and secondary explosions only added fuel to the fire. The returning pilots, flying at only 3,000 feet, stated that they could still see the smoke from the refinery when they were sixty miles away.

The story on this attack doesn't end here. Once the North Korean hold on the Pusan Perimeter was broken after the Inchon Landing, it didn't take long for the UN ground forces to capture Wonsan in October 1950. Intelligence personnel interviewed the senior manager of the refinery along with some of his engineers. They related the story that the refinery had been hit five times prior to the big *Valley Forge* strike on 18 July, and during the previous attacks only three bombs had hit within the confines of the facility and none were effective enough to cause a decrease in production. However, after the attack on the 18th, they stated that the entire refinery was a pile of twisted steel and rubble and that any hope of repairing it enough to get back in business was impossible. Their figures showed that 12,000 tons of refined products had gone up in flames and smoke. This included the main power plant, water tanks, and storage buildings, cracking plants, boilers, air compressors and coke furnaces. It proved to be one of the most effective and thorough air strikes of the war.

During the critical days in late July 1950 when the 24th Division was fighting hard to hold the key communications centre at Taejon, the entire 5th Air Force, along with B-29s based out of Okinawa, were concentrating their efforts close to the front lines. This was very unusual for the big bombers to be delivering ordnance that close to friendly troops. Far Eastern Air Force (FEAF) records show that close to 62 per cent of all sorties flown in July by the USAF were for close battlefield support. The emphasis was shifted over to close air support of the troops because most of the targets had been destroyed up in the extreme northern areas of North Korea. The USS *Valley Forge* had aircraft concentrated around the 38th Parallel, which was interfering with any North Korean efforts to bolster their push against the Pusan area. Navy F9Fs, ADs and F4Us took out bridges and shot up anything that moved on the roads and rails. At the request of Lt General Walton H. Walker, commanding general of 8th Army, the aircraft carriers of Task Force 77 began an unusual mission of providing tactical air support for ground troops that were barely hanging on to the Pusan Perimeter. The Navy's emphasis on interdiction would be put on hold for about sixty days until after the Inchon Landing. Saving the UN's foothold on the peninsula suddenly had top priority over everything.

Initially, this was handled by the USS *Valley Forge*, but when the USS *Philippine Sea* (CV 47) began combat operation on 5 August, this only intensified the enemy's problems. The *Philippine Sea* and USS *Badoeng Strait* (CVE-116) were the first carrier reinforcements to arrive in theatre and their focus was strictly on hitting the enemy along the perimeter. CVE-116 was carrying Marine F4U Corsairs on board and that would continue for three combat cruises. Records from the *Philippine Sea* state that its Air Group-11 pounded the North Korean forces with thousands of tons of bombs and rockets during those first days of operations and they logged as many as 140 effective sorties per day when they were in that area.

The *Philippine Sea*'s air group had two well-seasoned F4U-4B Corsair squadrons on board during its first cruise. They took part in just about every strike carried out by Air Group-11. One of VF-113's pilots was Ensign Robert 'Sport' Horton. He relates some of the early missions he flew long before the Chinese entered the war and even before the Inchon Landing:

> One of the missions I recall took place on August 13, 1950 (four F4U Corsairs were lost during the first 10 days of August). This mission gave me my first baptism under fire. We were ordered to destroy the Rising Sun Oil Refinery, located within the city of Pyongyang and it was heavily defended with a ring of anti-aircraft batteries. My Corsair was armed with a 500-lb bomb, eight 5-inch HVARs plus 900 rounds of 20-mm ammunition. During my first bombing run, the AA was so thick, visually, you could walk on it! I figured that if the pilots

ahead of me could make their bomb runs with little or no apparent damage, I could too! I made a perfect run and did some strafing as we pulled back to the carrier. To my shock when I climbed out of the cockpit, I discovered I had forgotten to arm my bomb because the arming wire was missing, which meant that the bomb probably hit the target but did not explode. More than likely, that unexploded bomb caused some psychological problems for anyone that was working close to it!

Later on in our tour, the weather had turned cold and there was snow up close to the Yalu. We found a bunch of enemy troops in the snow and they were apparently playing dead. There were no strafe marks in the snow around them, so no one had been shooting at them. After communicating with one of our Skyraider pilots, we decided that he would dive on them first and release his two napalm bombs and I would follow right behind with my 20-mm guns. When those troops saw the napalm release, they jumped up and started running straight into my 20-mm fire. We did receive a lot of small arms fire on those passes and when I returned to the carrier, my Corsair had quite a few small holes in it. Every one of the missions we flew up north was dangerous because of the intense ground fire. When the Chinese came in, they brought a lot more high calibre weapons in an effort to protect their supply convoys.

The *Valley Forge*'s air group kept the heat on the North Korean's effort to support their advancing troops. The successful first strikes on 3 and 4 July were only a preview of what was to come. Evidently, the first attacks against the airfield at Pyongyang did not prove to be an expensive lesson for enemy air operations because they continued to operate from that base. Intelligence reports indicate that they probably had no choice because the rapid push down into the southern portion of the peninsula made it more difficult to attempt support because of the greater distance and the fact that UN air power increased every day.

On 16 July, the *Valley Forge* emptied its decks as multiple strikes were ordered over a wide area in North Korea. A Panther sweep with at least two divisions hit the airfield at Pyongyang and found two rows of single-engine prop types parked about thirty yards apart. After several strafing passes, the parked fighters were full of holes but none burst into flames. The indication was that they had no fuel in them, which meant they couldn't be moved further north. Nevertheless, those fighters were rendered useless and many were still parked in the same place when the UN troops captured that airfield a few weeks after the breakout at Pusan. Panther pilots reported that they encountered no anti-aircraft fire during their firing passes.

The strikes flown on the 16th lasted from first light to last light. The turnaround time was extremely fast in that each aircraft had to be immediately re-armed and refuelled and then positioned for launch in single division strength or more. The highlight of the day's operation was a strike that began at 1700 hours by a large number of Corsairs and ADs. The latter were loaded with 1,000-lb bombs, while the F4Us were loaded with rockets and 500-lb bombs. It was a major effort to hit the oil refinery at Wonsan. Once over the target, one division of Corsairs peeled off first, making their runs with rockets and 20-mm cannon, which started several small fires.

This was immediately followed by the Skyraiders, which dropped everything they had on the first pass. With smoke filling the air, a final division of Corsairs made one last pass with all of their rockets. Seconds later, a number of secondary explosions rocked the area. On the way back to the carrier right off the coast, they spotted several small boats and they got hosed with 20-mm rounds. The pilots later reported that the only anti-aircraft fire they faced on the entire mission was some 20-mm and 40-mm fire from a small gunboat that was anchored in Wonsan Harbour. The sorties flown on the 16th were just a clear view into what each of the carrier's daily routine was providing that the weather cooperated.

August proved to be a very difficult month for UN ground forces as they tried to hold on to a small area in the southern tip of the peninsula. This was known as the Pusan Perimeter. The North Korean generals that were calling the shots were putting immense pressure on their field commanders to push the defenders off the peninsula and into the Sea of Japan. Fortunately, by this time, friendly air power had built up to the point that the invaders were facing a suicide mission in order to complete their orders. During the third week of August, Admiral Joy sent a message to General MacArthur stating that enemy targets above the 38th Parallel were too lucrative to pass up and indicated he wanted to lift the strict close air support orders in order to conduct strikes against targets in North Korea. The carriers had been consistently sending their photo-reconnaissance aircraft out, with escort, to keep an eye on what was going on north of the 38th. Two days later (25 August), Admiral Joy received an urgent request from the 5th Air Force requesting 100 per cent effort from all carriers on Close Air Support (CAS) because the communists were preparing to launch an all-out attack across the Naktong River and they needed all the help they could possibly get.

The situation was so desperate that all available B-29s were still being used to hit enemy concentrations around the perimeter. A few days before the urgent message was sent from 5th Air Force on 16 August, ninety-eight Superfortresses 'carpet bombed' the enemy build-up area north-west of Waegwan, where some 40,000 North Korean troops had gathered. They dropped 850 tons of bombs in an area that was 7,000 yards wide by 13,000 yards long. The next day, these same forces launched one of the heaviest attacks of the war right through this same area. It only went to show the tremendous pressure being put on the field commanders of the NKPA to finish it.

The retreat by the South Koreans and UN forces to the south was so quick and unexpected that most of the roads, bridges and rail lines were left intact. If they had been destroyed in a slow orderly retreat, it would have been much more difficult for the North Koreans to sustain their forces during the August push. However, Navy aircraft combined with Marine planes played close attention to the enemy supply efforts south of the 38th. In the meantime, planes from the *Valley Forge* were launching a minimum of two major strikes a day against targets on both sides of the Parallel. Their photo reconnaissance aircraft were accompanying the strike force to bring back pictures of the actual damage done to targets and, if need be, the bombers were sent back the same day or early the next to finish the job.

On a major strike in August, aircraft from Air Group-5 on the *Valley Forge* spread out over North Korea in search of any rail traffic. The first target that the VA-55 Skyraiders spotted was a locomotive hidden under some camouflage netting. One well-placed 1,000-lb bomb destroyed the target and as they moved several miles to the north, they came on a rail tunnel with plenty of room to skip bomb. The first of these went slightly to the right while the second AD skipped his 500-lb bomb into the tunnel opening where it exploded. It was a short tunnel because in seconds a lot of debris and smoke shot out the exit to the tunnel. Before the mission was over, they had tried to skip bomb six tunnels, but that was the only one that was successful.

From mid-October until the harsh winter set in, one of the main objectives for the carrier air groups were the many bridges that spanned the Yalu River. Lt (jg) Bill Gortney, of VF-51, comments on this:

> We ran into many problems in trying to take those bridges out. We lost one of our pilots on a mission that was based on a stupid decision by 'upper management'. They wouldn't allow our aircraft to bomb parallel to the bridges (90 degrees), which made it next to impossible to get a solid hit on them. One of our pilots was strafing some gun emplacements close to the bridges and when he finished and pulled up, his wingman was gone. We never saw any signs of a crash, so we never knew what had happened to him. I think that was the only loss we had in the squadron during that cruise. I believe we had about a 10 per cent loss rate in the air group and most of these were from the F4U and AD squadrons. When it came time for us to pull off the line, a little before that even, the real cold weather had set in and we had no winter gear with us, which included survival suits in case we went down in the water. I did get a couple of pairs of winter underwear and when we got the survival gear (Poopy Suits), they were all too big. They were miserable to fly in.

As Navy and Marine air power continued to build up, the number of strikes north of the bomb line increased. Maybe the emphasis was being put on targets up in and around Pyongyang and further north because the enemy felt relatively safe in bringing a large number of their fighters as far south as the captured airfield at Kimpo. This was short lived because when the plans for the Inchon Landing had been finalized, the Navy started concentrating on areas within a twenty-five-mile radius of Inchon and Kimpo. One of the first strikes was a major effort by F9F-3s from VF-51 and VF-52 against Kimpo, which was ten miles west of Seoul. Their arrival was totally unexpected and the pilots noted several burned out Yaks scattered out that been hit by Air Force Mustangs a few days previously. By getting down low they detected approximately ten enemy fighters heavily camouflaged along the perimeter of the parking area. Within minutes, most of these were on fire and assumed destroyed. A short time later, after the UN forces had re-captured Kimpo, the area was scattered with hulks of burned out and destroyed Yaks and Il-10s. These same F9Fs also laced several large oil storage tanks with 20-mm rounds, and when they exited the area the fire and smoke could be seen for miles.

Before the North Korean Army had been totally routed far above the 38th Parallel, they did have a reasonable number of prop fighters that had been given to them by the Russians long before the war started. As UN air power increased, these fighters were flown further north to airbases in and around Pyongyang. As it got impossible for them to fly south of the Yalu River, they started camouflaging them on the edge of the airfields, and in some cases they were towed as far away from the parking area as possible and covered with hay. At that point they learned just how destructive a

20-mm cannon can be. On many of the fighter sweeps off the carriers, the Panthers would come in low looking for stacks of hay. When they strafed these, some would blow up, revealing the remnants of an Il-10 or Yak-9. It didn't take long for the few remaining flyable aircraft the NKPAF had to fly to the safety of Manchuria.

One of the most unusual aerial kills by a Navy pilot occurred on 4 September 1950. What made this kill so unique and one-of-a kind was the fact that it was a Russian aircraft flown by a Russian pilot, probably coming out of an airbase in Manchuria. The Navy pilot credited with the kill was Ensign Edward V. Laney, a Corsair pilot with VF-53 flying off the *Valley Forge*. The kill was listed as a Russian Ilyushin Il-4, which was a World War II twin engine bomber. It was equipped with a manned dorsal gun turret.

On this day, Ensign Laney was due to fly the very early mission, which was a strike against targets in the Sinanju area, along with armed reconnaissance against any targets of opportunity. When he recovered back on the *Valley Forge*, he was also assigned to fly a second mission of the day which was a Combat Air Patrol (CAP) over the carrier that was in the Yellow Sea out from the Inchon area (although the famous amphibious assault on Inchon was still eleven days away).

He remembers the details of that second mission:

Lt Dick Downs was the flight leader of a four plane CAP mission over the Task Force. I was his wingman flying an F4U-4B (Bu No. 97485). Our area of patrol was a little west of the *Valley Forge* at about 10,000 feet. The picket destroyers were doing their job when they radioed they had two airborne targets at about 70 miles west heading east. Our CAP was vectored out to the west and when the two intruders were out about 40 miles, one of them turned north, but the second one continued on at between 30 and 40 miles from the Task Force and our carrier.

Our flight was directed to go down and identify the intruding aircraft. It was a twin engine bomber type with no visible markings. As Lt Downs approached the aircraft, its gunner fired on him at which time Downs climbed back up to where I was. Seconds later we received a radio transmission that said 'Geronimo', which was the Admiral's call sign directing our flight to go down and identify the bomber and try to get him to turn away and if he fired on us again, to shoot it down! The intruder was now approaching the 25-mile safe zone around the Task Force and at that point the Russian pilot increased his speed and continued toward our ships. Lt Downs peeled off and led the attack and as he got close, the gunner opened up on him again and he returned fire, but his rounds barely missed.

At that point, Ensign Laney went right in behind Downs and the gunner fires at him also.

I returned fire with a short burst from my 20-mm and the rounds went into the right wing around the engine, which promptly separated from the Il-4, quickly followed by the right wing and then the tail. At least one of the crew was able to survive and one of our picket destroyers picked him up. It was one of the pilots and he was definitely Russian. After landing back on the *Valley Forge*,

I was promptly helicoptered over to the Flag Ship where I was questioned about the shoot down. My gun camera film proved that the gunner on the Russian bomber was shooting at me. I was sure that it was an Il-4 because that was the only twin engine aircraft with a single rudder reported to be in that general area.

Many years later, some Russian historians published an article in one of their magazines about that incident. It turned out to be a Douglas A-20 Havoc that was one of many that had been given to the Russians operating in that area during the final weeks of World War II and they were flown by Russians against the Japanese. It was uncanny that a World War II Corsair would shoot down an American-made aircraft almost six years after it had been given to the Russians! If you take a look at a picture of the Il-4, you can easily see the similarities between the two aircraft.

For quite some time after the Korean War ended, the period that spanned from 25 July 1950 to the Inchon amphibious assault on 15 September 1950 has been studied intensely by the military. This was especially true in the mid to late 1950s when there was always the chance of the Cold War producing another similar situation. There have been two conclusions reached concerning this period: the Pusan Perimeter could never have been held and with the carrier's mobility all targets deep into North Korea were effectively hit by the air groups. This not only included all the transport types, but the emphasis was on carrier aviation and its ability to interdict the flow of supplies and put just about any target in North Korea within easy reach. Also, the gunfire from the destroyers and cruisers during those early days took a heavy toll on enemy movements along the coastal routes. However, according to Admiral Joy, the Navy's most unspectacular role was carrying personnel and supplies to Korea. General MacArthur stated to the Admiral:

> The vital role played by the aircraft carriers can't be overemphasized. Had you not employed the carriers as you did in sustained support of the 8th Army, Congress would think twice about further appropriations for the construction of aircraft carriers.

Another factor that made it easier for Navy air power was the fact that the North Korean Air Force made very little aggressive effort to support their troops even in the first days of the war. They were quickly wiped out and what few of their aircraft that survived retreated to bases in the extreme north-west Korea or into Manchuria. When naval or USAF aircraft tangled with them, it was all one-sided. The fact that the opposition's aircraft disappeared early made it a lot easier for naval fighter-bombers to inflict heavy damage on the enemy efforts to push the UN off the peninsula. All of this encompassed the time frame mentioned above and it set the stage for a complete rout of the North Koreans once the Inchon amphibious assault had been successful. Now it was a matter of the Navy moving their carrier air groups north and destroying anything that could be of value to the enemy.

CHAPTER TWO

Total Rout of the North Korean Army

The brilliant Inchon Landing carried out by the Marine Corps on 15 September 1950 proved to be the move that broke the back of the Soviet-trained North Korean People's Army. The 8th Army planned to initiate a breakout from the Perimeter as soon as the Marines had a foothold at Inchon. The move was brilliant and by this date the Navy was in position with some big carriers and the Marine Corsairs were also ready for heavy close air support of their troops. The USAF, hampered by the lack of airfields, was putting a maximum effort from airbases in Japan such as Itazuke, which was the closest base to Korea. The Navy had a distinct advantage because of the mobility of their air groups. With such a concentration of air power in a small area, the North Koreans had no chance of preventing the breakout or of an orderly retreat back above the 38th Parallel. 'It was a massacre in motion in the best target rich environment imaginable,' as one of the Navy F4U pilots explained it.

The biggest mistake made by the invading enemy forces was not to have pushed the UN forces off the peninsula quickly. American intelligence reports that were released at about the time the enemy efforts were at their zenith around the Pusan area stated the North Koreans probably had thirteen infantry divisions on the line and they were supported by at least one armoured division and two armoured brigades. This was broken down into eastern and western sectors. They had about 47,000 troops on the northern/eastern side of the Perimeter and 54,000 troops on the western side. This gave them over 100,000 troops against a much smaller UN force that was supported by one of the most aggressive air-to-ground campaigns in military history. When the 8th Army broke out of the stranglehold immediately after the Inchon Landing, one has an idea as to how massive the North Korean retreat was and what easy targets they provided for Navy and Marine fighter-bombers at that time.

The meagre forces that held on against overwhelming odds bought enough time for the US military might to build up just as it had happened in the Pacific in early 1942. From the Navy's point of view, the *Valley Forge* and *Philippine Sea* bought enough time for two more carriers to arrive on the scene when the North Koreans were in a disorganized retreat. The USS *Boxer* (CV 21) and USS *Philippine Sea*'s aggressive air group's efforts were not limited to just targets around the 38th Parallel. They dealt severe blows to anything south of the 38th (the disorganized retreating NKPA and all the way up to the Yalu River)!

The USS *Boxer* had been ordered to pull off a rush job, which delayed their entry into the war by hauling 145 North American F-51D Mustangs from the States to Japan. This was a critical request due to the severe shortage of USAF prop fighter-bombers in the Far East. However, the *Boxer* got down to serious business when they finally reported to Task Force 77 on 15 September. Instead of the normal complement of eighty-seven aircraft in its air group, it carried ninety-six aircraft. Carrier records state that the breakdown was as follows: sixty-four F4U-4s, eighteen AD-4s, one AD-4Q, three AD-4Ns, three AD-4Ws, three F4U-5Ps and one HO3S-1 helicopter. There were three explanations for the overage: the desire to augment the strike and ground support effort to the maximum, the reported unavailability of replacement aircraft in the theatre of operations and the expected low average availability of F4U-4 aircraft assigned, due to age. (The majority of these Dash-4s were on their third service tour.)

Flying combat operations off crude airstrips in South Korea proved to be dangerous at best, but the Navy pilots had to face some very difficult situations every time they launched and recovered and weather just added another dimension to the dangers. However, when the carrier strikes were over for the day, there were still some dangers lurking in the shadows. Ensign Elmer Tollgaard was an F9F-2 Panther pilot flying with VF-111 off the USS *Philippine Sea* during its first cruise (1950–51). He relates a freak incident that could easily have been fatal. He remembers the details:

> We were assigned to Air Group-11 and it was during one of our busy periods, but the missions for the day had been completed. On the *Phil Sea*, there was a dormitory style room as was on most all *Essex* class carriers. It was called 'Boys Town'. Flying Midshipmen and junior Ensigns of the Air Group lived in a bunk bed style room with a few mirrors and wash basins for quick clean ups.
>
> Approximately 25 young men lived in this room, which was located one deck above the hangar deck forward of the No. 1 elevator. At any time, there would usually be someone sleeping, reading, playing cards or cleaning up. On this particular day, there was an F4U Corsair on the hangar deck, facing forward just aft of the No. 1 elevator. A mechanic was working on it and evidently accidentally hit the firing trigger and the guns were armed and ready to fire. Several rounds of 20-mm ammo penetrated the elevator and 'Boy's Town' bulkheads and continued on through into the foc's'le. Rounds went through several racks, mirrors, sinks and lockers!! One of our Ensigns had just finished washing and combing his hair and was leaving the area just as the rounds came through the bulkhead. It was a miracle that no one was injured. There were others in that room at the time and none were hit. It was lucky for everyone that was in that area!

As the carrier force pulled up to full strength and the close air support in the Pusan area came to a close, the naval air groups were able to get back to what they did best and that was armed reconnaissance and interdiction. On most days when the weather was decent, the decks were emptied at least twice a day as most of the strike aircraft had multi-missions to fly. The only exception was the specialized detachment aircraft that did their work at night and they were all prop types. This put undue pressure on the maintenance and ordnance personnel because a lot of the aircraft came back with battle damage. Keeping the in-service rate at its peak was tough.

In a declassified document issued in the fall of 1950, the problems facing jet maintenance were put in writing and it pertained to all carriers on station. The following is quoted *verbatim*:

> Considerable concern has arisen about occasional surges in engine RPM during flight. These surges are frequently accompanied by momentary indications of fuel pump cut out. It has been observed that the fuel pump warning light will come on momentarily with rapid advancing of the throttle control. In as much as there is little or no information available to the squadrons on this, difficulty has been experienced in trouble shooting these problems. Operational and combat damages account for the major portion of the work load of the structures section. However, the presence of very capable and skilled personnel on each carrier makes the loss of flight hours a minor problem.

Prior to the Inchon Landing and all the way through the Chosin Campaign, the eyes of the fleet remained with a handful of camera-equipped photo-reconnaissance Corsairs from VC-61 on each of the carriers. They were mostly equipped with the F4U-4P during the early days and the composite squadrons quickly moved into the jet arena with the camera-equipped Panthers and Banshees. It was these brave pilots that set the stage for what the Navy air group's role would be once the war became stagnant after the Chinese entered the war. This, basically, was the information on the complex rail networks that linked Manchuria with the front lines along the east coast of North Korea.

One of these pilots was Lt (jg) Ray Hosier. He was flying missions prior to Inchon and on into the Chinese intervention with Air Group-11 on the USS *Philippine Sea*. He was probably the only F4U-4P pilot to make a low pass over the big airfield at Antung, Manchuria, when it was jammed with MiG-15s (this was right before the MiGs began crossing south of the Yalu River). He participated, along with some Marine photo-recce aircraft, in getting pictures for the Inchon Landing and he was the first pilot to land at the newly re-captured airfield at Kimpo on 18 September. He gives a rundown on what his schedule was like after the breakout at the Pusan Perimeter and on into the Chosin Reservoir situation and then on into 1951 when the push was on to stop the Chinese troops from consuming the entire peninsula:

> On September 30th, I photographed a six-strip map of Pyongyang at 16,000 feet with light Anti-aircraft fire.
>
> Our Corsairs were equipped with 20-mm guns in the wings and we carried about 800 rounds, which gave us an opportunity to go after targets of opportunity when we finished our photo run. Most of the time, we shot up all of our ammo against anything that moved. Our favourite targets were trains and warehouses and with the war less than four months old, there were still some targets moving during the day. Anything north of the bomb line was considered fair game! On a mission I flew on October 11th, my engine cut out over 20 times, which sent me back to the USS *Leyte* (CV 32) before I got in serious trouble. The maintenance guys corrected the problem and I launched again as we were in great demand because of the pre-strike and post-strike photos we had to get.

The Chinese started showing up south of the Yalu River in early November and the MiG-15s were getting more aggressive. My log book shows that on November 10th, I was sent up into the extreme northwest corner of Korea to photograph Sinuiju, several bridges and the MiG airfield at Antung. On one of the missions over Antung, I was jumped by a MiG-15 and we exchanged fire. Fortunately, we both missed and the fact that the MiG was not very manoeuvrable at very low altitudes enabled me to exit the area safely. Two weeks later, one of our carriers was headed back to the states after its cruise was over. They had the newer F4U-5Ps that were sixteen inches longer in the nose (supercharger) and they had cameras that rotated electrically but the two that we got were shy of the electronic gear that made this a possibility. Our Dash 4Ps were just about worn out by this time.

The USS *Valley Forge* ended their first combat cruise in early December 1950, which was about the time the war abruptly changed course. The carrier's two Panther squadrons (VF-51 and VF-52) had done an outstanding job over targets in North Korea. Lt (jg) Bill Gortney looks back on some of the things they experienced:

After our early strikes, we learned that anytime we popped our speed brakes, which were hydraulically charged, that they took so much hydraulic pressure and oil that it would safety our 20-mm guns! So we would find ourselves on

The USS *Valley Forge*'s air group first entered the war with major air strikes against airfields around Pyongyang on 3 and 4 July 1950. On the 4th, they lost three Skyraiders in operational accidents, but none was lost to enemy ground fire. The ruggedness of the AD is shown here with pilot Lt John Leverton standing in the huge hole in his VA-115 Skyraider. (*John Leverton*)

a strafing run, wanting to slow down, pop our brakes and the guns would refuse to fire! Pax River and the Grumman engineers got together and flew out to where we were. They brought a fix for the problem. The F9F was never thoroughly tested at Grumman or at the Navy Test Center. Fortunately, we got the problem solved and our Grumman Rep was great as he helped us out with several other problems.

With Air Group-5 working up close to the Yalu River, there was always the threat of encountering the swept wing MiG-15s.

We flew a lot of strafing missions far to the north and the only time I can recall running into MiGs was when we were hitting a target close to the south side of the river and we saw some of these fighters off in the distance. One of our guys identified them as the North American F-86 Sabres, but at that time, there weren't any of them in theatre, so we got out of there fast. Our F9F-3s did not have any ordnance carrying capabilities except for the 20-mm cannon. On one of these missions, we were strafing a series of big fuel storage tanks and it was a memorable experience to see the huge holes that we could open up in those tanks with our guns!

By the time that the NKPA had been pushed north of the 38th Parallel, General MacArthur was already discussing the possibility of pulling off an amphibious assault at either Wonsan or Hungnam to cut the enemy's retreat, thus not allowing them to regroup. This suggestion was presented to Admiral Joy, who did not agree with the idea because both harbours were heavily mined and it would be disastrous for any ships trying to enter them and in addition there were not sufficient numbers of landing craft to handle what would be required. The proposed landings at Hungnam would have been at two different locations that were in close proximity. Admiral Joy stated that there were not enough minesweepers in theatre to handle one landing, much less two. Navy and Marine air power was sufficient to handle what was required of them, but there was nothing they could do about the mines. Most of these mines had been furnished and implemented by the Russians prior to the beginning of the Korean War. Two weeks after the Inchon Landing, the wheels were in motion for plans to hit Wonsan with an amphibious assault, but due to the dangers involved, as pointed out by Admiral Joy, and the rapid advances of UN ground forces, those plans were shelved.

By early December 1950, the UN ground forces were looking across the Yalu River into Manchuria. The war appeared to many of the ground troops to be all but over. Lt (jg) Hosier continues:

I flew my Corsair into the Wonsan area and landed at the big North Korean airfield at Yonpo on December 16th to deliver some photos. The weather was very bad as it was most of the time during the winter months. At this time, the *Phil Sea* was operating in the Sea of Japan in an effort to support the Marines that were pulling back due to the hordes of Chinese that were pushing south. We were pretty far to the north and on one mission, I decided to fly a little further up and get a glimpse of the Russian base at Vladivostok because I wanted to be able to say that I had seen it and I was down low below their radar, so they couldn't detect my approach. As you might guess, things were rather loose at that time in the war and there was a lot of confusion because the war had taken a drastic turn for the worse.

On one of Hosier's longest flights (3.2 hours) up in the extreme north central area of North Korea, he experienced some higher calibre anti-aircraft fire. On one of these missions, he was taking pictures of some highway bridges and caught a 40-mm shell in the right wing root that did considerable damage to the rib and skin. When he got back on the carrier, he told his plane captain to patch it up and paint over it and not to tell anyone because he didn't want to miss any of his missions. Hosier ended his action-filled tour with 109 carrier landings and over 90 combat photo-reconnaissance missions over enemy territory. The other pilot in his VC-61 detachment that was in competition with him for most missions flown, Lt (jg) William Moffit, ended up with 111 carrier landings and one more mission than him. Their tours came to an end when they flew their F4U-4P photo-reconnaissance aircraft over to the USS *Valley Forge* (CV 45) from the *Philippine Sea* (CV 47) for their return home on the *Valley Forge*. The *Philippine Sea* stayed on in theatre with a fresh Air Group-2.

The USS *Leyte* (CV 32) was on station between September 1950 and February 1951 with Air Group-3 on board. Their first loss was an F4U-4P from VC-62 on 7 October.

Aircraft from the USS *Valley Forge* work over an area close to Kunsan, South Korea, on 6 August 1950. These buildings housed North Korean equipment and troops. At this time, most of South Korea had been captured by the enemy forces and all of the ground action was centred on the Pusan Perimeter. (*US Navy*)

When the Chinese entered the war in November, the air group's tempo picked up considerably. During the month of December, when the group's tasking was at its peak, the air group lost five aircraft. One of the most dramatic losses occurred on 12 December 1950 when Lt Commander Ralph Bagwell, the commanding officer of VA-35, went down in his AD-3 Skyraider after hitting a power line far behind enemy lines. There was no chance to rescue him and he quickly became a POW. His wingman on that mission was Ensign Richard A. Cantrell who relates the details of that mission:

> The weather over North Korea was always miserable during the winter months and December was no different. Our mission on that day was to get down as low as we could and hit targets close to the city of Huichon, which was far behind enemy lines. The clouds were down so low, we didn't have much room to work and I can remember the skipper stating 'I'm going down on the deck today so don't anyone follow me!' Seconds after sending that radio message, Lt Cdr Bagwell nosed his AD over and went down to tree top level in search of targets. It was a dangerous move for even the most skilled pilot. So intent was his search that he failed to see, until it was too late, the electrical high tension

Ensign Richard Cantrell poses in the cockpit of his AD-3 on the deck of the USS *Leyte* prior to flying another mission. He was flying wing for VA-35's commanding officer when he witnessed the CO's aircraft run into a electrical high-tension line and crash on the banks of the Chongchon-Gang River in December 1950. Note the bombing mission symbols painted on Cantrell's Skyraider. (*Richard Cantrell*)

wire directly in the path of his Skyraider. When he hit the wire, his AD went out of control and crash landed on the banks of the Chongchon-Gang River. He had no altitude and there was no way he manoeuvre to find a safer place to belly in. One of the other Skyraiders in our division was close by and the pilot, Ensign Eldon Jacobs, stated that the engine tore loose flipping the plane over on its back and when that happened, the vertical stabilizer broke off. Lt Commander Bagwell crawled out from under his aircraft and waved his arms to let everyone know he was uninjured.

The fourth member of the division got up to altitude and radioed the information to the nearest airfield, which immediately got a rescue helicopter in the air in an attempt to get the pilot out. Ensign Cantrell set up a tight circle over the downed pilot, while pinpointing his location of approximately ten miles south of Huichon. The downed pilot sought refuge from the bitter cold weather beneath a nearby railroad bridge while he waited on the helicopter to arrive. Ensign Jacobs had already signalled him that it was on the way. An hour went by and the chopper was more than a third of the way to him, when suddenly from the opposite side of the bridge, a green-clad Chinese soldier brandishing a rifle sprang out and surprised Lt Commander Bagwell. It was a shock and in a matter of minutes the area was swarming with Chinese troops that seemed to come out of nowhere.

Cantrell continues:

> It was very disheartening to watch Bagwell being taken prisoner and not being able to strafe the Chinese for fear of hitting our commander. It was with great reluctance that one of our division pilots had to radio the helicopter to turn around and return to base! We stayed close and they marched him off in a southerly direction towards a bivouac area that had at least 500 Chinese troops in it. We didn't dare make a strafing run because Lt Commander's life would have been a possible forfeit! As an aside, the normal tour of duty for a commanding officer of a Navy squadron is about 26 months. Bagwell was in his 26th month as CO of VA-35 and he went down on his 29th mission! He had led us on numerous dangerous and successful missions against just about every type of target that was heavily defended up on the Yalu. He was instrumental in setting up an aggressive mission schedule to support the Marines during the Chosin Reservoir campaign. Fortunately, he survived his POW experience and has made some of the VA-35 reunions. All of the pilots and support personnel in VA-35 had a very special bond and it was because of the calibre of leadership provided by Lt Commander Bagwell!

The heavy ordnance hauler for the *Philippine Sea* during its first cruise was VA-115 with its AD-4s. During the disorganized, rapid retreat by the North Korean forces, it was operating in the Yellow Sea after supporting the Inchon operation. The air group's orders were to seal off all of the transportation routes coming out of Manchuria into the western section of North Korea. At that time, the orders were clear that they were not to bomb on the Manchurian side of the bridges and that was where the gun emplacements were. Several Skyraider pilots have commented that their bombs sometimes 'missed' the bridges and went long into the guns that were shooting at them from the north side of the river. These guns were not just limited to the bridges as they were based all along the river up in the north-west corner that would soon earn the name of 'MiG Alley'. Lt (jg) John DeGoede was an AD pilot in VA-115 and recalls an incident after a bridge strike in that same area:

> We were headed for those same bridges that were pouring supplies and equipment from Manchuria into North Korea. My wingman and I set up our dives from altitude and on the way down I stated that this time on pull out, we would stay low, head west and follow the river rather head south. We released our ordnance and made a sharp turn to port skimming about 20 feet over the river and heading back toward the Yellow Sea and the *Phil Sea*. After clearing out of the target area, I glanced over at my wingman Lt (jg) Harry May. A steady stream of tracers was coming at him from the south side of the river as we barrelled along. I radioed and told him that there were a lot of guns shooting at him and he replied 'What in the hell do you think they're doing to you?' I glanced over to my right and sure enough, I was getting as much attention from the north shore as he was getting from the opposite side. Fortunately, they were shooting high and we moved out of it in a few minutes and made it safely back to the carrier.

Soon after this mission, General MacArthur flew out to the *Philippine Sea* to address the pilots. They all gathered on the hangar deck in uniforms, ties and jackets. He told them that he knew of the hazards of not being able to return enemy fire when it was coming from the Manchurian side of the river. He stated that his hands were tied and that the politicians in Washington were running the war, but he did not say anything negative about President Truman in his speech. He concluded his talk by telling the air group that they still had to bomb the bridges on the Yalu because it was the only way to stop the enemy from supporting their troops. After all, the North Koreans and Chinese had absolutely no support from the air, so they had to depend on the rail and road bridges to be able to continue.

Beginning in mid-October 1950, Corsair and Mustang pilots that were working against targets at very low altitudes reported seeing hordes of enemy troops south of the Yalu River, but these sightings were ignored at HQ in Tokyo. It was estimated that tens of thousands had crossed the river with about 400,000 poised north of the river. Pictures taken by the photo-reconnaissance F4U-5Ps and RF-51Ds pointed this out. At first, it was presumed that some Chinese had come across to help the remnants of the North Korean forces get safely into Manchuria, but with the number that were in plain sight, this theory was quickly thrown out of the window. Now, the order was given for the Navy air groups to concentrate on attacking the bridges that spanned the river as that appeared to be the main conduit for the influx of Chinese troops.

Captured Chinese troops helped identify at least four Chinese armies that were on Korean soil. During the first week of November, Admiral Struble received the following dispatch from Vice Admiral Joy:

> General MacArthur considers it urgent that the over water spans on the Korean side of the international bridges along the Yalu and Tumen Rivers

be destroyed because of heavy use by the enemy to supply their forces. The Manchurian territory and air space under no circumstances must not, repeat not, be violated. You have been assigned the mission of attacking the two bridges near Chongsongjin. The USAF is fully committed in the area of Sinuiju.

This set the stage for Navy and USAF operations for the remainder of the war. The attacks on the big power plants, located on the river, would come at a later date.

Lt (jg) DeGoede recalls a mission he flew using napalm, which almost proved to be his last one:

> We were sent out on a close air support mission using napalm. This required getting as close to the ground as we dared to, in order to leave a swath of fire about 40 feet wide and 100 yards long. As I made my approach into a narrow valley, I though to myself… if this napalm bomb does not release, this plane will not make it over the mountain in front of me! IT DID NOT RELEASE! Just so you know, crashing with napalm still attached is a certain fiery death! Knowing that I was going to crash, I radioed that I had had it! My past did not flash in front of me; instead I was trying to understand why there was no snow on the mountain ridges because there was snow covering the lower elevations. I was so close to the ground that I could see the small rocks that lined the top of the ridge. My plane stalled just as I reached the top of the mountain and lucky for me, there was a steep drop off on the other side, which allowed me to build up speed and recover from the stall. I climbed back up and made another run and this time, the napalm released. We were able to help the troops on the ground by taking out a lot of the enemy troops, so the mission was a success.

A significant number of the Navy and Marine pilots that were shot down or had to bale out or ditch due to mechanical problems survived the ordeals. When questioned about any memorable missions, the ones that stand out most vividly are the ones that relate to their rescue after going down. They credit survival training, the determination and skill of the ResCap (Rescue-combat air patrol) pilots and helicopter pilots with an emphasis on good luck! (ResCap indicates the top cover for any rescue operation where a helicopter is trying to get in and extract a downed pilot.) A number of these survivors were flying in the late autumn and winter of 1950, which indicated most were involved during the Chosin Campaign and the few months immediately following.

During World War II, winter survival gear for the aircrews was not such a major issue, although the winter of 1944/5 in the European and Mediterranean Theatres proved to be very hard for the Air Corps, but the Navy carriers were focused in the Pacific and cold weather was not a factor. The aviators that did a brief stint in the Aleutians could attest to how important cold weather gear was, but facing the bitter cold winter weather over North Korea could not have been anticipated because very few, if any, had experienced it and flying off the deck of a carrier up in the northernmost reaches of the peninsula proved to be a memorable experience. During that first winter of the Korean War in 1950/51, it was evident that this should be addressed immediately. The matter of survival equipment was constantly in a state of flux during this period. Even after the bitter experiences over the Chosin

Reservoir, it was impossible to state that one particular kit of equipment was the ideal solution.

The first major problem to be solved was that of a survival kit to be carried on all strikes over the beach by one of the aircraft in the flight. By improvisation and pleading with the various supply officers, a kit was formulated that consisted of the following: sleeping bag, soap, warm clothing, carbine, rations, gloves, cigarettes, first aid kit, toothpaste and brush, machete, .38 calibre ammunition, a survival booklet and a radio transceiver. This kit gave a tremendous boost in morale to all the pilots, knowing that it was available to them in the event they were shot down. Fortunately, with an excellent recovery system by helicopter, the kits were never dropped to pilots and the efficiency of the actual gear could not be evaluated. As the winter months approached, more cold weather clothing was included in the kit.

During the warm summer months, the standard flight gear was a summer flying suit with extra pockets sewed on, and a Mae West with signalling mirror attached, along with the standard gear of flares, whistle, dye marker, shark chaser and flashlight. As winter approached, an exposure suit, long woollen underwear, extra gloves and boots were added to the list. Since it was impossible to dress adequately for both land and water survival, most pilots chose to prepare for water ditching depending on the survival kit if forced down over land. Consequently, the first thing a crippled Navy aircraft would do over land was head straight for the nearest water and comparative safety.

CHAPTER THREE

Enter the Dragon

There were some elements of UN ground forces that could look down on the Yalu River and there were rumours flying about that the war would be over by Thanksgiving and the men would be home by Christmas 1950. The Inchon Landing had supposedly won the war. But, this was not to be and it would have been very disheartening if those troops could have looked into a crystal ball and found out that the war would not end for another thirty-two months! In late October and early November, numerous F4U and F-51 pilots had reported that the Chinese were pouring across the Yalu River, and as these reports made their way to Tokyo General MacArthur refused to believe that the reports would have any effect on the outcome of the war. Two weeks later, he would find out the hard way. With the Navy having several top carriers working far up the peninsula, their aircraft were relentlessly pounding anything that moved and the USAF had called two major B-29 bomb groups home because there were no targets left for them to bomb. Later on in the war, it was estimated that the Chinese troops numbered at least 275,000 on North Korean soil by late October 1950. With the winter conditions that far north in November and the Chinese wearing their white winter uniforms, it would have been impossible for low-flying photo-reconnaissance aircraft to determine the extent of their numbers.

Ensign 'Boot' Hill, flying Panthers with VF-112, recalls what his unit was doing at the time the Chinese began showing themselves south of the Yalu:

> In early November 1950, the Chi Coms were pouring across the river using the bridges at Sinuiju. On the 10th, we launched a major strike to bomb and destroy the bridges using both Corsair Squadrons (VF-113 and VF-114) along with our AD squadron (VA-115). Our two Panther squadrons (VF-111 and VF-112) had the task of providing top, middle and low cover for the strike force. Our orders were not to cross north of the river, yet Antung Airbase was only 9 km north of the bridges. The weather was clear and very cold and you could see for ever. The Skipper's Division was assigned Hi-CAP and from 28,000 to 36,000 feet, we could plainly see the MiG-15s line up, take off and climb out on their side of the Yalu to altitude and then turn south toward the river and our strike force.
>
> The MiGs wanted to get at the props and it was our job to prevent it. The F9F-2 was the best fighter in Korea, at that time, but with a straight wing, we could not out dive or out climb the MiG. But, if it stayed around, we could easily out turn it, so, we engaged four of them over a 10 minute period and afterwards, my gun camera film showed several HEI hits on the starboard side of one MiG's fuselage. After developing the film aboard ship later that day,

all of the frames that contained any MiG pictures were forwarded straight to Washington. This had been the first all-jet engagement in air warfare history. It was the same day that Lt Commander Tom Amen made his MiG-15 kill and a first jet kill for the Navy.

Several major newspapers published articles on the front page of their papers, indicating that this was the highest, altitude-wise, jet battle in history with some of the action exceeding 32,000 feet. Of course, two months later, this would change drastically when the F-86 Sabres arrived in theatre, as some of their air battles with the MiGs would easily exceed 35,000 feet on a regular basis.

Hill continues:

Two days after the big battle with the MiGs, we were up in that area again. The encounter lasted a long time with no one getting in any kills and by the time we broke it off, we were all very low on fuel. We didn't have enough to return to the carrier, so we had to land on a beat-up, pock-marked short 3,800 foot runway at Wonsan. All eight main tyres were blown during roll out and until Marine assistance arrived, our four F9Fs took rifle hits from a small group of NKPA troops that the Marines had left in isolation on the northern tip of the area close to the runway. It was a deadly serious time with the Chosin Reservoir and the evacuation of Wonsan and Hungnam. We were the only jets to land at Wonsan during the war. I believe that 95 per cent of the strikes and recce hops flown by Air Group-11 during November and December 1950, were in support of the Marines coming out of the Reservoir and their evacuation to safety. I can also tell you that during our initial series of strikes against the bridges up on the Yalu, we did not lose any ADs or F4Us due to MiG-15 action.

A short time later, Ensign Hill was catapulted off for a mission on a two-ship road recce mission hunting for any targets of opportunity. The other pilot, flying lead, was Lieutenant Robert 'Chili' Chilton. He would be second to launch behind Hill, but had a serious problem with a fuel control malfunction. The backup was an Ensign Stollenwerck who quickly took off to join the other Panther. To send two ensigns on a mission like this was unusual, and if Hill had not already launched the mission probably would have been scrubbed. This gave Ensign Hill the lead as they went feet dry in search of anything on the roads or rails. They were loaded with 5-inch ATARs (special anti-tank rockets) and a full load of 20-mm AP and HEI ammunition. As they reached an area south-west of Wonsan, they spotted a locomotive with several box cars moving into a short tunnel that was no more than 150 metres long. They immediately initiated an attack and caused a series of secondary explosions that caused fire, debris and people to fly out of both ends of the tunnel. Evidently, that train was loaded with ammunition and troops. Both pilots were called to the bridge when they returned to the *Philippine Sea* and congratulated by Admiral Ewen.

For every Navy, Marine or Air Force pilot that dropped napalm or strafed at the required low altitudes, they all had some remarks to make about getting hit with small arms fire. Ensign Don Horton, flying with VF-113 in Corsairs commented:

In early October 1950, the carrier air groups were pounding targets far up in the north-west corner of North Korea. This post-strike photograph shows the bomb craters over an area that had been a major rail/road junction for the enemy. Several strikes by AD Skyraiders had completely turned the area into a wasteland. (*US Navy*)

Flying down low was always dangerous because you were well in range of enemy troops with their rifles. I taught myself to always fly my F4U in a slight skid after coming off of a strafing run because it tended to confuse the people shooting at me because at that time, your aircraft was most vulnerable. The tactic worked because my plane took less hits on those runs. On one strafing pass, I heard a loud pop and saw my bullet proof windscreen shattered. One more inch to the right and I would be missing my right ear. On one mission, one of our pilots flew into the ground and crashed through a house. His Corsair had evidently been hit with some accurate small arms fire. We immediately started a rescue procedure and after his rescue, we strafed what was left of his plane until it was burning and then we returned to our carrier. Fortunately, we were close to the coast and were able to keep enemy troops away from him until the helicopter got him out. It could easily have ended tragically.

On 8 November 1950, two carriers from Task Force 77 launched strikes against the numerous bridges connecting Manchuria with North Korea. These included rail and road bridges that were pouring supplies and equipment southward to support the enemy offensive. Between 9 and 21 November, naval aircraft logged a total of 593 effective sorties against the bridge complexes that spanned the Yalu River. The heavy hauling capabilities of the AD Skyraiders helped the strike forces drop 232

On 9 November 1950, the commanding officer of F9F squadron VF-111, Lt Commander William T. Amen, was leading an attack against bridges on the Yalu River. They were jumped by MiG-15s and he shot one down, becoming the first Navy jet pilot to score a kill against the new swept-wing MiG-15s in the war. In this picture Plane Captain Bob Owens points to Amen's Panther, which has had the MiG symbol painted on it. The squadron operated from the USS *Philippine Sea*. (*W.D. Davidson*)

tons of bombs on these targets. The bomb loads were made up of 500-lb, 1,000-lb and 2,000-lb GPs. Records from the USS *Valley Forge* state that the strike force they launched consisted of sixteen Corsairs, twelve Skyraiders and eight Panthers. At the time, there were three big carriers assigned to this mission with the other two being the USS *Philippine Sea* and the USS *Leyte*.

In examining this force more closely, the strategy was for the first wave to go in consisting of eight F4Us assigned to hit the anti-aircraft positions, and this was followed closely by eight F4Us dropping 500-lb VT-fused bombs against these same gun emplacements. (VT represents Radio Proximity, which means the bombs had the capability to explode right before they hit the ground. This was the most effective way to kill the gunners that were manning the anti-aircraft guns.) Within a minute or so after this, the Skyraiders began to peel off into their dives against the bridges with their blockbuster ordnance. Damage to the bridges was heavy and these attacks were repeated on the 10th, 12th, 14th, 15th, 16th, 18th and 21st. Attacks on the area after the 21st were sporadic but just enough to discourage or delay any repair efforts by the enemy. As these attacks started to taper off, Navy pilots reported a huge increase in anti-aircraft fire originating from the Manchurian side of the river. This created a big problem for the strike planners as hitting targets in Manchuria was strictly frowned upon. When the enemy realized the imposed restrictions, all of the gun emplacements were moved to the north side. B-29 bombing missions against targets on the south side of the river would receive the full brunt of the guns and searchlights that cropped up on the north side.

The bridges in the Sinuiju area were the most dangerous because they were the closest to the MiG base at Antung. Putting the Navy F9Fs in close proximity to the MiG-15s was bound to evolve into a clash between the two aircraft and that is exactly what happened. The first Navy jet pilot to score a MiG-15 kill was squadron leader Lt Commander W. Thomas Amen of VF-111 from the USS *Philippine Sea*, flying a F9F-2. He recalls the events of that memorable mission on 9 November 1950.

> Our original plan of attack divided our twelve Panthers into three groups: four to clear the area of MiGs and go in with the F4Us, four to cover the Skyraiders and the remaining four to cover their pull out and withdrawal out of harm's way. We launched at four minutes past nine that morning and headed straight for the bridges. We made it in exactly 29 minutes and our timing was perfect as we joined up with the slower prop types at the planned time. Down below us was the town of Sinuiju, which looked about the size of Taejon, and that bridge looked as strong as the Golden Gate Bridge in California! Across the Yalu was the huge MiG base, which we could plainly see, but we couldn't see well enough to tell what was parked on it, but a few minutes later, we would find out!

The leader of the bomb laden Skyraiders, Commander Deacon, pushed over at exactly 10:00 a.m. The sky looked like a combination of smallpox and measles, but his division pushed right on through it with their aircraft buffeted about from the anti-aircraft bursts. He commented:

> I pulled out of my dive, circled to the left to watch the bomb drop. I had only seen about eight bombs explode when these big orange tracers came walking up my stern. There was only one thing to do and that was to turn into him, head on and slug it out. It was a swept wing MiG all right, coming through us like a bolt of lightning. I fired on him, but missed. The others in my division took up the fight, trying to line the MiG up … props versus MiGs, what a sight!

At this early stage of the fight, Lt Commander Amen radioed to the AD division enquiring as to where the MiG was, but there was no answer. Ten seconds later, a voice came on the radio, stating that the attacker was right behind the F9Fs and coming on fast. Amen continues:

> I looked over my shoulder and there he was, a shiny swept wing banking toward me coming in at my 7 o'clock. I immediately turned to meet him head on with my wingman Ensign George Holloman close behind me. The other two pilots in my division were barrelling in at full throttle. At that time, the MiG started to climb almost straight up to about 15,000 feet until he levelled off. All of this action had been taking place down very low at about 4,000 feet.

There at the base of the cloud cover, he started to arc and fishtail. In the climb, my wingman and I both got off a couple of ineffective bursts of 20-mm at him.

We kept right on his tail as we had no other choice because if we had let up, he would have gained the advantage. It was really the hounds after the fox in the sky! With at least a 100 knot speed advantage, the MiG could have got away flying straight and level. But, every time he turned, we closed the gap, shooting as we closed. The other two pilots in the division, Lt (jg) Carl Dalland and Ensign Earl Reimers, fired two bursts without scoring any hits, but apparently they scared him into a dive and at that time I climbed right on his tail!

Down we went at 400 knots … 450 … 500 with my guns wide open. I had him bore sighted and my rounds looked like they were dead centre but since this was the first real dogfight I had ever had, I wasn't sure I had him. Suddenly, my aircraft started to buffet as the nose was trying to tuck under. I put on my dive brakes and quit shooting. The MiG's dive angle had increased to 40 degrees. I knew I was finished chasing him and wondered how much faster he could go before he started falling apart. As we passed through 3,000 feet, the MiG flipped on his back and I thought that the pilot was either crazy or he had one of the best fighters ever built. Then, all of sudden I could see mountains coming up fast and then I saw trees and rocks and by some miracle, I pulled out with about 200 feet clearance. At that time, my wingman shouted out 'You Got Him!' The MiG had gone straight in and exploded and as I looked back it seemed that I had started a forest fire.

Carrier records state that there was a large turnout of personnel on the deck as the returning Panthers began landing. There was a celebration on the deck that would rival Mardi Gras. Amen commented that 'there hadn't been anything like this since the latter days of World War II and the fact that our air group had bagged the first MiG-15 was special'. The results on the bridge attacks on that mission seemed to take a back seat to the MiG kill. Reports showed that four of the Skyraider pilots had scored direct hits with five near misses. When the dust settled, the bridges were still standing, although heavily damaged, which meant that the air group was be giving them a return visit the next day.

The role of Navy carriers and their air groups remained constant for the duration of the war. It was almost an identical routine day after day: close air support and interdiction with endless repetition. Once the NKPA had been driven far above Pyongyang, the carrier ops shifted over to Korea's east coast. With the entry of hordes of Chinese troops into the war at the beginning of one of the most bitter cold winters in years, the tempo of sorties was increased to try and stave off the huge gains the Chinese were accomplishing on the ground as they marched steadily southward toward the 38th Parallel. General MacArthur ordered both the USAF and naval air operations to intensify their efforts on enemy communications, assembly areas and endless troop columns. The Chinese paid a very heavy price in December 1950/January 1951, but they were able to reverse all the gains that the UN ground forces had made, and before long the front lines were right back where they had been when the war started.

The USS *Leyte* (CV 32) was the fourth major aircraft carrier to arrive in the Far East to support the UN efforts. It was too late to support the Inchon Landing as it sailed into Sasebo Naval Base on 8 October 1950 with its Air Group-3, which had the standard one squadron of F9F-2s, two squadrons of Corsairs and one of the AD-3 Skyraider. It also had the usual detachments of specialized aircraft such as the AD-4N and F4U-5P.

Records from the *Leyte* state that it began combat operations on 10 October with several assigned secondary targets, while its photo detachment (VC-62) did some low-level work over the Songjin area. The pictures taken by their F4U-5Ps were used to brief a major group strength strike the following day on the 11th. For five consecutive days, they flew 472 offensive sorties and 56 defensive sorties. They were the key air group to destroy any efforts by the enemy to reinforce the area or retreat to the north. The *Leyte*'s aircraft fired 93,000 rounds of .50 calibre ammunition and fired over 2,200 rockets in this effort. This set the tone for the next 18 days with relentless strikes against anything in the way of the ground forces advancing on Wonsan and Chongjin. Their objective was to destroy any communications and transportation facilities in this area. The *Leyte*'s F9F Panthers also ranged out on wide fighter sweeps to the north of these cities and some were as close as twenty miles south of the Manchurian border. From 10 to 29 October, Air Group-3 logged a total of 1,185 sorties.

This photo explains a lot of what the air groups had to go through to keep a target completely out of business. The main bridges in the centre had been destroyed on the initial attack. A bypass was quickly built and it was also destroyed. Finally, a third road bridge was hastily built (far upper right) and it was destined for destruction the next day after this low level run by a photo plane from VC-61 got this picture back to the mission planners. (*Ken Kramer*)

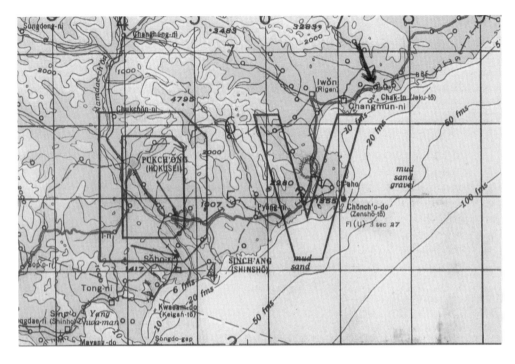

The map with the arrow in the upper right shows the exact location of this main rail line close to the east coast of North Korea. The photograph was taken by an F9F-2P photo ship from VC-61 on the USS *Essex* not long after a strike flown on 19 November 1951. The rails have been cut in two places but the nearby village was probably supporting a large conscripted work force that would have the rail cuts repaired in hours. (*Ed Laney*)

The *Leyte's* scoreboard for those nineteen days in October was impressive and proved to be in line with what other air groups were accomplishing at about the same time. North Korea was a target-rich environment during the disorganized retreat of the North Korean Army and the entry of the Chinese hordes into the war, both of which had no air support. Air Group-3 recorded fifty-one boxcars and two locomotives destroyed, along with twelve warehouses, several barges and eight trucks, among several other targets. The number of enemy troops killed or wounded from the strafing runs was not recorded as it would have been an estimate only.

Up to and including the Chosin Reservoir battles, there were many recorded heroic incidents and a great number of unrecorded deeds of bravery. You could say the same for just about any war that the United States has been involved in. However, there was one that occurred on 4 December 1950 that should be mentioned in every book that involves naval aviation history. It involves a couple of F4U Corsair pilots that flew combat with VF-32 off the USS *Leyte*. Ensign Jesse Brown, the Navy's first black aviator, and Lt (jg) Thomas Hudner were the key players in this story. They were part of a division of F4U-4s that were flying close air support for the Marines that were trying to finish their evacuation from the Chosin Reservoir in the middle of the Chinese Army. The weather was typical for Korea in December. The mountainous terrain was covered with ice and snow and as Ensign Brown dropped down to about 1,000 feet to try and spot some of the enemy troops, his engine cut out. He had evidently been hit with some accurate ground fire that had caused fatal damage to his engine. He was too low to bale out and he didn't have any power so he could not clear the high mountain ridges that were on all sides.

With only seconds to figure out what he had to do, he noticed a small area that was relatively level, so he made a wheels up dead stick landing. What may have looked smooth from the air wasn't actually that, but the snow helped soften the crash-landing. However, Brown's Corsair took a heavy beating during the landing to the extent that the front of the cockpit was jammed back toward Brown and he was pinned in. Ensign Brown's wingman, Lt Bill Koenig, circled low over the downed fighter and noted that Brown was waving at him with the canopy open, indicating he was OK. The other two Corsair pilots in their division were Lt Richard L. Cevoli and Lt (jg) Thomas Hudner. With Lt Cevoli flying above the other two Corsairs, he radioed for a rescue helicopter that was at least fifteen minutes away from their location. Meanwhile, Hudner circled the wreck at treetop level and made the decision to try and land as close to Brown as he could with hopes of getting him out of the cockpit and into the helicopter when it arrived.

The temperature on the ground was a minus 30 degrees and the Chinese troops were somewhere in the general area, so time was of the essence! Hudner put his Corsair down on the ice-covered rocks and came to a stop about 100 yards from Brown's aircraft. When Hudner jumped out and went over to him, he saw that Brown was alive, but only barely and his aircraft's engine was smoking, so Hudner started packing ice around the cowling. He also told the helicopter crew to make sure they had an axe with them as he wanted to try and hack the metal fragments that were trapping Brown in the cockpit. The chopper arrived and it didn't take long to see that the axe would not do the job. Brown was losing a lot of blood as he drifted in and out of consciousness.

The entire rail system in North Korea was a maze of tunnels, which allowed plenty of protection for the trains during the day. This scene was seventy-five miles north of Wonsan on the east coast. The decisive rail cut was done by either a 500-lb or 1,000-lb GP. This was also the work of Air Group-5 from the *Essex*. (*Ed Laney*)

Both pilots tried everything they could, but it was evident that nothing would free Brown and the light was fading rapidly. With the amount of blood that he had lost, it was certain that even if they could have got him out, he probably would not have made it back to friendly territory alive. Thus, Lt (jg) Hudner made the toughest decision of his young life and that was to leave him. Before they left the site, Brown had died. Both of the pilots barely made it out before total darkness had set in. For his heroic efforts, Hudner was awarded the Medal of Honor by President Harry S. Truman on 13 April 1951. Also in attendance at the ceremony was Mrs Daisy Brown, widow of Ensign Jesse Brown.

The fifth big carrier to join Task Force 77 in the war was the USS *Princeton* (CV 37) with its Air Group-19. Prior to the war, the carrier had been deactivated but, on 28 August 1950, she was recommissioned and rapidly put to work getting its aircrews ready for combat. Finally, on 5 December 1950 she was in position off the Korean coast and ready to commence operations. The *Princeton*'s first assignment was to fly against critical targets in and around Hagaru. Air Group-19 launched 248 effective sorties against these targets with great success. This pace continued as the battered Marine ground troops fought their way to the coast in the famous Chosin Reservoir Campaign. Finally, on 11 December, the Marines had reached the coast at Hungnam and started their evacuation onto waiting ships. Every carrier that was in the area covered this operation like a blanket and the support also extended to

The map shows the location of the small bridge and tunnel along the coast just north of the Korean village of Yongdae-dong that was hit by Corsairs from VF-53. The bridge was damaged and in a difficult location to be repaired quickly. The mission was flown on 19 November 1951 off the carrier USS *Essex*. (*Ed Laney*)

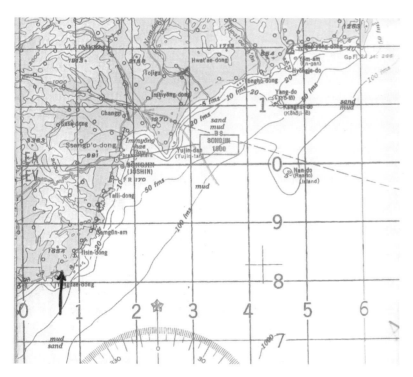

These Panther pilots flew off the *Essex* during the famous attack against the bridge complexes in the narrow neck of the Korean peninsula. They were flying the F9F-2 at the time when James Michener was on board. These strikes led to the famous movie *The Bridges at Toko-ri*. (*Ken Kramer*)

Marine Corsair units that were land based. The losses inflicted on the Chinese troops were extremely heavy. Marine records state that the evacuation was completed on 24 December, with all equipment and personnel safely out of harm's way.

During the month of December, the Chinese learned a valuable lesson but it was very costly in manpower. Evidently, even though they had monitored the war closely, they did not understand the devastating capabilities of air power in the air-to-ground role and their mindset was that overwhelming manpower could win in any situation. Once they tried to trap the Marines up on the frozen Chosin, their ground troops became exposed to relentless attacks from Naval and Marine air power. By the last days of December, the Chinese had started to practise the art of camouflage and most of their movements were restricted to night-time. Estimates state that during the final two weeks of December, air power was credited with killing at least 6,700 enemy troops. Navy aircraft were responsible for a good percentage of this because they remained in close proximity to the action, thanks to their mobile carrier force.

While the North Korean Army had been routed and pushed as far north as the river, they were not finished by any stretch of the imagination. By Christmas 1950, the Chinese had come to the rescue of the defeated North Korean forces. With such overwhelming numbers, they started pushing the UN troops back toward the 38th Parallel. At this time, the emphasis was placed on close air support over the front-line positions. The Navy had concentrated on the north-west corner of

North Korea because that was where the majority of supplies and equipment had come across, but with the ability to carry out missions from either coast, the carriers had a significant presence on the east coast due to the Marine evacuation from the Chosin area. Still, there was a large amount of land mass up in the far north-east corner that had lacked attention. American intelligence had picked up that there was a big shift from the west coast to the east coast by the enemy because there were still many bridges intact and the rail lines were pretty well intact. Reconnaissance flights up in the extreme north-east showed that at least one full division of North Korean troops was using the rail system there to move south to join their Chinese allies.

In an official memo from Admiral C. Turner Joy to Vice Admiral Arthur D. Struble concerning the importance of taking out all of the major rail lines in the north-east section of the peninsula, he stated:

> Rail routes on the northeast coast between Wonsan and Chongjin are of continuous value to the enemy as a major route over which supplies, equipment and troops are being transported to immediate battle areas. The enemy's known capability for quickly effecting temporary repairs to the damaged portions of this route can be seriously impaired by deliberate, methodical, total destruction of all piers, spans approaches and embarkments of each vital bridge in each critical area. The enemy cannot accomplish makeshift repairs when nothing remains upon which to make them. Naval air power and naval gun fire are good weapons to accomplish this job.

Thus, the die was cast on what the carrier air groups were expected to do. Naval records for aircraft losses during the period from January to March 1951 show that the USS *Philippine Sea* lost seven aircraft, the *Valley Forge* lost eight, the *Princeton* lost eleven and the Leyte lost only one. A few of these losses were due to operational problems in the extreme weather conditions.

From that point on, the rough winter weather conditions were constantly slowing deck operations, but the air group continued to fly interdiction missions as often as they could. Their purpose was to help make it impossible for the Chinese to gain any momentum with their human wave offensives that required a lot of food, ammunition and supplies. The Princeton's aircraft recorded fifty-four rail cuts between Pyongyang and the front lines and thirty-seven highway bridges destroyed. This, along with the weather, also had an adverse effect on Chinese troops. Air Group-19 records state that all of this damage was done between Pyongyang and routes connecting with Sinanju, Kachon, Sunchon and the trans-peninsula line. By 4 April 1951, the front lines had pretty well stabilized so air power had put a huge dent in the enemy efforts to overrun the peninsula. With this stalemate, the *Princeton* unleashed her aircraft against the Hwachon Reservoir area.

With the exception of brief periods of replenishment, the *Princeton* kept the heat on anything that moved until early August when it departed the Far East bound for the States, arriving in San Diego in late August. It should be noted here that the first cruise for the *Princeton* was split, when after six months into that one, they picked up another complete set of squadrons and the air group was designed as CVG-19X. This put the *Princeton* back in the action from 31 May 1951 until early August. Some records count this as a second cruise, but it did not have the duration of a normal one.

The USS *Essex* started its first cruise in the war in June 1951. To historians and many of the pilots, there are two things that stand out on that cruise. First of all, the famous writer James Michener was on board and was allowed to sit in on the strike briefings for one of the most heavily defended bridge complexes in North Korea. The information he gathered at that time led to a best seller and movie entitled *The Bridges at Toko-ri*. The second standout was that its Air Group-5 had the first F2H-2 Banshee squadron to ever see combat on board (VF-172). Carrier records for 16 September 1951 reveal the worst day that the Banshee would have in the entire war. On the 15th, the weather over most of the target areas were bad, so combat ops were curtailed, but the following day they were able to get most all of the group's aircraft out on strikes. As the *Essex* was recovering the planes from the last strike of the day, one of the Banshees with air brakes extended made a final approach at 1823 hours. It was BuNo 124968, which had been involved in a mid-air collision prior to its return to the ship. Under these circumstances, its landing was delayed to allow all the rest of the aircraft to recover just in case the disabled Banshee fouled up the deck.

When the pilot touched down, his fighter became airborne again, which caused it to jump over all three barriers, finally landing forward on the flight deck with nothing in its way but parked aircraft! It crashed into two Banshees and two Panthers, which immediately burst into flames. There were three killed, four missing and sixteen injured in the accident. In total, VF-172 lost four Banshees that day and VF-51 lost two F9F-2s. It was a disastrous day for the air group. As would be expected under combat conditions, the decks were cleared, both catapults tested and flight operations continued at a normal pace the following day.

One of the Corsair pilots, Lt Clayton Fisher, that was on that *Essex* cruise in VF-53 recalls the tragic accident involving the Banshee crash on 16 September:

> I was just returning to the carrier after an interdiction mission late in the afternoon and found out that our recovery on the deck was going to be delayed because of an emergency landing attempt by one of VF-172's Banshees. That aircraft had a damaged aileron from a slight mid-air collision with another Banshee while flying in formation. We circled the *Essex* watching the final approach as the plane touched down okay, but the tailhook was not down and it crashed into a parked F9F and crushed to death a chief petty officer, also killing the pilot. A wing tip fuel tank on the F9F exploded spewing flaming fuel into other aircraft that had just been taxied forward by VF-51 pilots that had been rushed out of their ready room to man their planes. One Panther was blown off the flight deck into the water. That pilot was Lieutenant John Moore who survived with deep burns on his face and ears. I think a couple of sailors were killed on the flight deck catwalk and others suffered multiple burns. It was just getting dusk and flaming gasoline was flowing like a waterfall from the flight deck into the water! It was a terrible tragedy!

Lt John Moore was an F9F pilot on the *Essex*. At the time this situation began playing out, he was in the wardroom with several other Panther pilots discussing the mission they had just returned from when the squadron duty officer rushed in and told them that a Banshee was in trouble and was returning to the ship. He needed them to get up to the flight deck immediately and help taxi their Panthers to the forward part of the deck as the aft section had to be cleared for the crippled Banshee. Lt Moore survived the tragedy that followed and he explains what happened:

> Six of us jumped up and rushed top side and by some miracle, I remembered what the skipper had told us many times. He said that every time we climbed into the cockpit, to have all of our flight and survival gear on. For this situation, it seemed foolish, but I went ahead and got everything on, including my Mae West. I got in the cockpit and was told the Banshee was three minutes out. Our deck hands were frantic in making sure we moved quickly and I caught a glimpse of a speck on final approach and it was the Banshee. My plane was the last one to start moving to a forward position and as I moved into the new parking area, I was on the very edge of the deck and from the cockpit, I could look straight down about seventy feet to the water.
>   As I climbed out of the cockpit, I heard the shriek of the crash whistle. I glanced back and saw the Banshee touch down and bounce over the crash barrier headed straight for my plane! I knew he was going to crash into me and I had a split second to decide whether to jump into the water. I took too much time and suddenly there was fire everywhere and as I closed my eyes tight, I felt my plane tumbling on its side onto the catwalk. The next sensation was one of falling through a ball of fire. I hit the water and popped right back up on the surface. The carrier was skimming past me at about 20 knots and suddenly I was engulfed in burning gasoline. I had inflated my Mae West, so I couldn't duck under the water for safety. I started splashing the water around me and the flames started moving away from me (I learned this in survival training). In a few minutes, the ship's helicopter was hovering over me and I was rescued.

Moore survived and went on to become a prominent test pilot in the Navy, while logging a lot of time in the F7U Cutlass and the North American Vigilante.
  Lt Fisher's division of F4Us helplessly circled the carrier as light was rapidly fading. Finally, they were ordered to recover at K-18, which was the nearest land base in South Korea. It would be a night landing.

> We had to circle while flare pots were lined along the left side of the Marston Matting (PSP). When you make your first landing on the 'beach' after making carrier landings, you feel like you're extremely fast when you touch down. The tyres really 'sing' rolling down on the mat. When you rolled off the mat to a parking area, the props kicked up enormous clouds of dust. We put on our oxygen masks to escape the dust. The next morning, the *Essex* returned to normal flight operations. After returning to our carrier, everyone pitched in to clean the dirt off of our Corsairs. Our CAG was Commander Marsh Beebe … CAG stands for Commander Air Group … The air groups themselves were referred to as CVGs. Commander Marsh Beebe and I flew over to a base in South Korea to pick up half of the cortisone available to help treat all the burns suffered by the personnel that were on deck.

Flight operations off the coast of North Korea were always hampered by the harsh winter weather conditions. This snow-covered deck was on the USS *Essex* with VC-3's night fighter Corsairs in the foreground. This photograph was taken in the winter of 1951/52. (*National Archives*)

The main duties of Air Group-5 on the *Essex* was almost a carbon copy of what was expected of every group. In declassified records from the carrier it states: 'The primary mission of CVG-5 was the support of United Nations ground forces.' This assignment was divided into two parts: the interdiction of enemy lines of communication and close air support around the front lines. Whenever indicated by sightings or photo-reconnaissance sorties, the group is sent out to destroy the enemy's supply build-up points. Also, the group's Corsairs were sent out to spot for naval gun fire support along the east coast of North Korea. The All Weather detachments carried out anti-submarine patrols (ASP) coverage for the ship in the task force. The night hecklers (F4U-5Ns and AD-4Ns) were sent out to take out anything that moved on the roads and rails in their sectors. The photo detachment (VC-61) performed low-level photos missions that determined the next targets and also post-strike sorties to determine the extent of damage to targets that were hit by the air group. The air group was also responsible for the all-important combat evaluation of the new F2H-2 Banshees serving with VF-172.

Most of the pilots and carrier personnel that have been interviewed state that looking back on all of those days and missions, they all seemed to have blended into one and that most were repeats of all the others. Each carrier, on station, was

The USS *Essex* carried the first F2H-2s into the war during its first cruise in 1951/52. They participated in the famous strikes against the 'Bridges at Toko-ri'. The Banshee had two Westinghouse J34-WE-34 turbojet engines that gave it a cruise speed of over 450 mph and a range of close to 1,700 miles. These F2H-2s were assigned to VF-172. (*Frank Glendinning*)

There were two versions of the F2H-2 used in the Korean War, the fighter-bomber and photo-reconnaissance types. This Banshee was from VF-172 and heading back to the USS *Essex* after a strike in North Korea. It was armed with four 20-mm cannon and could carry a bomb load of up to 3,000 pounds. (*Frank Glendinning*)

targeting whatever was being prioritized: interdiction and/or close air support. The photo detachments were either taking pictures of targets in the pre-strike mode or post strike mode. If you read the daily operational histories of any squadron during that war, they are all very similar.

A good example of this is to describe the events of a specific squadron during one month of their combat cruise.

The USS *Bon Homme Richard* (CV 31) did two cruises in the Korean War. On their first cruise (1951), they had two squadrons of F4U-4s on board and one of these was VF-874. A thorough review of that squadron's history for the month of July 1951 revealed the following facts that could probably be matched to all the other Navy Corsair squadrons that were in theatre. They deployed with twenty-six pilots and an average of fourteen aircraft in service and two that were down at all times. The squadron flew an average of twenty-two to twenty-six sorties a day and each flight lasted approximately three hours. The usual character and composition of flights assigned were as follows. Close air support of front-line troops averaged about two flights daily and consisted of two Corsairs and two Skyraiders. Bridge strikes consisted of one or two each day and they were made up of four F4Us and four ADs. Most days also included naval gunfire spotting for the cruisers and destroyers that were in close to the coast, also one anti-submarine patrol that was escorted by VF-874's Corsairs and the same for the photo-reconnaissance missions up north, which had to have an escort.

The average load carried by the squadron's F4Us consisted of a 150-gallon napalm tank and six 100-lb GP bombs, fused .01 nose and non-delay tail fuse. The aircraft that were assigned to the bridge strikes carried one 500-lb GP bomb and six 100-lb GPs or one 1,000-lb bomb and four 100-lb bombs. The usual set-up was to put VT nose fuses in all bombs and non-delay tail fuses. On the missions of naval gunfire spotting, one 500-lb GP plus six 5-inch HVARs were used. In addition to these loads, each Corsair had a full load of ammunition for its guns and a full external fuel tank.

The mission breakdown was as follows: for that time period, there were 314 missions flown by VF-874 pilots, which equated to 210 armed reconnaissance, 35 close air support, 8 combat air patrols, 28 naval gunfire spots, 24 anti-submarine patrols and 9 flights classified as miscellaneous. During this time, the air group was tasked with hitting well-defended Chinese assets above Pyongyang, which led to a lot of battle damage. At first, most of the anti-aircraft fire originated when the planes were below 1,000 feet (napalm/strafing), which accounted for 90 per cent of the damage, but as they got into mid-July the intensity increased dramatically and the squadron noted that all of the air group's aircraft were getting shot at from all altitudes and the weapons included 40-mm and 5-inch guns. This was an indicator of the damage that the air group was inflicting on the enemy supply lines. The USAF also indicated that during this period, their F-80s and F-84s were on the receiving end of much higher calibre guns that the Chinese had started bringing in.

This changed the bombing strategy somewhat in all of the air groups. It became necessary to change from a loose column type of attack to a coordinated attack system utilizing tactics developed in World War II. Starting bombing runs from 8,000 to 10,000 feet, the bombers would dive in out of the sun if possible and begin their strafing runs from the higher altitudes. The F4Us released their first bombs (VT fused) on marked anti-aircraft batteries (from photos taken by the F9F-2Ps

ADE3 Felix Norris, a plane captain in VF-791, checks out his assigned F4U on the deck of the USS *Boxer*. The squadron was part of Air Group-101. This was in the summer of 1951 during the carrier's second combat cruise. The assigned pilot to his Corsair was Lt John White. The squadron was a reserve unit out of NAS Memphis, Tennessee. (*Felix Norris*)

The F4U Corsair was very effective in a low-level dive with these 5-inch HVAR rockets. These were normally used to attack North Korean armour, rail traffic and bunkers. They had a velocity of approximately 1,350 feet per second (410 m/sec). The effective range was as far out as 5,000 yards (4,570 m). (*National Archives*)

of VC-61). This would be closely followed by the ADs dropping their bombs on the main target. The recovery from the bomb runs would be made away from the gun emplacements. This procedure helped diminish losses, but there were several instances where the pilots had to ditch or bale out after taking damaging hits on these heavily defended targets. Loss records for July 1951 show that the USS *Bon Homme Richard* lost two Corsairs, while the other carriers (*Boxer*, *Princeton* and *Valley Forge*) combined lost a total of eleven Corsairs. A couple of the latter ones were the F4U-5Ns from VC-3 detachments.

Not only were bombing runs made at higher airspeeds with low pullouts being forbidden, new rescue procedures were developed. The following is quoted from Air Group-102's operational doctrine dated 1 August 1951:

> When a pilot had to ditch or bale out, two planes would be immediately assigned by the strike leader to stay close to the pilot and observe his position and what the situation demanded. Two aircraft would be assigned to intercept and contact the nearest helicopter in the area and escort it back to the downed pilot. The remaining planes would orbit over the general area of the pilot, with one pilot relaying all information to the fleet as it developed. As soon as the pilot was definitely pinpointed, four aircraft would form a continuous orbit around the downed pilot making diving runs out of phase and strafing the area to keep the enemy from reaching the spot or firing at the downed pilot. As the helicopter would approach the pilot, this orbit would be lifted so the chopper could have free movement and at that time, the pilot would fire a smoke flare to assist the helicopter in locating the exact position. When picked up, at least two aircraft would fly escort while the remainder would be free to return to the carrier.

This system worked almost to perfection as most of the downed pilots that were not seriously hurt were rescued. The biggest criticisms in rescue operations came from the jamming of radio frequencies with unnecessary transmissions and inadequate information being given to the fleet and helicopter pilots. By the end of the trial period, the squadrons in Air Group-102 were enthusiastic about the rescue rate accomplished by the helicopters.

The primary mission of the carrier air groups was interdiction because they would move up the coast and have easy access to targets deep in North Korea. In February 1951, the Chinese had pushed far to the south and all air assets were told to concentrate on slowing them down and supporting the friendly troops. This lasted until September because the Chinese were constantly trying to mount an offensive. With at least three air groups concentrating on this plan of action, their success was so great that the surge of Chinese troops to the south was finally stopped and soon the front lines became stabilized close to the line where the war had started. On 20 September 1951, Far East Air Force (FEAF) ordered Task Force 77 to slack off on their close air support duties because the Marine Corsairs, Panthers and Skyraiders were more than able to take over that role. The primary reason for this decision was the overwhelming resources of the Chinese and their ability to move unbelievable amounts of supplies and equipment at night to keep their troops in a position to maintain their stance and perhaps mount a sustained offensive to gain new ground.

BU 765 518   R.R. BYPASS
BU 765 517   HWY BRIDGE
SORTIE: 067
DATE: 9 JAN. 1952
VALLEY FORGE CV-45

The problem with taking out key bridges was the fact that the enemy would rush hundreds of conscripted labourers in and have the repairs completed in hours. This post strike photograph taken by an F9F-2P from the USS *Valley Forge* in January 1952 shows the bypass that has been put in place since the bridge was destroyed. This allowed truck traffic to resume operations at night. (*Donald McNaught*)

Bear in mind that all their efforts were done with absolutely no support from the air. There was one factor that gave the Chinese soldiers a distinct advantage – they were conditioned to function with the bare minima of food and basic comforts that UN forces required. Many of the Chinese POWs were captured wearing only thin coats and tennis shoes with weather conditions hovering below the freezing mark.

It became Task Force 77's responsibility to take out anything that moved north of the bomb line for about 300 miles and this covered just about all of North Korea up to the Yalu River, with carriers unleashing their strike forces from both the east (Sea of Japan) and from the west (Yellow Sea). Operations from the east coast proved to be very dangerous due to the steep mountains and deep valleys that contained all of the road and rail traffic. The Chinese made sure these were well defended with an emphasis put on the main rail line from Yangdok to Samdong-ni. The one big break that the air groups received on these strikes was that on the extreme eastern coastline the mountains tapered down to a small segment of flat land where a lot of the roads and rail lines were situated. Most of the construction was due to the Japanese when they occupied Korea before World War II. This area was easy pickings for the Task Force because it was within firing range for the big guns of the heavy cruisers and battleships. The damage inflicted on these east coast rails and roads was so vast that the enemy shifted the emphasis from north to south re-supply efforts over to the west coast, which proved to be tougher on the naval and USAF interdiction operations because they contained less mountainous areas where the bridges usually spanned shallow river/creek beds. If a bridge was knocked out, it was easy for communist labourers to build a bypass within hours of the original bridge being destroyed.

Once the Chinese forces became entrenched in the war and the front lines had begun to stabilize, American intelligence began to understand why the enemy's logistics system was as aggressive and well defended as it was. It was determined that the average Chinese soldier required only about ten pounds of supplies per day to stay in an effective fighting mode. In other words, one of their divisions consisting of 10,000 men needed only 50 tons of supplies per day, and with what seemed like an unlimited number of vehicles and rail cars, this proved to be an easy task. The problem that air power had with this was to keep the supply level from exceeding this amount because anything above and beyond this would mean a surplus that could sustain a major offensive. These figures were broken down even further to show that 48 per cent of this was food, 22 per cent was clothing and weapons, 10 per cent pertained to petroleum products and the remaining 20 per cent was ammunition. With this determined, the mobile Navy carriers were given the task of roaming far up the peninsula and doing everything they could to reduce this flow to below what they required.

The maps of Korea carried by all of the pilots were broken down into grids that carried two letters such as 'DV' or 'CV' or 'DA' etc. These were vital in locating a target from the air. A Corsair pilot who was in the second F4U squadron (VF-783) on the USS *Bon Homme Richard* explains a harrowing mission he flew in one of these sectors (BC) during the cold November 1951 period, which was during the first combat cruise for the carrier. His first comments give details on the launch and recovery sequences (*modus operandi*) for the main strike aircraft types. The pilot was Lt (jg) Walter Spangenberg Jr.

> The *Essex*-class carriers operated on a 1.5-hour cycle time for the F9F Panthers, with the F4U and AD prop types on a 3-hour 'double cycle'. The AD could do this on its 326 gallons of internal fuel with no need for drop tanks, but the F4U carried only 230 or so gallons of internal fuel and needed a drop tank to provide a safe margin of fuel for the usual 45 minutes or so of circling at the end of the flight while waiting to land. One very experienced F4U pilot got so bored doing this that he dozed off and flew into another Corsair that was in formation and lost his vertical stabilizer. This caused him to have to ditch alongside the carrier because he didn't have any rudder control to safely land on the deck. The greatest penalty for the F4U in this type of operation was that the drop tank required the most capable external store station on the belly of the aircraft, so we were then limited to the six wing stations, each with 250 pounds capacity for ordnance.

Geographically, the Korean peninsula changes from reasonably flat country in the south to very rugged, mountainous country to the north. Since most of the carrier air groups were focused on targets up north, they were facing the most dangerous terrain on the peninsula. This put the main roads and rail systems down in the

All of the attack aircraft on the carriers were very accurate in delivering the 5-inch HVARs against ground targets. These rockets are being loaded on an F4U-4 Corsair on the USS *Valley Forge*. Note that the aircraft already has been loaded with bombs. (*Frank Jones*)

The USS *Princeton*'s first cruise in the war was between 9 November 1950 and 29 May 1951. This photograph was taken during the early days of that operation. The 'B' tail code on this Skyraider indicates it was assigned to VA-195. (*National Archives*)

This image demonstrates how dangerous it was to be working on the deck of a carrier when it was getting ready to launch aircraft. VC-3's night fighter Corsairs have been loaded and have started engines while deck personnel move in close. They often launched right before last light in an effort to catch enemy truck traffic on the move. This picture was taken on the USS *Princeton* in 1952. (*Wayne Russell*)

The USS *Princeton* steams towards its station off the coast of North Korea with most of Air Group-19's aircraft stowed on the deck. The F4U-4s on the deck were assigned to VF-192 and VF-193. They also had one squadron of F9F-2s and an AD-4 squadron assigned during that cruise. The gun crews are at their station even though there was very little risk of an air attack. (*Wayne Russell*)

The *Essex* had one full squadron of Corsairs (F4U-4Bs) in its air group during its first cruise in 1951/2. This F4U Corsair from Navy squadron VF-53 shown here, shared the decks with one squadron each of Skyraiders, Banshees and Panthers and all were part of Air Group-5. (*Frank Jones*)

The USS *Antietam* (CV 36) carried out one combat cruise during the Korean War (8 September 1951 to 2 May 1952) with Air Group-15 on board. All of their full squadron attack aircraft carried the 'H' on the vertical stabilizer. This AD-4 was assigned to VA-728, which operated off the *Antietam*. (*National Archives*)

The Skyraider on the right was a specialized All Weather night attack AD-4W assigned to Detachment 'G' of VC-11 on the USS *Bon Homme Richard* on the carrier's first combat cruise in 1951. The F4U-4 Corsair on the left was assigned to either VF-783 or VF-874. (*Bill Barron*)

The USS *Princeton* takes time out from it station off the coast of North Korea to take on supplies at a Japanese Naval base. The AD-4s on deck belong to VA-195, which was part of Air Group-19. This picture was taken in 1952 about midway through the *Princeton*'s third combat cruise in the war. (*Bill Crouse*)

The USS *Essex* (CV 9) is shown here taking on supplies and giving their personnel some shore leave while at the Japanese naval base at Yokosuka. The F2H-2 Banshees on the deck were with VF-172, which was the first Banshee squadron to see action in the Korean War during the carrier's first cruise in 1951. They were part of Air Group-5. (*Frank Jones*)

This VF-52 Panther received battle damage on a mission and its pilot was able to make it back to the Boxer safely. It is being pushed toward the elevator to be taken to the lower deck for maintenance and repairs. This was on the final combat cruise of the *Boxer* in 1953 when Air Group-1 was on board, which included three F9F squadrons (VF-52, VF-111 and VF-151). (*Jerry Stipanov*)

A close-knit group of F9F Panther pilots pose for a picture on the deck of the USS *Boxer* (CV 21) during the carrier's second combat cruise in the early fall of 1951. At this time, VF-721 was flying the F9F-2B. (*Norb Melsek*)

The USS *Valley Forge* moves into Yokosuka navy yard past the submarine net seen in the background. This picture was taken during the carrier's final cruise of the war in spring of 1953. The aircraft were assigned to Air Group-5, which had two squadrons of F9F-5 Panthers, one F4U-4 squadron and VF-54 flying the AD-4 Skyraiders. (*Bill Kelly*)

Once the Chinese got into the war, they brought a large number of higher calibre anti-aircraft weapons that the North Koreans did not have. This put more pressure on the F4U Corsairs and F-51 Mustangs when performing the low-altitude strafing attacks. This Navy Corsair suffered heavy damage and tried to make it to a friendly land base sometime in 1951 and didn't make it. (*Hayward Anderson*)

On the first strike that the *Valley Forge*'s air group carried out (3 July 1950), two of the F9F pilots from VF-51 scored kills over Russian-built Yakovlev prop fighters flown by North Korean pilots. This Yakovlev was caught on the ground at Kimpo AB during the Pusan break out. (*Al Wimer*)

Air Group-102's aircraft and personnel get ready for another long day of combat missions during the USS *Bon Homme Richard*'s (CV 31) first cruise in 1951. Its attack squadrons were identified with the 'D' on the vertical stabilizer. The Corsairs seen on the deck were assigned to VF-783 and VF-874. (*Bill Barron*)

When the Korean War started, the NKPAF had at least two fighter aviation regiments of Yak-9s. Each regiment carried an inventory of about forty-four aircraft. This Yakovlev was caught on the ground at a base in South Korea during the Pusan Perimeter battles. The F9Fs from VF-51 tangled with this type on 3 July 1950 when the *Valley Forge*'s air group attacked the big airfield at Pyongyang. (*Ernest Fahlberg*)

Although the TBM Avenger was obsolete at the end of World War II, it still had some purpose left as was proven in Korea. Both the Navy and Marines used them to shuttle supplies, key personnel, mail and battle plans. This picture was taken at Pohang AB (K-3) late in the war. (*Art Beasley*)

Corsairs from the USS *Essex* warm up during the carrier's second deployment to Korea. They were all assigned to VF-871, which was the only F4U squadron on board with the exception of the night fighter detachment (VC-3) that was flying the F4U-5N. (*Tailhook Association*)

During the final six months of 1951, the USS *Essex* (CV 9) was one of the major players in carrier operations against the Chinese logistics efforts with their interdiction missions. This F9F-2 Panther was assigned to VF-51, which was part of Air Group-5 during this period. The Panther squadron and both the Corsair and Skyraider squadrons carried the 'S' on the vertical stabilizer. (*Frank Jones*)

The USS *Bon Homme Richard*'s (CV 31) first combat cruise was between May and December 1951. Air Group-102 was its air arm with two squadrons of F4U-4s (VF-783 and VF-874) on board. The main strike force aircraft used the 'D' on the vertical stabilizer. This scene was at a naval base in Japan while the carrier was being replenished and the ship's personnel had some shore leave. (*Bill Barron*)

An element of F4U Corsairs returns from a mission right before they get into the landing pattern to trap back on the USS *Valley Forge*. This photograph was taken off the coast of North Korea in the spring of 1952. These fighters were from VF-653. (*Robert Balser*)

The USS *Boxer*'s final cruise of the Korean War was between late March 1953 and November 1953. The carrier was on station when the war ended. The carrier had one full squadron of AD-4s on board, which was assigned to VF-194. (*D.T. Ferrell*)

Deck hands move a VF-111 Panther forward after a heavy rain squall on the deck of the USS *Valley Forge*. During the carrier's 1951–2 cruise, ATG-1 had two full squadrons of Corsairs and two squadrons of F9F-2Bs on board with no Skyraider squadron except for the VC-11 and VC-35 detachments. (*Robert Balser*)

The AD-4s were heavily involved in the Korean War with at least one squadron on most of the carriers. When the war ended in late July 1953, there were four carriers on station off the coast and each had a squadron of ADs. This VF-194 Skyraider was assigned to the USS *Boxer* during that time. This formation is returning from a strike over enemy territory in June 1953. (*D.T. Ferrell*)

HMS *Triumph* was a key asset during those first few weeks of the war. It paired up with the USS *Valley Forge* in July 1950 to launch numerous air strikes against key targets in the Pyongyang area. In the pre-dawn hours of 3 July, the *Triumph* launched a dozen Royal Navy Fireflies against the Haeju Airfield. This Firefly is pictured at Suwon Airbase (K-13) in early 1951. (*James Dennison*)

On July 3, 1950, HMS *Triumph* sent nine Royal Navy Seafires, loaded with rockets, against multiple targets in North Korea, all of which were in and around Pyongyang. This Seafire was parked at a base in Japan in the summer of 1950. The Seafire had a top speed of 360 mph and was very effective in the close air support and ground attack roles. The HMS *Triumph* finished its combat stint after flying 360 sorties. (*Robert Dewald*)

There were numerous occasions where Navy aircraft received extensive battle damage but still made an effort to make it back to the carrier. This F4U from VF-871 ran into trouble once it touched down on the deck and flipped over. (*Wes Ralston*)

During a carrier's long deployment duty in the war, it was often taken off the line and pulled back to Japan for a brief R&R for the ship's personnel and to take on supplies and undergo repairs. Here, the USS *Philippine Sea* (CVA 47) is preparing to get back into action off the coast of North Korea sometime in the spring of 1953. The Corsairs in the background were assigned to VF-94. (*Bill Barron*)

One of VF-53's Corsairs recovers on the deck of the USS *Essex* after a combat mission. This photograph was taken in February 1952 towards the latter part of the carrier's first deployment. It was the only F4U squadron on board with the exception of the VC-3 detachment that was flying the F4U-5NL night fighter. (*Don Frasor*)

Strike aircraft on the USS *Bon Homme Richard*'s first Korean cruise used the 'D' on the vertical stabilizer. There were two F4U-4 squadrons in the air group (VF-783 and VF-874). The F9F Panther in the background was assigned to VF-781. (*Jettie Hill*)

One of the pilots from VF-154 on the USS *Princeton* is suited out and ready to fly a mission. The squadron was flying the F9F-5 Panther and was assigned to Air Group-15 in the spring of 1953. At this point, the war was rapidly winding down. (*Tom Randall*)

The USS *Princeton*'s final cruise took place from late January 1953 until 21 September 1953. It was one of the carriers on station when the ceasefire took effect on 27 July. It had two squadrons of Panthers and one each on the F4U-4 and AD-4. All of its strike squadrons used the 'H' on the vertical stabilizer. Its photo detachment flew the F9F-5P. (*Tom Randall*)

lower valleys, which placed the anti-aircraft gun emplacements along the ridges at a distinct advantage against any aircraft going down low to strafe and bomb. The life blood of the communist forces depended on the supplies flowing smoothly through this system. Without the special maps, it would have been almost impossible to pinpoint these targets without the help of the slow-moving airborne forward air controllers and they did not fly that deep into enemy territory.

The terrain maps of North Korea carried in the cockpit had an overlaid grid printed on them, so that any point on the ground could be defined by a two-letter designation for the grid rectangle plus a six-digit number that indicated the location within the designated rectangle. Using the phonetic alphabet then current in the Navy, the rectangle designated 'Baker-Uncle (BU)' was far to the north in the centre of the Korean peninsula. A target in an area such as this always caused some apprehension among pilots because the flight to and from the target would be long and over land where rescue by helicopter would be very difficult or impossible if they were shot down. The HO3S helicopter, then in use by the Navy, was relatively short ranged and could not hover at high altitudes.

Lt (jg) Spangenberg continues:

Late in November 1951, a strike was laid on in 'BU' against both a major railroad bridge and highway bridge which crossed a river valley between fairly high mountains both east and west. The bridges were defended by significant anti-aircraft artillery installations on high ground on both sides of the valley. Four of our ADs from VA-923 and four F4Us from VF-783 were assigned to do the strike. This area in North Korea was beyond the range of our F9Fs, which otherwise would have been used for flak suppression. In order to have a greater chance of success in a bridge mission, the aircraft would dive along the length of the bridge so that bombs dropped a little long or short would still, hopefully, hit the bridge. The communist gunners knew this, of course, and so had arranged their gun batteries accordingly. The strike was well carried out, with the fighters diving first on the flak batteries, followed by the ADs with their big bombs on the bridges. No casualties were suffered by the attacking aircraft and they all joined up for the long flight back to the carrier.

After some minutes of cruising along in loose formation, the flight was attacked from astern by two MiG-15s. They had been spotted moments earlier by one of the Corsair pilots and he radioed a warning immediately. Perhaps half of the flight had not heard the warning, however, because of the peculiar antenna patterns of the then brand-new ARC-27 UHF radio equipment in their planes. The flight scattered like buckshot with only a fraction of the pilots having any idea what was going on. The MiGs made one firing pass, hitting one of the Skyraiders and then they exited the area. I presume that they were at their extreme range from base and their fuel was running close. The flight regrouped around the stricken AD, which was trailing smoke as we headed for Wonsan Bay, where a helicopter was based on Yo-Do Island and could safely retrieve a downed pilot.

The condition of the Skyraider that had been hit was serious enough and it continued to lose altitude. However, the experienced pilot made it over the bay and baled out, only to land in some very choppy waters stirred up by high winds. The flight leader of the ADs organized a ResCap over the downed pilot while calls were made to the rescue people at Yo-Do. He also radioed for some relief as all of the aircraft in the ResCap force were low on fuel after that deep strike and they had to have enough fuel to get back to the carrier. The *Bon Homme Richard* was much closer than the nearest land bases in South Korea, so they only had one option. In a very short while, the relief flight arrived and the remainder of the original strike force departed for the carrier. The *Bon Homme Richard* had been monitoring the radio chatter during the MiG attack and had immediately, using radio silence for everything except the low frequency YE coded beacon, changed course and moved closer to the returning force, thus cutting the distance they would have to fly. The YE coded beacon operated at a very low frequency, allowing the carrier to monitor the path of the friendly aircraft without giving away their position. This allowed the carrier to move closer to the returning force, which cut down the risk of any running low on fuel.

All of this had caused some fuel and navigation anxiety in the returning aircraft, but they found the carrier headed eastward at full steam. They made a quick circle as the *Bon Homme Richard* turned into the wind and all recovered safely with fifty knots of wind across the deck. The downed pilot was rescued and returned to the carrier in good shape.

These four Skyraider pilots posed for a picture just minutes before they launched from the USS *Essex* (CV 9) for another mission over North Korea. Left to right are: Lt (jg) E.A. McCallum, Lt Harry Zenner, Ensign Don Frazor and Lt W.L. Burgess. They were flying the Skyraiders with VF-54 in September 1951. (*Bill Burgess*)

During the period from October to November 1951, there were eleven Navy Skyraiders (all models combined) lost in theatre. Most of these were the bomber versions that suffered extensive battle damage on missions. On 26 October, the USS *Essex* launched its VF-54 Skyraiders against several selected targets along the east coast of North Korea. The squadron had been on a streak of good hunting against the rail lines and tunnels. On some of these, they had skip-bombed 500-lb GP bombs into the tunnels, catching locomotives hiding there. The resulting explosions blew out both sides of the tunnel. Lt (jg) William Burgess was one of the pilots that were flying that day and he had already destroyed several targets before his luck ran out. He recalls that day:

We were going after rail cuts and any boxcars or locomotives we could find. The day before, I had scored a direct hit on a bridge bypass, which put it out of business. All of our rail cuts on this day had been between Chungjang-ni and Hamhung.

As we approached Hamhung, I spotted an intact bridge and realized I had a chance to add another one to my total and as I glanced at my chart, I saw that it was one that was defended by radar-controlled Triple-A [Anti-Aircraft Artillery]. My request to go down and hit it got immediate approval. My wingman, Ensign Don Frazor, stayed close to me as we moved up to 10,000 feet and started the long dive toward the bridge. I was set up to bomb the bridge from north to south with the sun in the west. Not long into my dive, I saw what I thought was sunlight reflecting off the water, but it wasn't. Just as I placed my gun sight on the bridge, I heard a loud thump and my aircraft flipped over instantly. It took a couple of seconds for me to realize what had happened and I fought to get it right side up. Smoke began to fill the cockpit so I opened the canopy and headed straight for the coast.

As Burgess got clear of the target area, the smoke was getting heavier coming from under the instrument panel, but there was no heat or fire, so he continued on toward the sea with no intent to bale out until he was over safe territory. What had happened was that two 88-mm explosive rounds had hit his Skyraider. One round had exploded on the bottom of the engine and the other had blown a gaping hole through the wing root beside the cockpit. Minutes later, Burgess looked at his oil pressure gauge and it was steadily dropping. If he was going to make the coast, he would have to increase power. On top of this, he had a 1,000-pound GP bomb still on one of the racks and when he tried to release it, nothing happened. The explosion had severed the manual release cable, and with this added weight his stall speed would be messed up when he tried to ditch in Hungnam Harbour. His only option was to set up the normal switching configuration: left inboard, nose/tail (fusing), master arm on and hit the 'pickle' button. To his relief, the bomb dropped off, which increased his chances for a safe ditching. If the bomb had stayed on, with the additional weight and drag, the aircraft would have started to cartwheel when it touched the water and the only way to walk away from that was with a lot of luck. With the coast in sight, the *Essex* was still another 100 miles out to sea, so trying to make it there was out of the question.

Burgess continues:

Just as I radioed Ensign Frazor that my oil pressure gauge was reading zero, his engine quit. Fortunately for me, my props stopped with the upper two blades being in the 10 and 2 o'clock position, which gave me good forward vision. One of the other pilots in my division had already alerted the ships in the vicinity what my situation was and the rescue regimen was already in motion. The destroyer USS *Conway* was close by and they were in position to respond almost immediately. However, the biggest problem was that North Korean shore batteries were strung out along the cliffs that surround Hungnam Harbour. As the destroyer came into the harbour, they opened up on it and my position would be well within their range. Fortunately, there was a division of VF-53 Corsairs led by a good friend, Lt Ed Laney, close by and they came in and worked over the gun positions with their 20-mm guns. This took a lot of pressure off the ship that was coming in to help me when I ditched.

My Skyraider was losing altitude quickly, so I went through the checklist over the radio: armament switches off, parachute harness unfastened, survival vest unbuttoned, shoulder harness locked, mags off, canopy open and locked, flaps down full, tail hook down. I was facing a strong tail wind, which meant that I would have to ditch at a much higher ground speed, which posed more of a problem. But on the bright side, if I hadn't had the wind at my back, I would never have made it to the coast! The water was coming up fast and when I felt the tail hook dragging the water, I pulled hard on the stick to make a final flare to slow the plane down. Suddenly, there was a huge spray of water and I was thrust hard against the straps, going from 145 knots to zero in about three seconds.

The Skyraider settled quickly and the water was up to the windscreen as Burgess struggled to get out of the cockpit. Once free, he started swimming as hard as he could still wearing all of his gear and shoes. He had heard that when an aircraft sinks, it could suck the pilot down with it, so he had to distance himself. Exhausted from the frantic swimming, he looked back to see if he had gone far enough, but with all the weight on him, he had only swam about eight feet. The plane slipped under and he did not feel anything that could have taken him down. He had a lot of trouble getting his Mae West inflated, along with his raft. The choppy waters combined with the water temperature of 56 degrees did not help. It was mandatory to wear an exposure suit when the water temp was 55 degrees, but on this mission, he did not wear one. Burgess's fingers were numb and he was having a lot of trouble getting the dye-marker packet open. He recalls:

Thanks to the effective strafing runs by VF-53 Corsairs and Ensign Frazor circling overhead to guide the destroyer in, I had a fighting chance. The skipper of the destroyer decided to make one more run at me as the shore batteries had quieted down. He came in at eleven knots and passed within three feet of me. They tossed a knotted rope over the side and I was able to grab it and they hoisted me up on the deck. I was lucky because so many Navy pilots drowned in their chutes or froze during the cold winter months before help arrived.

There were numerous US aircraft that were brought down by cables stretched across some of the narrow valleys. The first of these occurred in the early fall of 1950 when an Air Force F-82 Twin Mustang ran into one while looking for targets down in a valley north of the 38th Parallel. The wreckage and bodies were discovered when the UN forces pushed north after the Pusan breakout. The Navy and Marines were no exceptions, but on many of these incidents the damage did not bring the plane down and the pilots used their flying skills to bring their aircraft safely back to home base.

3 September 1951 was a very busy day for Air Group-5 as they were hitting a number of targets over enemy territory. The Operations Officer for VF-54 (equipped with AD-4s), Lieutenant Frank Sistrunk, was hit by anti-aircraft fire while bombing a bridge. As he pulled out of his bombing run, his Skyraider was smoking and he headed straight for the east coast and safety, which was thirty miles away. Halfway to the beach, his aircraft was seen to take a nose dive from an altitude of 2,000 feet. His wingman indicated that the plane went into the ground and exploded, and there was no indication that Sistrunk tried to bale out. He was listed as KIA (killed in action). It was not known if he had been hit by ground fire or if a cable had done the damage. Ensign Neil Armstrong was an F9F-2 pilot with VF-51, which was also on the *Essex* during its first combat cruise. He had a very close call on that same day. He was flying in the vicinity where VF-54 was flying and while on a low-level attack in some mountainous terrain, he ran into serious trouble with a cable that was strung out over the valley he was in. He recalls the mission:

I was flying as wingman for Major John Carpenter when I struck a cable on a rocket run and I don't recall what the target was. It sliced off six to eight feet of my right wing tip! We immediately headed south across the bomb line toward Pohang airbase (K-3). Major Carpenter and I discussed the situation and concluded that the minimum speed at which my aircraft would be controllable would be unpredictable. I could have tested it at altitude, but more than likely would lose control and be forced to eject. If the aircraft went out of control while in the landing pattern, ejection would likely be fatal.

On the other hand, if I kept the aircraft at a high and controllable speed on final approach, it would likely not be stoppable on the short K-3 runway, which if I remember correctly was at about 5,000 feet. We concluded that the best option was to eject at altitude in a controlled situation and land in the water near K-3. That is what I did. The ejection was performed in straight and level flight at about 15,000 feet. The ejection seat was of the old 22–24 g 'shotgun shell' powered variety. An onshore wind carried me inland where I landed in a rice paddy. That ended being lucky for me because I later learned the bay there at Pohang was filled with mines! I was quickly returned to the *Essex* on one of the COD [Carrier Onboard Delivery] aircraft. I only suffered a slight injury to my lower back, which happened as I ejected. I returned to flight status a week later.

The next day (4 September) VF-51 was out again in force. This time, fate dealt another heavy blow when two of its pilots were listed as KIA. Lt (jg) R.K. Bramwell was hit by flak and never had a chance to pull out of his dive. On that same mission, Lt (jg) J.J. Ashford went down for a rocket attack. He was hit and went straight into the ground in a violent explosion. This triggered the belief that all of the gun emplacements in that area were automatically or electronically controlled. Both pilots were listed as KIA. Up until this date, the air group had destroyed seven bridges, ninety rail cars, twenty-five trucks, numerous ox carts and over two hundred enemy troops. All of these at a cost of five pilots killed, one aircrewman killed and ten aircraft lost. The more sophisticated and higher calibre anti-aircraft emplacements being brought in by the Chinese were starting to extract a heavy toll.

The following day, the USS *Boxer* relieved the USS *Bon Homme Richard* and both the *Boxer* and *Essex* continued to pound the enemy behind the front lines. Records show that Air Group-5 sent out the entire force on 6 September to concentrate on bridges. On that day, they logged thirty-three sorties against them and recorded four direct hits and nine near misses. Intelligence gained from the past three days indicated that the Chinese were moving large numbers of troops towards the bomb line. On both the 5th and 6th, pilots reported at least 2,500 enemy troops were sighted and attacked, but enemy manpower was so overwhelming that this hardly put a dent in their southerly movement.

There were many events that happened in the war that involved naval aircraft. But if you had to narrow it down to just two major operations, the efforts of carrier aircraft during the Chosin Reservoir Campaign would rank as one and the other would probably be the attacks on a series of bridges that were enhanced and immortalized in the eyes of the general public because of the movie *The Bridges at Toko-ri*. The latter was one of the most well-planned operations of the war and it was centred around Air Group-5 on the USS *Essex*. While the movie did give it a 'Hollywood make-over', the facts still speak for themselves. Well-known author James Michener was on board the *Essex* for six weeks and this was during the time of the strikes in which he was allowed to sit in on the planning and crew briefings.

Actually, this operation included a series of bridge complexes that were located in the narrow neck of the Korean peninsula. These were critical in the movement of supplies and equipment down into the front lines. They were located above a line from Wonsan over to Pyongyang, far north of the 38th Parallel. The Navy was given the job of knocking out the bridges that were as heavily defended as any target in North Korea. Using B-29s to do the work was not an option because you had to get down low to ensure accuracy. The communists used forced labour from nearby villages to quickly repair road and rail damage from bomb strikes. In most cases, the repairs were done in a matter of hours because thousands of civilians were available, but this pertained mostly to areas that were easily accessible. The bridges in the 'Toko-ri' complex were in mountainous areas where quick repairs would have been out of the question due to the terrain. So, taking out these bridges would have a lasting negative effect on Chinese troops at the front. Previously, all efforts to take these targets out had proved to be futile.

In late 1951, the Navy began looking at the idea of using all three main aircraft types (F4U, AD and F9F) against the same targets in a coordinated attack at the same time. In the past, they would send a couple of divisions of the same type to do the job, but with little success. The mission planners were desperate to cut down on the losses in these attacks and to destroy the bridges. This strategy fell squarely on the shoulders of the squadron commanders on the *Essex* and their operations personnel. Initially, it would be Air Group-5 carrying out the attacks. Author James Michener was allowed to sit in on the planning of these coordinated, integrated strikes against all these bridges that were located in relative close proximity. The American public would come to know these as the 'Bridges at Toko-ri'. In the case of the *Essex*, there would be four aircraft types hitting these targets because one of the Panther squadrons had been bumped off at the last minute and the first squadron of F2H-2 Banshees to fly combat replaced them (VF-172). The toughest part of the planning was to make sure that all of the strike aircraft arrived over the target at the same time and this was crucial.

This was a unique situation because of the timing. The first strikes carried out by the USS *Valley Forge* against the airfields in and around Pyongyang in early July 1950 proved that it was going to be difficult to get the timing right because, on that strike, the F9Fs launched last and still got to the target way ahead of the main prop force. One of the Panther pilots that flew on the first of these bridge attacks was Lt (jg) K.C. Kramer who flew Panthers in VF-51. He comments on what he witnessed on these missions:

> Up to this point, this had never been done because jets operated under a totally different schedule. We didn't have aerial refuelling in those days, so a jet mission might last only about one and a half hours. On the other hand, the prop aircraft could remain airborne for over four hours, so this new type of mission required an enormous amount of detailed planning. All of our four squadrons had to arrive over the target at the same time. The big Skyraiders were the key because of the big bombs they could carry. Because they were the slowest of the attacking aircraft, they would launch first. Next would be the F4Us followed by the F9Fs and, finally, the F2H-2s. The Panthers were armed with fragmentation bombs and would be the ones to protect the attack force from the anti-aircraft batteries located all around the bridges. The timing had to be perfect because the gun emplacements had to be attacked just seconds before the bombers came into range.

The Panthers were slightly underpowered so they were limited on the size and quantity of bombs they could carry. Getting them off the deck was a problem because the *Essex*'s hydraulic catapults wouldn't let them have the heavy loads. So, the F9Fs usually carried four 250-lb GP bombs or four 260-lb frags. The latter of these was the weapon of choice for taking out manned guns during these integrated attacks.

Kramer continues:

> Before we launched the first strike, all of the pilots involved would gather for a detailed briefing that included up-to-date photographs of the bridges they were to bomb. All of the gun positions were clearly marked and each F9F pilot was assigned specific gun positions, which we identified by key landmarks that were memorized, and these marked photos were taken by us in the cockpit. When we got over the target and located our targets, we peeled off and went after them. The F4Us were also assigned this task and they followed closely behind us. There wasn't a single gun emplacement that didn't have an aircraft assigned to it.

Thanks to the fragmentation bombs, some of the guns that were bunched in close to one another were taken out or disabled with one bomb. Lt (jg) Kramer continues:

> Once we got over the bridges, the flak was extremely heavy! The enemy knew what we had in mind and they threw everything they had at us. If I remember correctly, there were at least 20 bridges in this extensive complex. Also, there was never any doubt that the big AD Skyraiders were the only aircraft the Navy had that could drop those bridges. They came in so low and slow before dropping their bomb loads that they were sitting ducks. With our new tactics, a lot of them were saved to fight another day because we did so much damage to the anti-aircraft batteries.

The squadron commander for VF-51 was Commander Ernie Beauchamp and he was the leader of the initial attack by the Panthers. His comments add to the picture:

> After about six weeks of integrated efforts against those same bridges, the air strikes went back to the old ways. In other words, the anti-aircraft threat was never brought up to the previous level they had been before the first strike and they were no longer considered a serious problem. The ADs and F4Us could get in and destroy any repairs that had attempted without sustaining heavy losses to them. The new coordinated tactics had worked the way they were designed to.

By early 1951, the concentrated attacks on the north-eastern communist rail system had begun to have devastating results. Every carrier that was working off the north-east coast (Sea of Japan) was part of this effort. The USS *Princeton* and USS *Essex* were key players in this action between January and June. The bridges in the 'Toko-ri' complex had been crippled to the point where they were not a key factor, but they had to be monitored every few days to see the extent of any repair efforts. On the morning of 2 March 1951, the CO of VF-193 (F4U-4s) operating from the USS *Princeton*, Lieutenant Commander Clement M. Craig, stumbled upon a major bridge that was untouched. His squadron had been bombing the Kilchu bridges when this target was discovered. Craig commented that:

> …we had been bombing other bridges along the rail route and were heading back to the south when we saw it. It was very long and high and a conservative estimate put it at 600 feet long with a maximum height of 60 feet. Five concrete piers supported six steel spans across the canyon. Adjacent to this operable bridge were an additional five piers of a companion, but incomplete bridge.
>   We also noticed that this bridge had tunnels at each end of the bridge. Actually there were two tunnels, which would eventually allow through traffic in both directions. This bridge was south of the Kilchu bridges, at which point three rail lines from Manchuria joined.

This immediately took top priority because if it could be taken down and kept down, the flow of southbound rail traffic over the eastern network from China would be seriously slowed down. It was also in a position where it would be extremely difficult to repair or bypass. Upon arrival back on the carrier, the mission planners set up a major strike against the bridge that afternoon. That attack produced only minor damage. The next morning, Air Group-19 unleashed an attack with eight AD-4s from VA-195 carrying the big bombs and the bridge was destroyed. The ADs were led by squadron commander Lt Commander Harold 'Swede' Carlson. From that time on, that area was referred to as 'Carlson's Canyon'.

Naval photo planes from the VC-61 detachments were essential in determining where the strike priorities should be placed. It didn't take long to realize what they were up against because it was apparent that the eastern network of rails and roads were the dominant factors in moving supplies north and south. This would be the focal point for the carrier's strike force for some time to come. It included 1,140 miles of track, 956 bridges and causeways and 231 tunnels. Due to the mountainous terrain, this translated into one bridge every 1.2 miles of track and one tunnel for every 5 miles of track. These tunnels were estimated to house about 1,200 feet of track, so the trains were relatively short in order to be able to hide inside these tunnels during the day. This network of rails, when working at capacity, could move 5,000 tons of supplies per day. Once the air groups started their campaign, this total was knocked down to less than 500 tons per day. Navy air power did its job and had just about eliminated the chances of a sustained major Chinese offensive.

Train activity, during the day, all but disappeared early on in the war and this was due to air power from all branches of the military. At night, the carriers only had a token force to stop nocturnal movements in their small detachments of F4U-5Ns, and specialized night-flying Skyraiders. The USAF was the dominant night attack weapon as it had large numbers of Douglas B-26 Invaders that divided North Korea into small segments and was able to keep at least one aircraft up in those sectors all night with one relieving the other. The Marines had one squadron of F7F-3N Tigercats and one squadron of F4U-5Ns that divided up whatever was left for their night missions. Even though the Chinese were able to move a certain amount of supplies by rail, regardless of what damage was done to their rail system, the network of roads also gave them a way to move supplies with their endless number of trucks. Intelligence estimated that there were at least 2,000 miles of roads in each half of North Korea with the busiest being inland from each coastline. The rail lines and bridges were a top priority for naval aircraft for the entire year 1951 and well in to 1952. It was this daytime interdiction effort from all the air groups on station that kept the Chinese from mounting a significant offensive.

The USS *Bon Homme Richard* was involved in two combat cruises in the war and the first one put them in action in the early summer of 1951 with Air Group-102 on board. They had two full squadrons of F4U-4s (VF-783 and VF-874). The *Bon Homme Richard* participated in the heavy interdiction campaign carried on by the carrier force between 1 May and 31 December 1951. This time frame included a total of seven carriers and air groups. The final stats show how costly it was due to the ever-increasing number of Russian-built anti-aircraft weapons being brought in by the Chinese. Seventy-four Navy aircraft were lost during this period and the *Bon Homme Richard* had the heaviest losses at twenty aircraft.

The success of any Navy air campaign depended on the service personnel and how high they could keep the in-service rate. Korea was no exception. Aviation Electronicsman 2nd Class Leon Bryant served with one of the Corsair squadrons on the *Bon Homme Richard* (VF-874). He remembers how dangerous it was to work on the deck during operations and what was involved in keeping the F4Us ready to fly the missions:

> I helped the pilots before take off with their radio problems and interviewed them when they returned from missions to see if they had encountered any problems when they were up. I was on the flight deck during most operations (day or night) and I witnessed most of the accidents that occurred there. A good percentage of my deck time was spent in the cockpit of our squadron's Corsairs doing checks and repairs.
>
> I also rode the brakes when they were moving aircraft around on the deck, which was very scary. When 're-spotting the deck' the technique was to hook a tow bar to the aircraft, tow it behind a tractor 'Mule' to get it rolling fast enough to travel on its own and then steer it with the brakes. If any of the maintenance crews were working in the cockpit at the time, they were expected to steer it when the tractor driver released the tow bar. Sometimes, they wanted the aircraft parked in one of the corners with its tail wheel within a few feet of the end of the flight deck. You would roll rapidly toward the fantail and at the appointed place hit one of the brake pedals and hopefully turn the Corsair through 180 degrees. The secret was not to panic and drive the aircraft off the edge of the fantail.

The forward visibility of the F4U was extremely poor because it sat at a sharp angle on its tail wheel and it was even worse when you didn't have a parachute to sit on. When one of the deck hands was in the cockpit during the moving process, it was necessary to rely on hand signals from someone that was standing nearby on the deck. At night, re-spotting the aircraft was far more dangerous because hand signals were replaced by a waving torch light.

Bryant recalls:

> The flight deck was made of steel, covered with about 1.5 inches of Douglas fir planking. After several months of continuous operations, the wooden deck became saturated with oil drippings from all those R-2800 engines, making it very slippery. Moving around on the deck with all of those engines running was extremely hazardous. We were told that if we fell, we were to lay spread eagle and not attempt to get up. An F4U could taxi over you if you were flattened out on the deck, but that 14 foot four-bladed prop could get you if you stuck your head or butt up too much. The F9F's also posed a danger as you could easy catch a blast from their jet engines as they taxied toward the catapult.
>
> The slippery deck meant that we lost a lot of tail cones chewed off by the pilot in the Corsair behind. Even with the brakes full on, the tyres would creep forward a few inches while sliding on the slick deck. This was exceptionally bad after a rain. The wooden deck would also shed splinters! The prop blast would blow slivers into your skin like you wouldn't believe. We wore helmets and goggles to protect our faces and eyes. Slamming a Corsair cockpit canopy shut was also dangerous and more than one crewman lost a finger. But, the

thing topside personnel feared most was an arresting cable parting. Sometimes they had to change some of the cables every couple of days if operations were constant. There were thirteen cross-deck pennants, as they were called, and if the pilot was lucky, he caught one of the first three or four cables. But, those aft cables took a brutal beating and if one of them broke under tension, watch out! Fortunately, I never saw that happen.

The USS *Boxer* (CV 21) was a major player in these efforts, especially on its second cruise because the dates coincided perfectly with the new orders. They were on station from March to October 1951. They had two F4U Naval Reserve squadrons on that cruise; VF-791 was a reserve unit that was based out of NAS Memphis, Tennessee, and VF-884, a reserve unit out of NAS Olathe, Kansas. Recalled to active duty out of civilian life, they proved to be extremely efficient and aggressive when it came to using the F4U-4 in combat.

VF-791's trademark insignia was the Confederate Flag and almost all of the pilot's helmets had the Rebel Flag painted on it. They were strictly focused on the tasks at hand and their statistics speak for themselves. Squadron records published at the end of their combat tour show that they flew a total of 1,250 effective sorties, equating to 3,600 hours of flying time. The list of target types was too numerous to list, but among some of the most noticeable was the total of destroyed targets: 175 bridges, 140 trucks, 20 supply dumps, 125 rail cars and over 500 miscellaneous buildings. As with every other Navy squadron that flew combat in Korea, it was impossible to get an accurate figure for the number of enemy troops that were killed or wounded. In seven months of action, VF-791 dropped over 750,000 pounds of bombs and rockets. Each of the squadron's pilots averaged about 60 sorties and their in-service rate was exceptionally high due to the long hours the maintenance and ordnance personnel put in.

Among the many assignments that both VF-791 and VF-884 performed was one that got very little publicity but was crucial for the naval gunships cruising right off the coast line of North Korea. It was known as a Naval Gun Fire (NGF) mission. The heavy cruisers and battleships had a lot of range for their big guns and the Corsairs would stay low over enemy territory in search of possible targets for them. Once something was spotted, the coordinates would be relayed to the ship(s) and they would start firing with the Corsairs giving out corrections on each volley. It was on one of these earlier spotter missions that VF-791 lost its first F4U of the cruise (April). It happened over the Wonsan area when one of the pilots was attempting a message drop over the cruiser USS *Saint Paul* (CA-73) that was working in Wonsan Bay. The pilot received a broken shoulder but was promptly rescued by an escorting destroyer. That afternoon, another of the squadron's Corsairs was returning from a spotter mission when his hook caught the cable and broke. It ended up halfway over the port side on the No. 2 elevator.

Fortunately for the pilot, his fighter was secured before it tipped over and he was unhurt. However, the troubles of VF-791 were not over yet on this type of mission because the next afternoon another of the squadron's pilots was up over Wonsan when a large calibre anti-aircraft round blew a hole the size of a basketball in his port wing. The flaps were almost knocked off and his hydraulic system was compromised. The pilot received permission to return to the carrier and when he arrived a large crowd was on Vulture's Row waiting to see a wheels-up landing. On his final approach, the pilot blew the gear down and was able to catch the wire, and the aircraft came safely to a halt. (The aircraft were equipped with compressed air bottles so when they had hydraulic problems, the pilot could use them to 'blow' the landing gear down.)

The Navy had some *Iowa*-class battleships in theatre. Probably the most famous of these was the USS *Missouri* (BB-63). One of the VF-791 pilots that had the honour of working as a spotter for it was Lt John White. The ship was armed with nine huge 16-inch guns that had a very long reach. Lt White recalls one of those missions in July 1951:

> At this time, the USS *Missouri* was working right off the coast around Wonsan Harbour. I had been assigned to work with the 'Big Mo' [one of several nicknames for the USS *Missouri*] and do some gunfire spotting for it. I remember there were several large warehouse type buildings scattered around the city of Wonsan that had managed to escape prior damage or at least it appeared that way from up on my perch a few thousand feet above the harbour.
>
> I had a grid in my possession with the city marked off neatly in squares, each having a number like C-4, B-1, D-5 etc. I easily made contact with the fire control on the *Missouri* and reported to them that I was over the city and harbour and was ready when they were. Using my grid, I easily located a large warehouse-looking building, matched it to the grid number and relayed this information to the *Missouri* and told them to fire away! In about one minute, after a huge explosion, the building completely disappeared. Their aim was right on and we continued this for the most part of an hour. The landscape looked much different after that session with the big rifles! What impressed me the most was how accurate they were and what enormous damage a gun of that size could do to a target!

The strategy laid out by the Chinese was to use their overwhelming manpower to push the UN forces back further to the south and it was air power that held the key to preventing this. Once the initial push by the Chinese had come to a halt, they were pushed back to just about the same area where the war started. They knew they could build up large concentrations of troops but they could not use them to their advantage if they weren't allowed to build up the required supplies, food and munitions to sustain a major offensive. Intelligence was aware that the first big push would be coming in late April or May 1951. Naval air power increased their efforts against anything moving south towards the lines and the ADs were hitting the front-line positions with the 1,000-lb and 2,000-lb blockbuster bombs that could penetrate into the deep bunkers that the Chinese had built. For several months, the air group's mission priority had been shifted to interdiction and they were paying a heavy price because of the number of gun emplacements that were set up along the key roads and rails. The Chinese had unlimited resources for these and they knew that without the firepower they would never be able to sustain a major offensive.

For the USS *Boxer* and Air Group 101, the close air support mission resumed on 2 May due to the first big spring offensive by Chinese troops. The two Corsair squadrons were spread thin as they strafed front-line positions and still worked the roads that led to the forward positions. The Air Force fighter-bombers were also in the thick of it, so the front-line areas were crowded with air traffic during the day, but the real action started at last light. This developed into a test of stamina and determination on both sides. Thousands of trucks were on the roads from the Manchurian border south to the front lines and return. While the F4U-5N Corsair detachments on the carriers (VC-3) were able to get in some interdiction/harassment missions, they lacked the numbers necessary to counter the enemy's efforts. The Marine night fighters and USAF B-26 Invaders provided the muscle that made a difference with each aircraft working a specific sector. All of these specialized aircraft caused a lot of damage to rail and road movements and, at first light, naval aircraft were out in air group strength taking out any stragglers and finishing off anything that was damaged by the night operators.

The effective use of US air power put a big dent in the first phase of the spring offensive and it bogged down. However, it wasn't over because on 17 May Phase II began, which re-defined the phrase 'suicide attack'. Waves of Chinese rushed toward the front-line positions of UN troops. This time, it evolved into missions that were close and personal. In other words, napalm became the weapon of choice, with some of the drops just a grenade's thrown from UN forward positions. VF-791 put two divisions of Corsairs up with napalm as early as they could launch. The first division, consisting of pilots Bowen, Davis, Lamb and Crouch, went in first and their targets were the ridges above the front lines that were crawling with intricate trenches filled with enemy troops. For his book *Enter the Dragon*, Australian author Russell Spurr went to Hong Kong and Macao years after the war and interviewed former Chinese Army veterans of the Korean War. They said the most feared and effective weapon they faced was napalm, which probably caused the death of more troops than any other weapon.

Three days into the offensive, the UN forces were holding their own and air power had weakened the chances of the enemy making significant advances, but reinforcements were pouring in from the Pyongyang area. On the afternoon of 20 May, VF-791 sent out two divisions of their F4Us and caught a large number of Chinese troops on the move out of Hong Chou, which was close to the front lines. The 'Rebel' fighters were carrying a combination of bombs and napalm, which killed the main force, followed by the finishing touch: multiple strafing attacks with their guns. As the Chinese lost ground, American troops gained enough ground to overtake the area that VF-791 had just hit. They counted at least 2,000 enemy troops KIA. This strike went down as one of the squadron's most successful missions and it brought the efforts of the enemy in that immediate area to complete halt.

The Memphis reservists had a sister squadron on that cruise that finished with impressive statistics. VF-884's 'Bitter Birds' cut a wide path across the peninsula with their Corsairs. Just like the other reservist squadrons that were on the *Boxer*, most of the pilots were World War II veterans with young families and were either just settling into new jobs or were finishing college. This scenario was repeated numerous times with all branches of the military and it also included National Guard squadrons in the USAF. Most of these units lost pilots MIA (missing in action) and KIA during their tours and very few, if any, got back with no losses.

VF-884 finished their stint on the *Boxer* and posted a list of their accomplishments that included over 2,200 enemy troops killed (confirmed), 842 buildings destroyed and 174 bridges taken out of commission. They lost six pilots from the original cadre they had started the cruise with. By the third week of October 1951, the squadron had logged more than 1,500 sorties, which allowed them to drop more than 370 tons of bombs, 65,000 gallons of napalm and fire 3,563 rockets. Their Corsairs were equipped with six .50 calibre machine guns, which fired almost 1,400,000 rounds at enemy targets.

One of VF-884's pilots was Lt (jg) Norman Edge who relates some of his more memorable experiences while flying combat over North Korea:

> One time, I literally shot myself down. A lot of our ammo was left over from World War II and the tracers were tending to explode (one of our pilot's wings was damaged when the tracer exploded at the end of his gun barrel, still inside the wing, peeling some metal on the leading edge of his wing back). I was strafing a target and, out of the corner of my eye, I spotted an explosion just ahead of me on the right. Within a minute, I noticed oil flowing over one of my wing flaps. The Corsair had two oil coolers (one on each wing), so I cut off that cooler as I had no idea how much oil I had lost, but knew it would be foolish to stay up any longer than I had to. I told my flight leader my problem and we headed back toward the carrier which, at that time, was in the midst of preparing for the next launch and could not take me back on board, so I had to go to another carrier (the USS *Bon Homme Richard*) that was in our vicinity. The mechanics soon found the problem; a piece of copper shell casing (from the exploding tracer) had come back into my oil cooler with enough force to cut it and cause my oil leak. I had almost shot myself down!

Working down low enough to clearly see an enemy gun emplacement and its gunner firing at you was common place. Lt Edge relates a very good example of just such a mission:

> On one of my missions, my flight leader and I were looking for a good target because I still had my napalm. After several minutes down very low, we spotted an undamaged building standing all alone. There was a machine gun next to it shooting at us, so we figured it held something important. I peeled off and made my drop and felt I got a perfect hit, but nothing happened as was often the case. My flight leader had followed me in order to shoot tracer rounds into the spot in order to ignite it if necessary, but he never saw the impact, so he didn't fire. I went back around and fired a burst at where I thought it hit and sure enough, the target ignited. It was a perfect drop; about 20–30 feet in front of the building, but the building remained unaffected. The napalm bomb had hit at the base of a big stump and the napalm splashed on both sides leaving a clear 'V' in the centre, which is where the building stood unharmed!
>
> That machine gunner and I traded shots and I think I got him, but I know he got me in the leading edge of my right wing. The round exited back in the fabric of my wing. As you probably know, the North Koreans never fired tracer rounds so one of the hazards was that we never quite got used to the fact that we never knew we were being fired on from the ground, which often

Communist trains had plenty of places to hide in the numerous tunnels that formed an intricate network in the mountains of North Korea. However, the Navy air groups gave this priority on almost all of the interdiction missions. This rail bed and tunnel entrance had been bombed so many times that there was no effort by the Chinese logistics personnel to try and get it back in working order. (*John Leverton*)

lulled us into a false sense of security, which led us into taking unnecessary chances. For most of our low altitude attacks, we were being fired on.

Once the Chinese became involved in the war, the number of anti-aircraft guns increased many times over because of the pressure that air power put on them when they were trying to move supplies and equipment into the front-line positions.

One of the biggest problems that the F4U and AD squadron pilots had was the fact that their rail cuts were repaired within hours and they had to constantly repeat those strikes. As time went by, the number of guns protecting the rail junctions increased every week. The maintenance officer for the 'Bitter Birds' of VF-653 was Lieutenant William R. Clarke. He describes one of those rail cutter missions flown on 11 March 1952:

We were briefed for a routine rail strike a little south of the Hamhung/ Hungnam area followed by an armed reconnaissance of the highway/roads to the north of that. We flew relatively low and in loose formation so as to afford better visibility and area coverage. We were looking for anything that moved or looked important. The terrain was rugged and when the road forked, two of us took one fork and the other element took the other route. We increased our altitude to improve on radio communication between our two elements. As we approached a hydroelectric plant, one of the pilots in the other element radioed he was getting some anti-aircraft fire and then he stated he had been hit.

We were not allowed to attack any of these plants as it was a political issue but he must have gotten too close. Seconds later, I heard that he was baling out and his wingman said that he did bale and his chute was on fire. It did not have a chance to open and he plummeted into the side of a mountain. My wingman and I headed immediately for the crash site, which was over 5 miles away. When we got close enough to see the burning wreckage, we started drawing accurate fire from around the power plant. We could not locate the downed pilot and his wingman said there was no way that he could have survived the impact. It was a tragic incident as he was a very good friend. Needless to say, a short while later, we were allowed to hit the plant and we blasted it to the ground along with all the gun emplacements that surrounded it!

There were at least a dozen Carrier Air Groups that did combat cruises in the Korean War. Many of these had Naval Reserve Squadrons on board because it had become apparent during the first six months of the war that they were going to need far more pilots than they had anticipated. A classic example of this was Air Group-15, which would conduct its first combat cruise on the USS *Antietam* (1951–2) and then a second cruise on the USS *Princeton* (1953). For the first one, the Navy called up several Reserve units: VF-653 from Akron, Ohio, VF-713 and VF-831 from Denver, VF-837 from New York and VA-728 from Glenview, Illinois. By the time the second cruise started, most of these squadrons would be redesignated numerically. VF-653, flying the F4U Corsairs, would be moved to ATG-1 and serve on the USS *Valley Forge*.

Whenever a Navy pilot was shot down behind enemy lines, it was a mad dash by other pilots to get to the area and provide cover (Rescap) until a rescue helicopter could arrive. This had priority over everything and because of this a large number of pilots were saved from POW status. The AD Skyraiders were the 'kingpins' for this type of mission because of their long loiter time and heavy ordnance-carrying capabilities. Lt Raymond S. Edinger was the XO of VF-653, flying the F4U-4s on the USS *Valley Forge* (he was promoted to Lt Commander during the cruise). He gives details about what was involved in a rescue operation on 8 February 1952:

It was my day off as I had flown the past two days, when the squadron Duty Officer alerted me to a 1030 briefing for an 1130 launch on a Rescap mission.

Our three night fighter Corsairs had rendezvoused with three AD-4N Skyraiders and with a helicopter from the Cruiser USS *Rochester* before dawn to effect the rescue of the downed pilot. In attempting the rescue, the overloaded HO3S-1 crashed, alerting enemy troops in the vicinity. This triggered some heavy gunfire from the surrounding ridges. One of the ADs was hit and diverted to an airfield in South Korea. Also, a Corsair piloted by Lt John McKenna disappeared after reporting he was hit and was on fire. Also, at about this time, Ensign Marvin Broomhead, a pilot in VA-194 (Skyraiders) was shot down and my second section was diverted to fly Birdcap over him. [Birdcap: flying top cover over a downed pilot to protect him from being captured while the rescue helicopter is en route.]

My wingman, Ensign Busch, and I flew to the site where the first pilot had gone down in order to relieve four pilots from the USS *Philippine Sea*. The Birdcap I relieved reported very little enemy resistance, but the previous Birdcap reported heavy fire from gun emplacements on the adjoining ridge, which they had bombed and strafed. We circled the area and couldn't see any activity but on the third low pass, Ensign Busch received small arms fire that damaged his Corsair. We continued to circle and occasionally strafed suspicious-looking movements, being careful not to fire too close to the crashed helicopter.

After a brief period, Lt Edinger and his wingman were relieved by a division from the USS *Philippine Sea*. At that point, Edinger took that flight leader down low over the crashed helicopter even though visibility wasn't too good. He told the leader that he would call out when he was directly overhead of the downed crewmen. At the moment he called out, he felt his Corsair lurch and the engine seemed to miss a beat. Seconds later, the leader called out that he had the target in sight and he also noticed that Edinger's aircraft had been hit and was losing oil.

Pilots from VA-115 get their briefing on the day's mission in the squadron Ready Room on the USS *Philippine Sea* (CV 47). This was during the *Philippine Sea*'s third combat cruise when the squadron was flying the AD-4s in the early summer of 1952. (*Pete Swanson*)

I continued up the valley slowly climbing and advised my wingman to call *Aboveboard,*the ship that was three miles off shore and coordinating the rescue attempt, and advise them of my predicament. [*Aboveboard* was a reference to the ship that was closest, which would be launching the rescue helicopter. They never referred to any specific ship by name, especially if they were in hostile waters.] With oil streaming from my left wing, I shut off the left oil cooler and continued to thread my way up the valley and over the mountain. When we reached *Aboveboard,* I was advised they had a longboat in the water and were ready to rescue me from a ditching alongside. By now, I realized the oil loss was hydraulic fluid and although the engine was running a little rough, all engine gauges were reading normal, so I would return to the *Valley Forge.*

With the carrier all set to receive a disabled aircraft, all of the planes already on the deck have been moved forward and the barrier had been elevated just in case. As Lt Edinger attempted to lower his gear with the emergency CO_2 bottle, it failed. That left him with a dangling landing gear and a hung 5-inch HVAR that may have been armed.

The Air Boss gave me the choice of ditching beside the carrier and being rescued by helicopter or coming aboard the carrier. Should I decide to try landing, he would have to land me last because there were still some of our aircraft in the pattern and, in that case, he would place a line of tractors, which were normally used to move aircraft about on the deck, behind the barriers. This was a precaution to protect all the aircraft that had been recovered and moved forward just in case of a bouncing tail hook and I didn't catch a wire.

On my first pass, due to no landing gear or flaps, I was too fast and had to go around. With encouraging words from the boss, I was able to make a landing on my second try. After touching down, several members of the ordnance crew chased the rocket, which had jarred loose during the landing and was sliding down the deck. They threw it overboard and the crash crew, in their white fire-resistant suits lifted me out of the cockpit in case my plane caught on fire. The best part of the entire affair was being taken down into the sick bay and given a dose of 200-proof liquid pacifier! Further examination of my Corsair revealed small arms damage to the hydraulic system and moderate damage to one cylinder in the engine. Also minor damage sustained in landing. Fortunately, I was on the schedule to fly the next day and I did!

The damage that VF-653 did to the enemy was impressive. Squadron records published six months after their return to the States indicated they had made 1,472 rail cuts, destroyed 175 bridges, 36 locomotives, 724 rail cars, 307 vehicles, 919 boats, killing over 1,100 enemy troop

The remaining four reserve squadrons would stay together and, after a five-month training cycle, they embarked on the *Antietam* for their first combat deployment. VF-713 was flying the F4U-4s, while both VF-837 and VF-831 would operate in the F9F-2s. The final full attack squadron on that cruise was VA-728, equipped with AD-4 Skyraiders. The USS *Antietam* (CV 36) had remained in reserve until the war in Korea started. Going through some reactivation preparations, she was able to go back into active duty in mid-January 1951. After going through a shakedown cruise and getting her Air Group-15 ready, the *Antietam* sailed for the Far East on 8 September 1951. When that cruise ended, the air group had logged close to 1,000 combat sorties. Lt George Schnitzer was an F9F Panther pilot who flew combat missions during that cruise. He discusses his experiences flying some of the CAP missions that could easily relate to just about all of the carrier deployments during that period:

> During a specific time frame that our carrier was on the line, our air group's Panthers flew a total of 52 combat air patrols and I was involved in five of them. The difficulties experienced during these flights by our division were not unique to us, but were typical. The *Antietam*'s controllers were very green and they had little understanding of the difficulties of another flight of jets where no altitude information was known. Flying at 30,000 feet, there were a lot of cubic miles of airspace within eyesight. Finding even friendly jets was difficult when looking down at them against a dark blue sea. When vectored out for a practice intercept, it was hard to get them to put us into a good intercept position. The controllers all too frequently vectored us directly over a flight to be intercepted. The best positioning for the CAP was 'up sun' about 5,000 feet above and at least 3,000 feet to the side of the 'bogey'. This happened only once in a while rather than frequently. The controllers also didn't realize the turning radius of a jet fighter at these higher altitudes. Their training must have been done using slower prop types. Interceptions of the F4Us and ADs were a lot easier and we had a great time zooming past them as they returned from their missions. Fortunately for the task force, we were operating too far away from active enemy airfields for them to be a serious threat.

Every aircraft carrier that served in the Korean War had specialized detachments on board with the exception of the jeep carriers. One of these squadrons was VC-35, which flew the AD-4N Skyraider. The unit had been formed up in late May 1950 at NAS San Diego. They would provide anti-submarine capabilities to protect the Task Force and they would also specialize in night strikes, electronic countermeasures (ECM) and some search and rescue. They were a deadly force to contend with during the hours of darkness. This model of the AD would have a crew of three, a pilot and two enlisted crewmen, which comprised a radar operator and an ECM/ASW operator who were positioned side by side in a small compartment behind the wings. These detachments would consist of four aircraft, six pilots and over three dozen enlisted types.

One of the VC-35 pilots was Lt William C. Raposa who was assigned to Detachment 'F' on the USS *Boxer* in 1951. He remembers a memorable mission that he flew over North Korea in early May 1951. It was one that ended up disrupting the entire early strike force that was getting ready to launch. He recalls:

> I'm hit and we're on fire back here!...These were not the best words a VAN Team-5 night intruder pilot flying an AD-4N likes to hear from an air crewman, especially over the middle of North Korea! My regular crew was on board this night and our patrol sector was due west of Wonsan toward Pyongyang and

then south toward the front lines. According to the notes in my flight logbook, we had catapulted from the *Boxer* at close to 2:30 a.m. with one 1,000-lb GP and eight 220-lb VT fused frag bombs. Also included in the mix were two flares and 400 rounds of 20-mm ammo. My usual wingman was flying loose trail with me. Both of us had our regular radar man on board.

It seems that only one hot round had found its mark, but Lt Raposa's Skyraider was lucky because the Chinese were using the Russian-built 12.7-mm quads that could put a lot of lead into a very small space.

Up until this time, on the mission, we had destroyed one truck, which must have been loaded with munitions because it blew up with spectacular explosion, eight ox carts moving south along a well protected road as well as a few assorted buildings. I remember the small calibre fire was intense along most of the route. All of our bombs had been dropped and well as both flares and I was strafing with the last of the 20-mm ammo when I pulled sharply to the right and felt the thump as my plane was hit with a high calibre round. A second later was when one of my crew in the back shouted out that we were on fire! After realizing we had been hit, I radioed my wingman and told him we were going to guard channel to broadcast a 'Mayday'. Continuing my turn back to the east, I was able to check out the engine, oil pressure, hydraulics and circuit breakers. Everything was OK, so I figured the damage was minimal.

Lt Raposa climbed up to 8,000 feet with full power and IFF (Identification: Friend or Foe) on emergency, he picked up a response from the heavy cruiser USS *Saint Paul*, which was on station about five miles east of Wonsan Harbour. They were still fifty miles inland at the time and Lt Raposa was trying to determine if it would be better to divert over the mountains to the closest friendly airstrip, which was at Kangnung (K-18), or continue back to the carrier. It had already been determined that the 12.7-mm round had exploded inside the rear compartment, but the fire was only from the round exploding in one of the parachutes back there. It hadn't been determined how badly one of the crewmen had been hit, so the decision was made to go back to the *Boxer* as quickly as possible in case the injuries were serious.

I had no way of knowing how hectic things were back on the carrier because our buddy carrier, the *Bon Homme Richard*, had not yet arrived on station and there was no ready deck available for emergency services. My radar man in the back said he could not determine how serious the injuries were to the other crewman, so we would make sure the medics were standing by on the deck when we landed. We had closed to about 10 miles from Wonsan and I could see the harbour ahead just as dawn began to break. Two of our F4U-5Ns from VC-3 had been recalled and were waiting for my wingman and me to show up so we could all fly out to the carrier together. They had been working targets on the roads running north of Wonsan.

Since the *Boxer* was a straight deck carrier, aircraft had been spotted aft of the landing area for the first launch and Lt Raposa's untimely return was causing

The USS *Boxer* was involved in four cruises in the war. This frozen scene was on the deck during a winter storm in February 1952. The Skyraider was assigned to VA-65. Regardless of the weather, the aircraft has been loaded with bombs and waits for the first sign of improvements in the weather. (*James Williams*)

quite a commotion. The solution was to move up the launch time, which would be better than having to re-spot all the strike aircraft forward to get a clear deck for the incoming four aircraft.

Lt Raposa continues:

> The *Boxer* was on a course of 045 and this gave me pretty much a straight in approach rather than a standard flat pass. We landed with no problem and the Air Boss shut me down in the wires so the medics and Flight Surgeon could get to our wounded guy and move him to sick bay. As I was being towed forward, the bullhorn blared out 'Pilot report to the bridge'. The Captain of the ship wanted a first-hand account of this incident since he had to modify the day's flight schedule. The Flight Surgeon came in as I was briefing the Captain and said the crewman was not injured and I was told that I should have diverted to K-18, but the fact remained that we still had a plane with a very big hole in it and a burned parachute. Most of the carriers in early Korea were still trying to perform World War II tactics with large day strikes and did not relish launching or recovering for just four night hecklers.

The atomic bomb was readily available during the Korean War and there is much speculation that there were B-29s standing by to deliver it had the need arisen. At the time, the Navy did not have a carrier-borne nuclear weapons aircraft capable of carrying one off the deck, but, then again, there is a question as to exactly what the Navy's role was in this puzzle. VA-115 was an AD-4 squadron operating on the USS *Philippine Sea* during their 1952 cruise. The pilots of VA-115 saw a lot of action, especially in the interdiction role. One of their pilots was Lt (jg) William 'Tex' Morgan. He recalls one of his missions and also makes a comment about the atomic bomb.

Douglas produced one of the most rugged aircraft made during the early 1950s in the AD Skyraider. It was the only carrier-based aircraft capable of delivering an atomic bomb in the event it was necessary. Scuttlebutt [a combination of accurate information and rumours] had it that we had one on board because a certain compartment was guarded by the Marines 24/7. There were several aircraft in the final stages of development that would have the capability to deliver a nuclear bomb off the carrier, but to my knowledge, none of these aircraft were available at the time of the Korean War and if they were, none served on carriers that were doing combat cruises off the coast of North Korea. We had practised a manoeuvre called 'Lob' bombing or 'Toss' bombing. This called for a steep dive aimed short of the target, an abrupt pullout, releasing the bomb on the pullout instead of the usual procedure of releasing it during the dive. The result was to toss the bomb onto the target ahead. The pilot then rolled over into a split-S to gain speed and clear the area ASAP to avoid the blast and fall out.

The power plants along the Yalu River in North Korea had been largely avoided for a number of political reasons until the spring of 1952, when a decision was made to take them out. On one such mission, we were briefed for a maximum effort strike coordinated (a word that always increased the tension during the briefings) with other air groups and the USAF. We were told to make only one run and stay south of the river because the target was heavily defended. As we approached the area at 10,000 feet, there was a lot of smoke from previous strikes and I could see heavy AA coming from all around the target. Seconds later, we had a good visual on our objective and I followed the Skyraider ahead of me in a 70-degree dive. Just as I was about to release three 2,000-lb GP bombs, much to my horror, I saw another plane coming in at 9 o'clock, flying straight and level right in my dive path! To remain in the dive risked a mid-air collision or hitting him with my bombs. In an instant, I thought of the 'Lob' procedure and pulled up sharply, releasing the bombs after a few seconds and lobbing them on to the AA gun batteries. With pounding heart, I rolled over and exited the area, thinking how lucky I had been and the same for whoever that other pilot was. My bombs hit in close proximity to the target, so maybe they did some good. It would have been tragic for two aircraft to run into each other during a bomb run!

Every carrier deployment during the war had at least one squadron of F9F Panthers on board. As previously mentioned concerning the first carrier to respond (USS *Valley Forge*), the experience level in jets was minimal at best. It was a learning process that came quickly to all the pilots that were flying them. Armed reconnaissance and combat air patrol missions were common among the Panther pilots and they used their 20-mm guns to perfection against anything they ran across. Lt George Schnitzer was operating from the USS *Antietam* (CV 36) with Air Group-15. He recalls the sequence of events that he participated in right after his carrier had come off replenishment during the last half of their cruise. These could easily have been a profile of any F9F squadron that flew combat during that period.

It was late February and the weather was still cold and unpredictable. We moved back into combat mode just hours after we had finished with replenishment. By noon, the cloud cover had moved in quickly and it was solid all over the northern part of the peninsula. Right before everything closed up, our division got off the cat for a quick mission with another division. We went down under the overcast and got in some good hits and, on the way back to the coast, we hit a string of boxcars that had been disabled by some of our Corsair night hecklers from VC-3. Before we left the area, we got in several good rail cuts, which probably caused the enemy a couple of days before they could use that route again. The flak was not very accurate, which helped us make some good drops. Just as we got back safely to the carrier, the real bad weather closed in and operations came to a halt. Two days later, the weather finally started clearing, which got us back in the air. My first mission that day was to fly CAP over the fleet and early that next morning, I was slated for an armed reconnaissance mission into some well defended territory. We were operating along the east coast and our entry point for feet dry was at Hungnam and we worked low all the way to Tongmungori. The area around Hungnam was laced with many Triple-A gun emplacements. As we passed over that area, we stayed high (above 20,000 feet) and maintained a high speed and constantly changed airspeed and direction because they were very accurate in tracking us.

A few minutes into our low level work, one of our pilots spotted some boxcars on a siding and before we went after them, we made sure it was not a flak trap. After determining that it was relatively safe, we destroyed all the boxcars and tore up the rails in numerous places. None of us spotted any flak, but there may have been some that were not using tracers. For one reason or another, many of our divisions were seeing lots of boxcars and for the next five days, our air group pounded the entire transportation system inland from Hungnam. When the surge was over, we had logged 291 sorties during that short period. Although we didn't lose any aircraft, many of them came back with numerous holes due to small arms fire. I think every enemy soldier fired rounds at any aircraft that was coming in low. For the next few days, both of the F9F squadrons' pilots had to stand alert, sitting in their aircraft for four hours at a time. Most of us lieutenants opted out of this duty due to our rank, so that left all of the Lt (jg)s and Ensigns. It would have been interesting if an emergency had come up and the alert birds were launched with all junior officers taking the intercept!

CHAPTER FOUR

Endless Interdiction and Close Air Support

When at least two of the big carriers teamed up to launch a full-strength strike against targets in North Korea, the end results was usually total destruction of their objective. By the late spring of 1952, the front lines had pretty well stabilized with some see-sawing back and forth. The Chinese still had a distinct advantage in terms of sheer manpower, but American air power did a great job of levelling the playing field.

One of these raids took place on 25 May 1952 when aircraft from the USS *Boxer* and the USS *Philippine Sea* launched an attack on Chongjin in the far north-eastern corner of North Korea. It was close to the East Korea Bay in the Sea of Japan and only fifty miles from the Chinese border. Intelligence reports stated that it was the third largest populated city in North Korea, so it housed a lot of war production in small factories and it was a major storage and supply centre for the Chinese military, which was desperately trying to build enough supplies to support a major offensive. Air power was putting a dent in these efforts and this strike by Air Groups-2 and 11 set them back on any plans for a successful push to the south. This strike was the second to be carried out, with the first being on the previous Easter Sunday. The ADs, F9Fs and F4Us dropped an impressive load of ordnance that was estimated to be around 230 tons on key assets. In addition, the battleship USS *Iowa* came in close enough to bombard these same targets with its big guns.

The fighter-bombers from both carriers logged over 200 effective sorties that day as they worked in seemingly never-ending shifts that kept aircraft over Chongjin most of the day. By early afternoon, the billowing columns of smoke from raging fires were so dense that it was difficult to select targets that had not been hit. The low-level photo reconnaissance that had been done the day before the attack revealed an abundance of enemy assets and the photo run the next day showed that four electric transformer stations had been levelled and a fifth one heavily damaged. A major radio station had been destroyed, along with forty-eight supply buildings and twenty-eight barracks that were housing Chinese reinforcements that were destined for the front lines. Some of these structures were protected with anti-aircraft gun emplacements and most of them were neutralized when the first wave of Panthers came in. Even though the war's end was still close to one year away, the Chinese knew that the chances of gaining ground were growing slim and when the ceasefire occurred, the line would be drawn right across where the front lines were.

Chongjin was also an important rail junction with a large number of boxcars resting on side tracks. After-strike film revealed that twenty-one of these railcars had been destroyed and the rails had been cut in thirty-two places. This strike, along with most of the others, was well coordinated. The F9Fs hit the gun emplacements as the Skyraiders were beginning their dives from altitude. One of the AD pilots from the *Philippine Sea*, Ensign George McCallister, scored direct hits with two 1,000-lb GPs on a fuel dump, which triggered a multitude of secondary explosions. In the meantime, a couple of the F4U pilots were talking with the USS *Iowa* and they directed its big guns to bear on one of the biggest transformer stations in Chongjin. They scored direct hits and that target disappeared in less than a minute. The Skyraiders were mostly armed with 1,000-lb bombs, which were more than capable of destroying anything within the target area. The last strike of the late afternoon was mostly carried out by the F4Us and a few F9Fs because there weren't enough targets left to bring the ADs back in at last light. When the last Panther set down on the *Boxer*'s deck, its pilot Lt (jg) Warren Brown recorded the 53,000th landing that had been made on that carrier. That figure included many years before the Korean War.

Just a couple of days before the second anniversary of the start of the war (25 June 1952), the UN forces decided to step up the pressure on the faltering peace talks and also send a message to China and the Russians. Task Force 77 would be a key factor in delivering the notice in the form of a massive attack on the big Suiho hydroelectric dam on the Yalu River. The US Secretary of Defense, Robert A. Lovett, summed up the new aggressive stance at a news conference where he explained that the decision to bomb the dam was made entirely on military grounds. He also let it be known that in an extreme emergency, such as an all-out strike or air attack by communist China's 2,000+ air force fleet, that they could expect full-scale retaliation against targets in Manchuria. At that time, Lovett also told the media that he did not see an end to the Korean War coming anytime soon, but that the United States was in it to the finish.

There was one factor about this raid that had to be taken into consideration. The dam was extremely close to three major MiG-15 bases in Manchuria and each was packed with these fighters. There was a huge complex of hydroelectric dams on the Yalu River in the heart of MiG Alley. The MiG-15s usually formed up into combat formations over that complex before coming south of the river. No fighter-bomber attacks could be carried out in this area without heavy top cover support from the F-86s. Navy raids were no exception because their fastest jet (F9F) was usually loaded with bombs or rockets, which would have made them defenceless against the lighter and faster MiGs. There was every expectation of some major dogfights developing once the Navy strike force got into the area, but, fortunately, the risk of losses was too great for the communist fighters to try and attack the bombers. Loss records for that day show that no F-86s were lost, so that was an indicator of very little action at altitude.

On 23 June, the attack commenced in the afternoon against the major power plants on the Yalu. It involved four carrier air groups hitting in waves that lasted until last light. They came from the following carriers: USS *Boxer*, *Bon Homme Richard*, *Philippine Sea* and *Princeton*. When the day was over, seven of the nine plants were destroyed and the remaining two were severely damaged. These facilities were heavily defended and the F9Fs and F4Us got in ahead of the Skyraiders and took out a large percentage of the threats. The key factor in the success of the mission was the ADs, carrying two 2,000-lb GPs and one 1,000-lb GP, which had the capability of destroying any target in North Korea, including these plants. Post-strike photos showed that initially there were forty-seven gun emplacements defending the plants. After the strike on the 25th, six of these had been destroyed and twenty-six had been damaged to the extent they were not a threat to the bombers. Fifteen others had had their crews killed or had been abandoned during the bombing. Loss records for this date show that only one F4U, from the USS *Bon Homme Richard*, was lost. It was identified as being one from VF-74.

On the evening of 23 June, the commander of Task Force 77 sent the following dispatch to all four carrier captains:

> At 1600 hours, this force commenced systematic destruction of Hydro Electric Plants along the Yalu River. Loss of these plants will constitute one of the most devastating blows dealt the enemy in the past two years. Retaliation is expected. Stand alert and be ready to take on all comers. Com 7th Flt very well pleased with the first operation of a four carrier task force in a long time and with the performance of all hands in carrying out the strike so well! Well done all ships and all planes!

Many of the military leaders felt that this strike should have been carried out a year earlier, but it was never approved. The Chinese suffered equally with the North Koreans because much of their power in Manchuria was supplied by these same power plants. Intelligence reports state that almost all of the power in North Korea was knocked out and the full extent of the effect on China was never fully known.

Around noon on the same day, more Skyraiders and F4Us from the *Boxer* had been rearmed and launched for a strike near the east coast, far from the Yalu River. A major truck park and supply centre had been located south-west of the city of Anbyon in Kangwon Province. While the afternoon strikes against the Suiho area were handled by other air groups, the *Boxer* unleashed about forty of its aircraft against this target. They encountered very bad weather most of the way, but as they approached the target the weather cleared. They estimated that 80 per cent of their ordnance hit the intended targets with some of the aircraft carrying incendiaries. This area was nestled in some of the most rugged mountains in North Korea.

The *Princeton*'s air group also had a hand in another strike later on in the day when they sent six Panthers into the Wonsan region to strafe Chinese troop concentrations and a new supply dump just south of the area. The Panthers, led by Lt Commander William A. Schroeder, attacked gun positions first and then methodically worked over the intended targets with great success. This was not a major strike, but it exemplified the quick response time the Navy carriers displayed when intelligence photos revealed a new, but temporary, target. Air groups carried out hundreds of these minor missions during the course of the war.

There is an old slogan that was made famous by a wrist watch manufacturer many years ago 'It takes a licking and keeps on ticking.' This could have been used as an endorsement by Douglas Aircraft Co. when they rolled the tough AD Skyraiders off the line. With the low-level missions the AD was assigned to fly, against some of the most heavily defended targets in North Korea, it is a tribute to their rugged construction that so many were able to limp back to the carriers, but many did not.

In April 1952, there were six Skyraiders lost out of a total of eleven Navy aircraft lost for that month. One of the pilots from VA-115, Lt (jg) Peter S. Swanson, from the USS *Philippine Sea*, was shot down on 10 April and he relates the details of that fateful mission. He was flying an AD-4 (BuNo 127863).

> It was a beautiful sunny day but the weather was still rather cool. In fact, the squadron was still required to wear the 'poopy suits' for strike missions.

These suits were bulky, rubberized coveralls that kept water from the pilot's body in case he had to ditch in the bitter cold waters off North Korea. It prevented hypothermia and eventual freezing to death. Swanson continues:

> Our mission this day was to strike North Korean gun positions located around Wonsan Harbour. Intel had proven that this was a major port for the enemy to receive supplies by small boats or barges under cover of darkness. It had high priority for us to blockade the harbour with mines and also have around-the-clock surveillance either by ships or aircraft. The enemy had dug tunnels in the hills around the harbour and laid rail lines into them on which they set flat railroad cars that had large guns mounted on them. They could roll them out and fire at any of our ships that were in range and then roll them back into the safety of the tunnels. My division's job was to try to bomb the entrance to the caves so they would collapse and not allow them to roll the guns out. Or, we would glide swiftly from altitude at the cave mouth and release our bombs or shoot our rockets so the warheads would bounce or ricochet into the entrance before exploding, thus destroying the weapon.

Swanson's division had just completed a series of bomb runs on the entrances to the caves and was in the process of pulling out to rendezvous and look each other over before proceeding on another run. They noticed that they were getting some flak, but it seemed to be light.

> As our four ships pulled up, one of the guys in my flight reported that I had a lot of oil coming from my engine and to check my oil pressure. My division leader asked me to report and at that instance, my engine surged slightly! I checked my oil gauge and noted a slight quiver and so reported. From that point on, my orders were to clean up (de-arm), set ordnance switches on safe, drop all unused ordnance, switch to main fuel and head straight for the *Philippine Sea* (it wasn't more than 80 to 100 miles off the coast). I did all of this as I turned to seaward. However, my wingman said the oil leak was now very pronounced and at the same time, I noted the oil pressure fluctuated and the engine slightly mis-fired. I announced to the flight leader that I thought I'd have to ditch and, according to my instincts, elected to do it soon, while I would still have some engine power available.

With that message, an entire network of Search and Rescue (SAR) actions was initiated. The flight leader relayed Swanson's ordeal on the ship/shore channel that was being monitored by the area SAR team, the *Philippine Sea*, 7th Fleet and more than likely…

the enemy. Things began to happen in sequence; first a message came through giving the coordinates of a landing site in the water that had been swept clear of mines, for just such an occasion, allowing surface craft to get in the area safely.

Swanson continues:

> They also gave me the wind and sea-state information to help me line up the correct approach and to give some indication of what impact would be like when my Skyraider touched down. I had already turned back towards the harbour and began looking for the ditching area. My flight leader eased power to level off and begin a descent and the rest of my flight moved to spot exactly where I was to ditch. Seconds later, I knew exactly where that was to be. At that moment, flight lead passed the lead to me so I could concentrate on the ditching. He pulled wide to the left and sat in close on my wing, matching power, attitude and altitude changes I made. He also began to go over the ditching check-off list, something we all had had drilled into us, and all of us pilots carried this list on our kneeboards.

The entire rescue operation was like something out of a textbook. The wind and sea conditions were moderate, the communication with all involved was flawless and the SAR effort was right on schedule. Swanson's power was steady, although the oil pressure gauge was almost down to zero. All he had to do was safely ditch, get out of the cockpit, get in the helicopter sling and eventually get back to his carrier. At 200 feet, he lined up on the ditching area directly into the wind.

> I lowered ½ flaps, dropped the tail hook (which would clue me exactly how high I was when I touched the water), locked my shoulder harness, locked open the Plexiglas canopy, tightened my crash helmet and ensured the visor was down, eased the prop pitch forward and, using trim tabs, set up a rate of descent of about 100 feet per minute and held it steady. Slowly the aircraft settled until the hook touched the water; then I eased the nose down and clipped a wave, which killed my flying speed.
>
> Immediately, my engine hit the next wave head on, which stopped me dead in the water, but not too violently. I had up to 30 seconds to evacuate before the plane would fill with water and sink. So, I released my safety belt, stood up with my parachute dangling underneath, which contained a stowed life raft. I stepped out on the wing, unbuckled my chute (but made sure to loop my arm through the chest straps so it wouldn't get away), inflated my life jacket and stepped into the water. My intention was to get out the life raft and get in it while awaiting rescue. Moments later, the chopper from the cruiser USS *Saint Paul* was overhead and I was signalled from above to abandon my chute and get into the sling being lowered from the helicopter. I was lifted up safely into the chopper and taken to the cruiser where I was treated royally. They took me over to my carrier and were given their reward of ice cream every time a ship returned a downed pilot.

The *Philippine Sea* wound up its third cruise in early July 1952 with Air Group-11 on board. According to the logbook of Lieutenant Arthur D. Gripton (an AD-4W pilot in the VC-11 Detachment), he flew the final mission of that cruise. It was a late afternoon mission (in BuNo 124079) that lasted 3.4 hours. As soon as he touched down on the deck, the Captain got on the bullhorn and announced to the ship's personnel that the last aircraft had just landed and it was time to go home. On the way back to the States, there was a stopover in Hawaii where the crew members had time to let off some steam.

The F2H-2 Banshee got its first test under fire during the Korean War. Lt (jg) Wayne J. Spence was one of the VF-172 pilots that flew it off the USS *Essex* on its first carrier deployment. While it saw a lot of missions over North Korea, it had very few chances to tangle with MiG-15s even though it was flying top cover for the slower prop types. He recalls some of the action he was involved in.

The new Banshees were very agile and carried a variety of ordnance with several bomb racks. The most common load carried involved four 250-lb bombs and four 5-inch HVARs or four 100-lb bombs on the outer four racks and 600 rounds of 20-mm ammo for the four cannons. When more complex targets were involved, we loaded up with two 500-lb bombs on the inside racks and four rockets or smaller bombs on the outer racks.

The Banshee could get up to an altitude pretty near what the MiG-15s could at 46,000+ feet. We could also easily out turn the MiGs with our straight wings and, with two engines, we had a built-in safety measure that could get us back to the carrier if one failed. We went deep into MiG Alley up on the Yalu River a couple of times in hopes of getting into some MiGs, but we didn't have any luck. I was flying tail-end Charlie on one of the flights and we were up pretty high and as we turned to head south, I looked up and there was a formation of MiGs above us, but none of them came down to our altitude. If they had, I would probably have been the first one they shot at. There was one interesting fact we learned about the MiG and that was he couldn't shoot at you if he was pulling negative 'Gs'. His guns were gravity fed and if one got on your tail, you could flip over and watch him in the mirrors and if he turned upside down expecting you to Split-S, you could start an inverted climb with negative 'Gs' and he couldn't shoot at you. If he stayed right side up, you could Split-S and he couldn't follow because of the tighter turning radius of the Banshee. We never lost any of our squadron's Banshees to MiGs.

There was an especially dangerous valley in Korea that is called the Bukka Valley today. It was about 20 miles north-east of Seoul. I believe it was called Changnim-ni back in the early 1950s. It was a key valley for the North Koreans and Chinese troops and their supplies because trains could deliver their loads within 10 miles of the front lines and the two railroad bridges in that valley were prime targets for our bombs. The Chinese had placed a dense array of anti-aircraft gun emplacements all over that area and it was very dangerous for the slower prop types to continue to keep those bridges knocked down, so a mission was planned using eight Banshees with each carrying two 500-lb bombs and 35 other aircraft to support the Banshees attacking the bridge. The support planes were F4Us, ADs and F9Fs who went in first to drop flak suppression bombs (Daisy Cutters) to get some of the gunners' heads down followed closely by our F2Hs attacking the bridges. It was a very successful mission.

According to records from the *Essex* on that first cruise, they arrived off the coast of North Korea on 21 August 1951. The Banshees launched their first combat foray two days later and it involved four F2H-2s, on an armed reconnaissance mission. Lt (jg) Spence was very interested in recording some of VF-172's history during that cruise and he indicated that they had twenty-four pilots assigned to the squadron and two would be lost in combat and two more with non-lethal injuries in operational accidents from the flight deck crash of 16 September 1951. Air Group-5 lost nineteen pilots to combat while conducting operations off the coast of North Korea. According to the Korwald Aircraft Loss Report, the *Essex* lost about fifty aircraft during that first cruise. This included all types including the specialized detachments that were in the air group.

The USS *Boxer* was on its third deployment in early 1952 with Air Group-2 on board and their station at that time was on the east coast. The Carrier Task Force usually operated with at least three carriers and ten destroyers that were screening for the fleet. Combine the strength of this force with the fact that there was at least a couple of jeep carriers operating with Marine Corsair squadrons along the west coast of North Korea and also a British carrier working off the north-east coast, and you had a devastating amount of air power that was constantly on the move up and down both coasts, usually at about 100 miles out. Lt (jg) Guy Lyons was a pilot in an F4U-4 squadron (VF-64) on the *Boxer* during that time. He gives some insight as to what both of the F4U squadrons of the air group were involved in during that period.

> Basically, the mission of Task Force 77 all during 1952 was to disrupt rail traffic on the east coast of North Korea where most of their rail lines were concentrated and also to provide CAS for the troops when it was needed. We preferred to go after major well defended targets such as electric power facilities, bridges, warehouses and enemy troop concentrations. This agenda probably extended on into 1953 also. The rail lines were divided into 20-mile segments for purposes of identifying and assigning target areas for the pilots. One section between Wonsan and Hamhung was identified as the 'Dagmar' area. There was a 'Jane Russell' area and other sections were identified with mostly female names. The 'Dagmar' area had open tracks and several tunnels. The North Koreans parked the trains inside the tunnels during the day for obvious reasons. Our Corsairs and the ADs dropped bombs to cut rail lines during the day and attacked trains the night fighters had isolated in the open areas by cutting rail lines ahead of and behind a train at night.

The F4Us from the carriers were not limited to the targets mentioned above because they also consistently attacked enemy assets within Pyongyang, Hamhung and the steel mills at Chongjin on the north-east coast.

Lyons continues:

> We made numerous raids against the complex of bridges that became known as the 'Bridges at Toko-ri', which was at the junction of three rail lines in the centre of North Korea. They were a difficult target in that they consisted of three rail bridges that intersected and crossed over each other at the bottom of a very steep canyon. This had to be one of the most heavily defended sites in

Korea! The USAF had tried carpet bombing the complex with B-29s but met with little success. The Navy attacked them with well planned dive-bombing missions using both Skyraiders, Panthers and Corsairs and this put the bridges out of commission for brief periods, but they were quickly repaired (about three days) and back in business. We had to go after them quite often.

I can recall some of our raids that were slightly north of Pyongyang and within reach of the MiG-15s. Some of our strikes brought out some big flights of MiGs but they were mainly spectators while staying at 50,000+ feet and they exited the area when the F-86 Sabre top cover came into the area. The Task Force Commander brought in a couple of Grumman F6F Hellcats (World War II vintage) with TV cameras mounted beneath the wings and which had controls that could be operated from a nearby chase plane. This set-up was very new at the time and these Hellcats could be considered forerunners of today's drones. Both of the F6Fs caught a wing tip on the canyon walls going in and did not damage the bridges. It was a good idea that was perhaps ahead of its time because it didn't work too well then.

During the summer of 1952, we received word that a Navy P2V, flying reconnaissance over the shipping lanes off the east coast of Russia, had been shot down. It was photographing rogue merchant ships delivering war materials to Vladivostok for transshipment into North Korea. The ships were identified and then barred from United Nations ports around the world. The Task Force 77 Commander dispatched the *Boxer* and several destroyers north

A heavily loaded AD-4N from Detachment-1 of VC-35 is readied for another night intruder mission over North Korea. This photograph was taken on the USS *Essex* (CVA 9) in 1952 during its second cruise with Air Group-2 on board. (*Tailhook Association*)

to an area east of Vladivostok. Our carrier operated in that area for a week while our Corsairs flew at 8,000 feet altitude on a north–south line off the big Russian port while staying outside the 12-mile international boundary limit. Our F9Fs flew CAPs up at 18,000–20,000 feet. Our F4Us were decoys but none of the Russian MiGs came out. After a week or so, the *Boxer* returned to the Task Force off Wonsan.

As has been said many times, the flight deck of an aircraft carrier is the most dangerous place to be, especially during flight operations. Lt (jg) Lyons recalls one of the incidents that ended rather badly and it was the result of a freak accident.

Late in our tour, one of the support guys was clearing the guns on one of our fighters on the hangar deck and a bullet discharged and ricocheted off the overhead and hit the gas tank of another aircraft close by. The resulting explosion and fire caused a lot of havoc. At least six people were trapped in the sick bay and died, including our flight surgeon. Some 35 people jumped overboard and may God bless the helicopter pilot that picked all of them up safely! The *Boxer* was back in operation the next day but it did cut our tour short and we returned to the States a month later after surviving a typhoon before we pulled out.

The USS *Oriskany* (CV 34) was an *Essex*-class aircraft carrier that did one combat cruise during the Korean War. After undergoing some major modifications in 1951, she finally departed for the Far East on 15 September 1952 with Air Group 102 on board. She joined Task Force 77 off the coast of Korea on 31 October. Her air group had two full squadrons of the newest F9F-5 Panthers, one squadron of F4U-4 Corsairs and one of AD-3 Skyraiders. They made a name for themselves with a considerable number of deep strikes in North Korea, as well as close air support missions over front-line positions during a period that the Chinese were trying desperately to garner enough supplies to initiate a major offensive against UN ground forces.

Of all the impressive statistics that Air Group 102 put on the books, none got the publicity that an epic encounter on 18 November 1952 did. It was a clash between several MiG-15s from the Russian base at Vladivostok and F9F-5s from the USS *Oriskany*. There were four Panther pilots from VF-781 involved: Lt Claire Elwood, Lt (jg) John Middleton, Lt Royce Williams and Lt (jg) David Rowlands. At the time of this encounter, the *Oriskany* was operating off the extreme north-eastern coast of North Korea near Chongjin, which put the carrier within easy striking range of any Russian aircraft based in or around Vladivostok. These four pilots were launched to form a protective shield over the *Oriskany* in case of trouble.

On this day, the weather was typical for mid-November in that it was cold and the overcast was sitting at about 500 feet. Visibility was bad below that because of the high winds and blowing snow. Mission reports state that visibility was between two to three miles. In a situation where you had two jets coming toward each other, that left practically no time to manoeuvre. There were three carriers operating in that area and all three launched strikes on enemy targets that were close to the Russian border. All the strikes went well, meeting only light anti-aircraft fire, and all aircraft returned to their carriers safely.

On the USS *Boxer*'s (CV 21) second Korean War cruise, Air Group-101 had one squadron of F9F-2Bs on board and they were assigned to VF-721. This photograph was taken during combat operations off the coast of North Korea during the summer of 1951. (*Gene Bazore*)

A fully loaded AD-4 Skyraider starts its take-off roll on the USS *Philippine Sea* (CV 47) in the spring of 1952. It was assigned to VA-115, which was part of Air Group-11. The AD had the capacity to haul an impressive load of bombs for long distances. (*Sam Wallace*)

The low-level strafing that the F9F Panthers did exposed them to heavy small arms fire. This F9F-2 received battle damage but made it back to the USS *Essex* (CV 9). It had to take the barrier because of hydraulic problems, as seen here. The Panther was assigned to VF-821 on the *Essex*'s second and final combat cruise in the spring of 1953. (*Jim Dodge*)

There were several F6F-5K Hellcat Drones used during the Korean War. They were TV guided to large targets such as bridges, carrying high explosives. This photograph was taken on the USS *Boxer* (CVA 21) in early September 1952. The TV camera can be seen under the right wing. (*Dick Starinchak*)

Lieutenant Guy Bordelon was a night fighter pilot assigned to the VC-3 detachment on the USS *Princeton*. He performed land-based duty at Kimpo AB to guard against the nightly Po-2 attacks on friendly airfields. During this duty, he bagged five enemy aircraft between 29 June and 17 July 1953 to become the Navy's only ace of the war. Note the red stars painted on the side of his Corsair at Kimpo. (*John Ferebee*)

Fully loaded AD-4 Skyraiders from the USS *Essex* head over the Sea of Japan towards targets of opportunity over North Korea. At this time in the early spring of 1952, VF-54 was flying both the AD-2s and AD-4s. This was during the *Essex*'s first cruise in the war. (*Don Frazor*)

The maintenance and ordnance crews hurry to turn this F9F-2B around for another mission. This photograph was taken on the USS *Bon Homme Richard* (CV 31) during its first combat cruise in the summer of 1951. The Panther was assigned to VF-781 with Air Group-102. It was the only F9F fighter squadron assigned to the USS *Bon Homme Richard* on that cruise, although the group's photo detachment (VC-61) was flying the F9F-2P. (*Bill Barron*)

One of the VF-51 pilots confers with his plane captain after a mission over North Korea. This was during the USS *Essex*'s first cruise, which lasted until late March 1952. (*Frank Jones*)

The USS *Cape Esperance* (CVE-88) was a heavy contributor to the war effort as it brought hundreds of much-needed fighters over from the States. This photograph was taken in November 1951 when the carrier brought over the first load of new F-86E models that were badly needed to fight the MiG-15s. They were destined for the 51st Fighter Wing at Suwon AB. (*Ted Coberly*)

The flight deck on any of the carriers was a dangerous place to be as seen here on the USS *Valley Forge* prior to launching a group strength air strike. The Corsairs shown here were assigned to VF-92 in the spring of 1953 as part of Air Group-5. (*Ken Brownell*)

The USS *Kearsarge* (CVA 33) performed one cruise in the Korean War, beginning in August 1952. Its Air Group-101 included one squadron of F2H-2 Banshees from VF-11. They were identified by the 'T' on their vertical stabilizers. This photograph was taken in the early autumn of 1952 while they were returning from a mission. (*Ed Mason*)

Navy Corsairs had a heavy attrition rate due to the low altitudes that they had to fly at. The Navy's first loss to enemy fire was on 19 July 1950 when one of the Corsairs was shot down. This VF-871 Corsair has just been hit with a round in its left wing as it continues to search for more ground targets. It was based on the USS *Essex*. (*Bruce Bagwell*)

Air Group-102 had one squadron that flew a combination of AD-3s and AD-4s on board the USS *Bon Homme Richard* (CV 31) during their 1951 cruise. This VA-923 Skyraider has been fuelled and loaded with bombs for the morning mission. The *Bon Homme Richard* was an *Essex*-class aircraft carrier launched in 1944. (*Bill Barron*)

This AD-4 was flown by VA-115 during the USS *Philippine Sea*'s third combat cruise in 1952. They were assigned to Air Group-11 during that period. This element of Skyraiders is returning from a mission with their pylons empty. (*Bill Morgan*)

The Douglas Skyraider proved to be exceptionally tough in the most hostile of environments. VA-923 pilot Lt Bill Barron points to a huge hole in his wing that was caused by a large calibre shell while over a heavily defended target. His aircraft has been brought below deck for repairs on the USS *Bon Homme Richard*. (*Bill Barron*)

Corsair pilots rush out to their planes for another mission from the USS *Essex*. On the carrier's first cruise, VC-61 was flying the photo version of the Panther (F9F-2P) and on the second cruise that detachment had converted to the Banshee (F2H-2P) as seen here with the standard 'PP' on its vertical stabilizer. (*Bruce Bagwell*)

The battle that raged in and around Suwon was disastrous for the North Koreans. This T-34 tank was destroyed with Navy aircraft firing 5-inch HVARs that were fitted with an armour piercing head. This was taken at Suwon in early 1951, several months after the Marines had liberated Seoul. (*Richard Merian*)

A bomb-laden F9F-2 from VF-51 heads for targets up north after a strike was launched from the USS *Essex*. The squadron served three tours in the Korean War, one on the *Essex* and two on the *Valley Forge*. (*Frank Jones*)

Ordnance crews mix the ingredients for napalm prior to a strike by these VA-702 Skyraiders that were operating from the USS *Boxer* in 1951. As part of Air Group-101, the squadron was flying both the AD-2 and AD-4 during the cruise. (*Len Gordinier*).

A couple of specialized Skyraiders line up for take-off from the USS *Valley Forge* (CVA 45) during the early spring of 1953. This was during the carrier's final cruise in the war. The tail code 'ND' was used by VC-11 on its AD-4Ws and 'NR' signified VC-35's detachment that flew the AD-4Ns. (*Bill Kelly*)

In early March 1951, the USS *Boxer* was docked at Pearl Harbor while en route to the Far East and its second combat cruise in the Korean War. The aircraft in the background were part of its VF-721 under control of Air Group-101. The tour would last until 24 October 1951. The personnel on deck were probably going to be dismissed for some brief shore leave before the carrier sailed. (*Len Gordinier*)

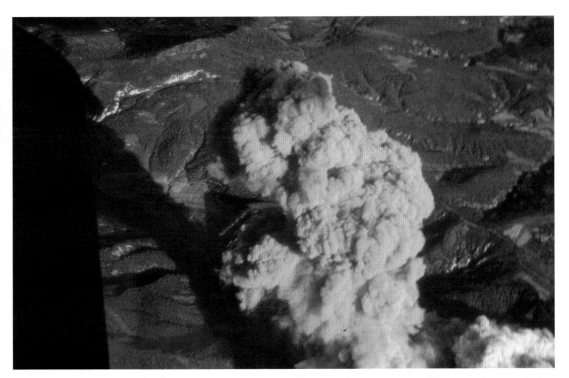

F4U-4Bs from VF-53 attack a huge enemy ammunition dump with great success. The secondary explosion was so big that the remainder of the strike force ranged out looking for other targets of opportunity. The squadron was operating from the USS *Essex* in 1952. (*Bruce Bagwell*)

The workhorse of the naval carrier force was the Douglas AD Skyraider. Each air group had at least one full squadron on board along with some specialized versions in detachments. The single engine AD could carry around 8,000 pounds of bombs and was armed with four 20-mm cannon. This photograph was taken on the USS *Princeton* (CV 37). (*US Navy*)

All of the carriers went through their supplies, fuel and ordnance at an accelerated pace and had to be replenished frequently. This supply ship, in the middle, is taking on two ships at once, including the USS *Bon Homme Richard*. Note the empty napalm tanks that are destined for the carrier's air group. This photograph was taken on the first cruise of the *Bon Homme Richard* in 1951, just sixty days into its cruise. (*Bill Barron*)

World War II era aircraft such as the Corsair and Avenger were very active in the Korean War, but the latter was not used in a combat situation. The TBM Avenger was the primary messenger/light cargo/mail carrier for the Navy. It shuttled back and forth between land bases in Japan, South Korea and the carriers. It was a welcome sight because it carried mail from home for the boat's personnel. This photograph was taken on the deck of the USS *Valley Forge* in 1952. (*Bob Balzer*)

Lt Henry Champion sits in the cockpit of one of the USS *Boxer*'s HO3S-1 helicopters during its cruise with Air Group-101 in 1951. All of the carriers had a detachment of HU-1s on board. Lt Champion flew combat with VF-791 in Corsairs during this cruise. (*Henry Champion*)

VF-781 flew the F9F-2B off the USS *Bon Homme Richard* during the carrier's first cruise in 1951. This model of the Panther was fitted with the underwing pylons that enabled it to carry a wide variety of ordnance. This view shows the 5-inch HVARs loaded and ready. (*Bill Barron*)

When each carrier deployment was completed and they returned to their home base, there was great fanfare with huge crowds to greet them. This was usually accompanied by a large sign displaying the Air Group's accomplishments during that cruise. This was the USS *Boxer* after one of its Korean War deployments. (*National Archives*)

Air Group-15 prepares to launch a major strike off the USS *Antietam* (CV 36) in April 1952. Notice the large turnout of carrier personnel that are waiting to view the launch. This photograph was taken during the final month (April 1952) of the *Antietam*'s only cruise of the war. (*Wayne Erdbrink*)

Air Group-19's aircraft are neatly parked on the deck as the USS *Princeton* nears port in Japan and the enlisted personnel are all suited out for a night of fun and relaxation. This photograph was taken on the carrier's third cruise in the war, circa 1952. The F9F-2s lined up are from VF-191. They were the only Panther squadron on board with the exception of the F9F-2Ps detachment with VC-61. (*US Navy*)

An HO3S-1 helicopter prepares to get airborne right before the strike force from Air Group-5 returns to the USS *Valley Forge*. This picture was taken in the spring of 1953 during the carrier's final cruise of the war. Each carrier had a chopper detachment from HU-1 on board. (*Hal Schwan*)

The USS *Kearsarge* (CVA 33) made one cruise in the war between the dates of 11 August 1952 and 17 March 1953. They had one full squadron of F2H-2 Banshees in their air group. The 'T' on the vertical stabilizer identified VF-11. The photo Banshees (F2H-2Ps) from VC-61 are seen in the foreground with the 'PP' tail code. Six weeks before the cruise was finished, the Air Group-101 on board was officially changed to Air Group-14. (*Gene Bezore*)

The second strike of the day was successfully launched and the four pilots mentioned above were flying the CAP with their primary responsibility being the USS *Oriskany*. Up until this time, the Russians or Chinese had not made any effort to penetrate close to any of the carriers that were on station. The Panther division figured they were in for another dull hour and a half orbit of the *Oriskany*. Launch time for this CAP was set for 1:00 p.m. and all four Panthers climbed up through the low lying overcast, breaking out into the clear at about 12,000 feet. While the F9Fs were still in the soup, the radar controller on the carrier radioed the division that he had bogies at eighty-three miles north flying on a course directly towards the Carrier Task Force. Lt Williams and the others were told to proceed immediately on an intercept course to cut the bogies off before they threatened the ships.

As the Panthers passed through 16,000 feet, Lt Williams stated that he had a group of contrails approaching his formation and, a few seconds later, seven MiG-15s flying line abreast of each other appeared at 35,000 feet or higher, which was way above the F9F formation. The flight leader of the VF-781 foursome was Lt Claire R. Elwood. This was destined to be a very dangerous and unique encounter because they were definitely Russian MiGs flying out of a Russian airbase. Before they closed, Lt Elwood's Fuel Pump Warning Light came on and the Combat Information Center (CIC) ordered him to report back to the carrier. His wingman, Lt (jg) Middleton, flew back with him, which was standard procedure in a situation like that when over enemy territory. Now, the odds were stacked in favour of the MiGs as a seven against two fight looked promising.

At this time, the MiGs passed overhead and were approximately forty-five miles from the *Oriskany*, but suddenly they went into a sharp turn to the left as if initiating a 180-degree turn to head back to their base. In the meantime, Lt Williams made the turn to follow them, continuing to climb while staying a distance behind the seven-ship formation. Suddenly, the enemy formation broke quickly back towards the two pursuing Panthers, while splitting up into two separate groups of four and three MiGs. Immediately the MiGs initiated a steep dive, which took them out of the contrails and visual contact with them was immediately lost by Lt Williams and his wingman. This prompted him to contact the *Oriskany* controller to get information on what the MiGs were up to, but he received bad news … the MiGs were no longer visible on the ship's radar!

This news made Williams initiate a slow left turn to point him in the direction of the last visual on the seven bogies. Suddenly they re-appeared, and this time it was a lot more serious as four MiGs, flying abreast, came down on the two Panthers with their cannon blinking orange on an aggressive firing pass. Williams immediately turned into the first four MiGs and positioned his fighter in gun range of the trailing MiG in the formation. He fired a short burst of his 20-mm gun at it. His rounds hit squarely on the MiG's fuselage and it started trailing smoke and debris as it fell out of the formation. Lt (jg) David Rowlands, Williams's wingman, followed the MiG down trying to get his guns and gun camera to function, but no luck. Seconds later, he gave up and immediately started a climb back to the same altitude as his element leader. In the meantime, the other three MiGs in the formation continued to climb above Williams to get in position to make another firing pass on him. Seconds later, they started firing their 23-mm and 37-mm guns at him from a distance that was definitely out of range as Williams turned into them and fired his 20-mm as the aircraft closed on each other at a phenomenal rate of speed.

Lt Williams stated:

> All of a sudden the other three MiGs joined the fight and I found myself dog fighting six of them. In the midst of all the rolling and jinking, I noticed one of the MiGs was locked onto my six o'clock. I turned hard causing him to overshoot me before he could score any hits on my aircraft.

After much manoeuvring, Williams got in position to shoot one of the MiGs and his high-explosive armour-piercing rounds impacted squarely on its fuselage. The disintegrating MiG was shedding pieces back into the slipstream and Williams had had to make a violent break to avoid the debris. He locked onto another MiG and scored hits on it. After scoring numerous hits on several of the MiG-15s, he was so busy trying to keep them off his tail that he didn't have time to follow each damaged MiG to see if it went down. But the fight raged on and in a couple of minutes he saw one of the MiGs on his tail, firing away. Just about the time he radioed the carrier that he needed help, a 37-mm round hit his Panther and exploded. His fighter was in serious trouble as he lost rudder control and had very little use of his ailerons, which left him with only one fully operational flight control and that was his elevators. This reduced him to 'porpoising' as a means of evasive manoeuvring as orange balls of fire passed above and below his fighter. His only hope was to make the cloud layer that was at 12,000 feet, which he did without absorbing any more hits.

Finally, Lt Williams began limping back towards the *Oriskany* and as he passed over a number of picket ships in the force, some began shooting at him, but that stopped after he got close enough for the gunners to recognize his straight-wing fighter. At this time of year, the Sea of Japan had frigid waters so baling out would be very dangerous. Trying to land on the carrier would be risky at best. He had more control of his F9F-5 at speeds above 170 knots, but he still had to try. The skipper of the *Oriskany* helped out when he lined the carrier up with William's final approach, so this cut down on trying to manoeuvre and line up the carrier deck and he was able to bring his damaged Panther down safely. He had expended all of his 20-mm ammo in the fight.

Officials from a top-secret agency were on a Navy cruiser close to Vladivostok when the lengthy dogfight was going on and they had monitored all the Russian radio transmissions. It was determined that only three of the Russian MiG-15s made it safely back to their base. Four of the fighters went down and all four of the pilots were killed. Lt Williams was informed of the results and, from what could be determined, he had shot down at least three of the MiGs but some sources show him with only one kill. He was also sworn to secrecy about the dogfight as it was a very sensitive issue.

There were many heroic actions carried out by pilots that flew combat missions in the war. Some of them were noted in detail while others went unnoticed. In a situation where one pilot got in trouble or was at risk, his fellow aviators swarmed in to help in any way they could. The emotions that drive this force can never be put in words and it is the same in many organizations such as law enforcement or the fire service. They are there for each other regardless of the risk. One of these acts occurred in April 1952 within the ranks of VF-112, a Panther squadron flying off the USS *Philippine Sea*. The key figures in this story were Lt (jg) Robair Mohrhardt and Lt (jg) Wally Carter. When an air group launched a strike, they usually sent two of their F9Fs up to protect the carrier and its support ships. This was to guard against a surprise air attack. On this day, Lt (jg) Mohrhardt was one of two Panther pilots patrolling over the Task Force when a critical situation developed. He describes the incident as it unfolded.

I was a young Lt (jg) flying a combat air patrol over the carrier when the ship called and said one of our squadron pilots was in serious trouble after hitting a well defended target. They gave me the directions to join up with him. I left my wingman Lt (jg) Jim Scott to continue to CAP and I headed for Lt (jg) Wally Carter who was flying the damaged F9F. He was on the CAG-11 staff, but always flew with VF-112. He had been flying escort on a photo mission when he was hit in the canopy and had suffered numerous cuts from the shattered Plexiglas. His eyes were affected and he could barely see, which caused him to become separated from the photo ship. I joined up with him, looked him over and did not detect any other damage except around his cockpit. He indicated that he could not see much other than the instrument panel, so that meant he could not fly on my wing.

I moved in close on his wing and started giving him directions; come left, come right, ease off on the power, start a let down, level off, etc. At the time we joined up, we were off the coast of North Korea and the closest friendly land base was at Kangnung (K-18). I guided him to that area and got him lined up with the main runway, with the crash crews standing by. Carter got his gear down and I stayed in close to his left wing until right before touchdown. We were lined up perfectly and right before his gear touched the runway, I told him to cut the power and I went to full throttle and headed back to the carrier just as soon as I saw that he was safely on the ground. The Marines at K-18 took great care of him and a few days later Carter was back on the ship. Without someone to guide him back to safety, there was no way he could have landed his plane. In this case, we both were very lucky!

As can de determined by the number of Naval Reserve squadrons that served in combat during the Korean War, they were a very effective force operating from the carriers. On the final combat cruise of the USS *Princeton* in the war, they had one AD Skyraider squadron that had its share of Reservist pilots: VA-155. Beginning in early February 1953, the *Princeton* was moving up the coast of Korea just like she had done over the past three cruises. Her Air Group-15 had the same mission assignment as it had had previously: close air support and interdiction. In addition to one Skyraider squadron, they had two squadrons of F9F-5s and the last Corsair squadron to see combat in the war: VF-152. The war had been a stalemate for months with the peace talks still bogged down and the Chinese trying everything they could to build up enough supplies to gain ground before the truce was signed. They knew if was just a matter of time, so they used every trick in the book to bring in hundreds of trucks to supply storage points and they were good at camouflaging these. However, low-

The USS *Princeton* at anchor off the coast of Japan sometime in the spring of 1953. The Corsairs seen on the deck were from VF-152. All of the regular strike squadrons on board had the 'H' on the vertical stabilizer. (*Robert Adkisson*)

level photo reconnaissance had also improved for the Americans and Air Group-15 had notched an impressive record of targets destroyed, especially rail cuts.

Lt (jg) John M. Sherly, a Skyraider pilot, flew two combat tours in the war. The first was on the USS *Princeton* during its 1952 cruise and the final one was immediately after the war ended, on the USS *Oriskany* (September 1953 to February 1954). He flew the AD-4 and AD-6 while logging fifty missions on each cruise. He comments on a few things that pertain to operations and missions he witnessed while on the *Princeton*:

> I was a member of VA-195 and we had a full complement of 28 pilots, one engineering officer and one ordnance officer. Our targets were almost always selected to break up the enemy's transportation and logistics system. It was constantly either bombing bridges or railroads and most of these were well defended, especially during the latter stages of the war. We also were called on many times to help the ground troops especially when the Chinese were trying to find weaknesses in the line and on a few occasions, I was a spotter for the big battleship USS *Iowa*.
>
> One particular mission that I will never forget was the second of about four attacks I participated in against the well defended power plants. This one was up on the Yalu River and the mission was sometime in July 1952. We launched with a maximum load of blockbuster bombs (2,000 lb) and approached the

One of the *Princeton*'s Skyraiders drops both of its 1,000-pound GP bombs on enemy troop bunkers on top of that ridge. The AD-4 in the distance had already released its bombs and they are seen exploding on target. Both of these Air Group-15 aircraft were assigned to VA-155 during the 1953 cruise. (*Robert Adkisson*)

target from 10,000 feet. Our mission was to knock out the facility's locks. I rolled over into a 45-degree dive and opened up my dive brakes to try and slow down to about 400 mph. As I passed through 2,000 feet, I punched off the bombs and forgot to close the brakes! This caused my Skyraider to 'mush' and I lost speed and found myself at about 200 feet over the river. There were hills on both sides of the river and the air was filled with tracers coming from every direction and they were very close. For a few seconds I thought I was going to buy the farm, but I got out of their range without a scratch. It was all small arms fire and if they had had heavier calibre guns, it might have been a different story. I pointed the nose up and went to full power as I headed back to the *Princeton*.

The bomb strikes against the well-defended power plants in 1952 were legend among some of naval aviation's finest hours in the Korean War. These targets had been off limits for quite some time for political reasons. One of the first big missions against the Suiho Dam up on the Yalu River occurred on 23 June 1952. It is recalled by a Corsair pilot, Ensign D.W. 'Ace' Jewell, who was flying with the 'Stingers' of VF-113, which was part of Air Group-11 on the *Philippine Sea*. He recalls that mission:

All of the aircraft in our group were assigned to this strike, which would be against all of the electrical power plants producing current in North Korea.

AD-4 Skyraiders from VA-195 score direct hits on a munitions factory in North Korea. The last division to drop their bombs had trouble with visibility because of the fire and billowing smoke from the secondary explosions. The squadron was part of Air Group-19 on the USS *Princeton*. (*John M. Sherly*)

Our ADs were loaded with 250-lb and 500-lb bombs while our Corsairs were carrying two 250-lb GPs and four HVARs and a full load of 20-mm ammo. Our assignment was strictly flak suppression while the Skyraiders dive bombed the main complex.

The day came and we found out it was a timed take out and all of the hydroelectric plants in North Korea were to be bombed at specific times. The launch went off without a hitch and with our commanding officer Lt Commander John Strane leading, we all joined up and proceeded towards the beach. VF-113 was to join up with VA-115 near the target before the attack started. We committed every Corsair we had that was in-service (14 out of 16). This equalled out to three divisions of four aircraft and one section of two aircraft. I was in the section of two on my division leader Lt Bob Taylor. In other words, I was 'tail-end Charlie'. The formation was loose as we hit the coast line. Our target was north and not far from the Yalu River. The weather became 2/3 cover with cumulus clouds and as we droned on, it was obvious that the skipper was searching for the reservoir and the dam. We were in a valley that led to a dead end, so we had to climb up through the cloud layer than back into another valley. I was too busy flying on my lead to really know where we were. Finally, we caught a glimpse of the reservoir in the distance and began a wide circle and after contact with the Skyraider squadron was established, we widened the circle. It was disturbing to glance over toward the big MiG airbase at Antung and see all those MiGs in the air practising touch-and-go landings! Now, my head was on a constant swivel because I had a feeling we were going to be jumped by some of those MiGs!

After circling the target area for at least fifteen minutes, the strike force finally lined up for their attack. The Corsairs went in first to knock out the gun emplacements, but there was no flak. For some reason they were silent. The remaining F4Us were ordered to hit a building that was assumed to be the office for the plant. But, you always have to anticipate the unexpected. As they were committed in their dives, the intensity of the Triple A increased. Ensign Jewell, diving hard, had all his switches on when the orange balls started coming up in thick waves. This tends to break one's concentration as Jewell had one eye on his leader and one eye on the target. With all the chatter on the radio and Ensign Jewell well into his dive, he salvoed all of his ordnance and before he started his pull out, he let go with a long burst from his 20-mm guns.

He continues:

The guys from VA-115 did a great job with their heavy ordnance with numerous direct hits. We pulled out low and fast, leaving smoke and flak behind. The building that we were assigned to was levelled. We pulled out much lower than the ADs, so we were in a heavy crossfire for a few seconds because we were below the ridgeline and the gunners were shooting straight across at us and they probably wiped out a few of their own. On the way back, there was a steady stream of chatter involved, those that had taken hits or were streaming hydraulic fluid. It sounded like mass confusion! We made it back to the carrier and as I taxied to the parking area and folded my wings, I gave the thumbs up sign to my maintenance chief and he responded with a violent thumbs down sign! I stayed in the cockpit as my Corsair was taken down to the hangar deck. When I exited the cockpit, I saw what the chief was referring to; there were 162 holes in my aircraft and fortunately the rounds had not hit anything vital. It took a lot of patches to get her back in the air!

The USS *Princeton*'s final cruise in the war was between January 1953 and September 1953. It had Air Group-15 on board with two squadrons of F9F-5s, as well as one Corsair and one Skyraider squadron. A week before leaving the States in early February, CVG-15 was transferred from Reserve Status to that of regular Navy Air Group, which meant that its squadrons would be redesignated as VA-152, 153, 154 and VA-155. Air Group-15's first combat cruise had been on the USS *Antietam* between September 1951 and May 1952. The carrier arrived off the coast of Korea in March 1953 and, possibly a bad omen, the first combat mission for the air group was scheduled for Friday the 13th! They did not lose any aircraft on that mission and they continued to fly daily and were pulled off the line on 1 April.

Within a very short period, the *Princeton* was back in action and CVG-15 set several records over the next four months. The first of these occurred on 15 June (about six weeks before the ceasefire) when they flew 184 sorties in one day. According to *Princeton* records, this was a remarkable accomplishment because it was achieved from the deck of a small straight deck carrier and at a time when

Lt George Smitman waits in the cockpit of his AD-4 Skyraider for time to start engines. He received the DFC on a mission he flew in March 1953 while flying with VA-155 off the USS *Princeton*. (*George Smitman*)

Lt George Smitman was hit while bombing a heavily defended target, and with his instruments shot out and his hydraulics damaged, he managed to bring his VA-155 Skyraider back to the USS *Princeton*, as seen here. The mission was flown in March 1953. (*George Smitman*)

night carrier operations were still considered anything but routine. The second outstanding record was set by VC-3 pilot Lt Guy Bordelon when he shot down five night hecklers while deployed to a land base. The third record was earned by having fifty-six days of around-the-clock operations between 1 June and 27 July (war's end). This feat was due to the fact that the USS *Philippine Sea* had some serious mechanical problems and had to return to Japan for repairs, which put the pressure on the *Princeton* to fill in the gap.

Lt George E. Smitman, a Naval Reservist, was awarded the Distinguished Flying Cross (DFC) for a mission he flew on 22 March 1953 in his VA-155 Skyraider. It was supposed to be a routine close air support mission and the target was a build up of Chinese forces close to the front lines. As he was making his first bomb run, his Skyraider took a major hit, which caused total failure of all his flight instruments. Despite the damage, he made repeated dives on the target area to make sure he expended all of his ordnance. It was noted that his attacks resulted in destroying four mortar positions, four supply bunkers that were easily destroyed by the 1,000-lb bombs. His smaller ordnance took out about 175 yards of trenches that were occupied by enemy personnel. In addition to this feat, he was able to fly his aircraft back to the *Princeton*, where he discovered that he could not lower his flaps or landing gear!

Lt Smitman circled the carrier while the air group landed the rest of its aircraft. Then he lined up the deck and made a perfect wheels-up landing with minimal damage to his aircraft. While numerous pilots faced this situation and landed successfully, there were many that did not. For expending all of his ordnance effectively against the target and making it back to the carrier with no instruments

Lt George Smitman makes his final approach to the USS *Princeton* after returning from a mission with his instruments and hydraulics shot out. He was flying with VA-155 in an AD-4NA (BuNo 126911). The mission was flown in March 1953. (*George Smitman*)

or hydraulics, he was awarded the DFC. VA-155 proved to be extremely effective against enemy troops and truck movements during those final weeks of the war, as was the entire air group. Navy aircraft loss records for the month of March 1953 show that the *Princeton* lost only one aircraft. The *Philippine Sea* lost six; the *Oriskany* lost three; followed by the *Valley Forge* with four losses. During that month, the Navy had four of its big carriers on line keeping pressure on the Chinese. When the truce was signed on 27 July 1953, the USS *Princeton* remained in the area and on 7 September got underway for San Diego to end a brilliant series of cruises in the war.

The USS *Boxer* probably contributed as much to the war effort as any other carrier because, in addition to its four combat cruises, it initially carried a deck full of USAF aircraft over to the Far East during the very early days of the war. Its final cruise started in late March 1953 with ATG-1 on board. VF-194 was one of the squadrons that flew the Skyraiders during the final months of the war and they had done a stint on the USS *Valley Forge* back in 1952 while flying in the F4U-4B.

By the time Ensign Thomas A. Smith, fresh out of flight training, entered the war on the USS *Boxer*, the air group was flying at a frantic pace, trying to bring the war to a successful ending. He relates some of his experiences while flying the AD-4NA with VF-194.

Our squadron was pretty well known when we got to the Far East because they had done an earlier stint in Corsairs with outstanding results. Many of our pilots were on their second tour and quite experienced and were a mixture of regular Navy, reservists and about a half dozen boot ensigns like me. Our air group (ATG-1) had, in addition to the regular squadrons, some composite detachments and our helicopter rescue unit, which picked up around eight of our squadron's pilots that suffered from failed launches. Of course, it didn't help that the Navy was experimenting with spark plugs that seemed to fail quite often. It didn't help matters that our AD-4NAs were loaded with about 5,000 pounds or more of bombs, rockets and 720 rounds of 20-mm ammo for almost all mission launches.

The straight deck carriers like we had in Korea required always landing safely by catching a wire. A hook skip or long landing meant going into a barrier (which, at least, meant an overhaul or at worst flying into the 'pack' … which was where the aircraft that had landed safely were when the barrier was dropped back down). If you did land into the parked aircraft, you were probably killed along with many others that were working on the deck. The ATG-1 pilots were pretty good about getting a 'cut' – signal by 'Paddles', the Landing Signal Officer (LSO) – or a wave off, which got you to power up and circle around for another attempted landing after getting into line again. Both 'cut' and 'wave off' were mandatory signals and all other signals were advisory. So that was the good news. This means, of course, that there is always some bad news. The pilots launching in the jets (Panthers and Banshees) didn't always make a successful catapult shot. The *Boxer* had one erratic catapult and the other one was pretty reliable. When a jet went in the water on launch, the cockpit frequently split open on hitting the water and, when this happened, it usually took the pilot to a watery grave!

As far as the ADs having trouble in getting off the carrier, they also had their share of problems. Many were loaded down with about 2.5 tons of ordnance and with the faulty spark plugs; several went right off the cat and into the sea. The aircraft had only four bolts holding the engine to the mounts and when the Skyraider went straight in nose first the engine would shear off ahead of the cockpit separating it from the airframe. The AD's fuselage would then float for a long time … up to a minute. This provided plenty of time to get out on the wing where the hovering rescue chopper could get a sling down and pull the pilot to safety. According to Ensign Smith, his squadron lost seven or eight ADs like that but never lost one of the pilots.

> Sometimes, when you got a bad launch, you could fly it out of this problem by using 'ground effect' (a wing's characteristic of pushing air down when very close to the water, thus pushing you up until you got sufficient air speed to retract flaps and start to climb). This usually took two to three miles before you could figure you had made it. I was one of those pilots that were fortunate enough never to have lost that battle! My first mission was a bummer! We were assigned to bomb a reservoir and I could not hear anything on my head set en route and by the time we were 'feet dry' I still couldn't resolve the lost communications problem before we started our bomb runs. Rather than hold outside the area, I chose to follow in the 'daisy chain' but not drop my bombs since I could not identify whether there were friendly troops nearby… still no communication!

After going 'feet wet', Ensign Smith dumped his ordnance and when he got back on the *Boxer*, he found out that his communication cord had been wrapped around a seat lever and had pulled out.

> Railroad bridges were frequent challenges; you were cautioned not to drop bombs if you were below 1,000 feet (over terrain), but it was difficult to hit anything that was only ten feet wide! You either hit it right on or missed and the bomb would blow up in the water. One time, after four of us had missed, I went down to about 500 feet and pickled one off on the bridge and while I nailed the bridge, it nailed me too! A piece of concrete went through my portside wing flap leaving a hole you could drop a basketball through! I immediately found that I needed almost full left stick to fly in level flight. It made an interesting landing back on the carrier. I had learned another lesson the hard way!

By the late spring of 1953, the Chinese were still pouring troops and supplies into the front lines in the hope of gaining more ground before a ceasefire was agreed. In a lot of instances, they threw their heaviest concentration of troops against the ROK lines in the hope of finding a weak spot. Ensign Smith relates one of the missions he flew in support of just such a thrust by the Chinese:

> Once, we were called in just after going 'feet dry'. Then our L-5 controller (Code named 'Top Hat') assigned us to a priority target. A vast Chinese contingent

had just crossed the 38th Parallel on the east coast and was threatening a vital area called Anchor Hill. Three thousand Chinese troops were in full charge to make it to a point where they would be in position to change the whole character of the east side of the Korean peninsula. They were up against about 3,000 ROK defenders. The ROKs were losing position quickly and 'Top Hat' gave us an assignment to bomb the enemy troops. We were carrying 250-lb and 500-lb bombs, which were way too heavy to ensure accuracy because of the friendlies that were in close contact with the enemy.

   We told 'Top Hat' that we would hit more than just enemy troops and he told us that the South Korean General had ordered us to drop all of our ordnance to ensure that the Chinese were stopped. We were told once again to hold off and the ROK General repeated his order: 'Take out the entire hill!' We did as ordered, but it was situations like this that didn't make the conflict any easier! At this date, we thought that the war was only a few days away from ending.

A significant number of very young Navy pilots undertook combat tours in Korea, especially during the final months of the war. This same situation was also prevalent in the Air Force and Marines. But, their superior training, compared with their adversaries, got most of them through safely. In 1953, the number of anti-aircraft guns placed along the key roads and rails posed the greatest dangers to aircraft that were flying the low-level bombing missions. Lt (jg) Sam Catterlin was one of those pilots that flew AD-4s with VF-194 off the USS *Boxer* on their final cruise in 1953. Almost all of his missions were CAS against Chinese troops that were well dug in.

   On one of the days that Catterlin's Air Group-1 was sending out its aircraft against a variety of targets, he recalls that his Skyraider squadron put up two separate efforts in the form of two four-ship flights against targets around the Wonsan area. It was one of his earlier missions when the adrenalin was really pumping. He remembers:

I was leading one of the flights of four AD-4s against several targets that were in close proximity to each other. We made our bomb runs while encountering a normal amount of Triple A and small arms fire. After the last of our ordnance had been expended, we climbed for altitude while turning toward the coast and return to the *Boxer*. Suddenly, one of our pilots that were in the division next to us called out 'I've been hit...I'm on fire!'

   The background sounds from his aircraft indicated exploding 20-mm rounds in their ammo cans. I immediately came on the radio and told him 'If you're on fire...Bale out!' It took a couple of minutes for him to respond to my suggestion and he stated that maybe he wasn't on fire. There was no further indication of exploding shells. We proceeded on back to the *Boxer* with no further problems. That pilot was Steve DeLancy and his Skyraider had a good size hole in the starboard wing just behind the 20-mm inboard gun. It was the only one of our ADs that were hit on that mission. When we finished debrief, the XO called me aside and told me not to tell these new pilots to bale out unless I was sure they were in serious trouble because they just might do it! Fortunately, no one in my squadron had to bale out during that cruise.

The drain on Navy squadrons and their personnel was constant as the war moved into its final year. The Reserve units had come in to help with a heavy commitment and all of these units did an outstanding job. There were some carriers that only did one cruise and they were also very successful. The Cold War in Europe was starting to build up a lot of tension and the Navy's obligation was to keep some of its carriers in a high-visibility mode, especially in the Atlantic and Mediterranean. Air Group-4 was based on the east coast out of NAS Jacksonville in 1952–3. They were equipped with two full squadrons of F2H-2 Banshees and one squadron of F4U-4 Corsairs (VF-44). Their only AD squadron was VA-45. The group was destined to do one combat cruise in the Korean War on the USS *Lake Champlain* (CVA 39). Each squadron in the group (not counting the specialized detachments) consisted of sixteen aircraft, twenty-four pilots and about a hundred enlisted men that maintained the unit. When alerted for combat duty, it was understood that their missions would primarily revolve around close air support for the front-line troops, although they would definitely get a taste of interdiction against heavily defended targets.

Ensign Joe Jannotta was a young pilot just out of flight training in that group and he recalls the rigid training involved in getting everyone ready for a cruise in the war.

When I joined VF-44 in January 1953 as its junior officer, preparations were in full swing to achieve combat readiness. It involved intense rehearsals: dive bombing, strafing and rocket runs along with carrier qualifications (both day and night). Several times we practised air strikes where 50 or more of our aircraft would roll into a full power dive from 15,000 feet converging on a target. This simulated strikes on those heavily defended power plants that had concentrated gun emplacements around them. We referred to these as 'group gropes' and this amounted to too many aircraft in a small piece of airspace. To my discomfort, the F4U-4, in a full power dive hits maximum speed for the airframe at about 450 knots. Once at this speed, it would behave badly with the stick jerking and banging against my knees.

In late April 1953, the *Lake Champlain* loaded its personnel and air group and weighed anchor out of Mayport naval base east of Jacksonville, Florida. At full steam, they arrived in Tokyo Bay on 5 June by way of the Suez Canal and Indian Ocean. They re-provisioned quickly and went straight into combat off the coast of Korea. The biggest indicator that the Chinese were trying for a last-ditch offensive before an armistice was the fact that the air battles over MiG Alley had escalated and truck movement at night was on the rise. The F-86s would register fifty-five aerial kills over the MiG-15s in June 1953 and UN aircraft lost during the month of June would total sixty-five. The losses of the latter reflect the intense anti-aircraft fire that was thrown up by the enemy as they tried to defend their assets.

Ensign Jannotta continues:

We were working with two other carriers and our Corsair squadron was very active. I usually flew one mission a day and sometimes two, which consisted of flights of from six to eight VF-44 Corsairs. Most of these missions were

close air support for Marines and Army troops. Typically, we made three
runs against various targets, which consisted of one 1,000-lb GP bomb and
two 250-lb GPs. We usually fired our .50 calibre guns as we went in to drop
our ordnance because this was effective in keeping the gunners' heads down.
We went in at a 70-degree angle for targets that had been marked by FACs
with smoke bombs/rockets. The Chinese used a lot of high calibre automatic
weapons against us and those rounds seemed like large orange balls floating
up toward us. I was only hit once in the vertical stabilizer, but I had no trouble
controlling my aircraft and returning to the carrier safely.

One of the memorable missions he flew turned out to be his thirteenth. It began
routinely as the twenty ships in the Task Force turned into the wind simultaneously.
The two squadrons of Banshees launched first and after the last one was catapulted
off, the Corsairs from VF-44 got the signal to start engines.

Our flight of six Corsairs was loaded and ready. We hit the prime and start
buttons resulting in banging, coughing and belching of black smoke as the
four bladed props took hold. Taking our turn from a densely parked group of
aft aircraft, we were directed to taxi forward, unfolding our wings and going
through the take-off check off list and passing from one brightly coloured
flight deck hand to another. Choreographing the movement of combat aircraft
on a carrier deck was a thing of beauty; perfectly coordinated and timed. Once
in place for launch, the flight deck officer began waving a small yellow flag
above his head, which was the signal for full power. After a quick scan of
my instruments, I saluted. His arm came smartly down pointing forward.
Releasing my brakes, down the deck I rumbled. Getting a fully loaded Corsair
airborne was a delicate proposition; once off the bow, I lost a few feet of
altitude picking up an extra knot or two to begin a climb. Gear up and flaps
are slowly bled (retracted) with a climbing turn to begin joining up with the
rest of my division.

The mission for VF-44 that day was close air support over the front-line positions.
When they took off from the Lake Champlain, the weather was fine but by the time
they went 'feet dry', it had deteriorated.
Ensign Jannotta continues:

After checking in with our forward air controller, we were advised to head
north to search for a break in the overcast that would allow us to get below it
and start hunting for targets on the main supply lines. For the most part, the
enemy moved their supplies at night, but when there was a heavy overcast,
they had their trucks on the move because the chance of encountering aircraft
was greatly reduced. We found a hole in the clouds and, to our surprise, we
dropped down right over a Chinese convoy that consisted of about a dozen
trucks all headed south. When they saw us, they scattered quickly, but it was
too late. We made several strafing runs and set six of them on fire and as
we continued to fly north, we spotted a couple of small bridges, which we
promptly knocked out. On getting back to the ship, I mentioned to one of our

pilots that I had just flown on my 13th mission on the 13th of June in Corsair #13. Fortunately for me, it was not on a Friday! That mission got a lot of media attention in news articles entitled 'Lucky 13'.

Weather over North Korea was always a major factor in how successful a mission was going to be. Fog at ground level was also a factor as it hid the targets from the air. VF-44 had more than its share of inclement weather and a memorable occasion is described by Ensign Jannotta:

> This turned out to be one of the most interesting missions I flew that did not involve combat. It was a dawn launch of six Corsairs and as our flight rendezvoused after take-off the weather had turned marginal and by the time we reported 'feet dry', a dense fog had enveloped that area providing a modest one-eighth to one quarter mile visibility. At this point, there was no chance of carrying out our mission or returning to the carrier. Instead, we descended to sea level and worked our way back to the shoreline in hopes of finding a friendly airfield, which was Kunsan (K-8). It had a runway of 4,000 feet made out of the PSP. After several tries, we found it and made a safe landing with full loads of ordnance still intact. We were all OK, but the next few days were miserable. We sat it out for two days, bedded down in aluminium barracks, eating canned beef and vegetables for breakfast, lunch and dinner.

At this time of year, the entire base was a quagmire of mud that was probably about six inches deep. It was a stark contrast to the conditions on an aircraft carrier. On the third day of waiting, the weather cleared and the VF-44 pilots were able to take off. However, not long into the flight, they were told to turn back to Kunsan because the fleet was still engulfed in dense fog. Finally, at about 1:00 that afternoon, the weather started to clear and once again they took off.

> We were so anxious to get back to the carrier that we did not top off our fuel tanks, which was a big mistake that could have had serious consequences later in the flight. For the next five hours, we were engulfed in bad weather with practically no visibility. We flew in tight formation and I kept my eyes locked on my section leader (wing separation of about ten feet). Getting separated from the flight would complicate an already tenuous situation. Back and forth we went at 200 feet altitude searching for a carrier...any carrier! Low fuel warning lights came on and miraculously a few minutes later, there was a break in the fog and dead ahead was the island of the USS *Lake Champlain*! Quickly turning to parallel the ship's course, each Corsair broke to the down wind leg in preparation for landing, with just enough gas for one pass. I was the last one to hit the 180 and began a turn to port. I made it on the first try! Typically, in a flight of six, there would be at least one or two wave offs. This time, we all made it aboard on the first try and if we hadn't, probably a couple of us would have gone in the water!

The USS *Lake Champlain* (CVA 39) did one cruise in the war and the dates were from late April 1953 until December 1953. They were on station when the war ended and maintained the vigil until it was time to return to the States. The carrier had Air Group-4 on board and, for the first time, there were two full squadrons of F2H-2 Banshees in the mix.

At this late stage in the war, the enemy was trying anything they could to gain ground or to deliver a decisive blow because they knew it was just a matter of time before it was over. One of the dangers faced by the carriers was the threat of being attacked, especially those that were working up near the Russian and Chinese borders. To remove the element of surprise, each carrier had a small detachment of the AD-4Ws on board. AT2 Jack Sauter was an aviation electronics technician in VC-12. He recalls some of his experiences while serving on the *Lake Champlain*.

> These aircraft were equipped with the General Electric APS-20 radar, which was an excellent warning system. Initially, these were mounted on the old TBM Avengers. When we got the AD-3Ws and 4Ws, our Composite Squadrons (VC-22 on the west coast and VC-12 on the east coast) took over the airborne early warning tasking. I was in VC-12 and we sent small detachments to Korea on the USS *Leyte*, USS *Bon Homme Richard* and the USS *Lake Champlain*.
>
> On our carrier deployments, our detachments were made up of three AD-4Ws, five pilots and about thirty enlisted personnel. What made these units unique was the nearly exclusive use of enlisted aircrewmen to interpret the radar and then vector the combat air patrol (CAP) aircraft to intercept the target. All of these controllers were aviation electronics technicians. If it appeared unusual to employ enlisted personnel for such a critical task, there was a simple reason. Carrier-based Airborne Early Warning (AEW) was developed at a time of great military austerity just after World War II, and there weren't enough officers either available or interested in the program. However, the enlisted types came through and filled the gap.

The kamikazes proved that the carriers had the potential to be vulnerable to air attack, especially after World War II when the jets became operational. If a carrier task force was operating close enough to land targets for their aircraft to hit, then they were close enough to be attacked by opposing forces. When the first large carrier (USS *Valley Forge*) was operating close to the North Korean coastline in July 1950, it made the case for having AEW planes overhead and on the alert. When the MiG-15s entered the war in large numbers in December 1950, it took the alert status to a much higher level. For some reason or another, the MiGs never liked to operate over water, thus they were never a real threat. However, Intel knew that there were some Russian twin engine jet bombers based at one of the bases in Manchuria, but they never ventured south of the Yalu River and were never a threat.

Jack Sauter recalls:

> As the Korean War progressed, Task Force 77 kept at least three and sometimes four *Essex*-class carriers on station off the coast while conducting daily combat operations. Since our modified version of the Skyraider had two crewmen seats in the rear compartment, and we often flew with only one operator in order to save our eyes, sometimes this meant carrying a passenger. Generally, it was one of our pilots or chiefs becoming familiarized with the radar, but in

some instances it was a high ranking officer getting in his flight time. On one of these missions, I had the Chief of Staff to Commander Carrier Division I, a four striper (Captain) sitting in back with me. That day consisted of flying a 50-mile circle around the task force perimeter and plotting all air and surface targets. The Captain was very inquisitive; had I ever picked up any bandits? Did I find it difficult to interpret this 5-inch screen, hour after hour, with no relief? The answer to the first question was no and the answer to the second was yes. Then he turned to me and said with great seriousness, 'I came along today to see for myself just how good our AEW was. I've always been uneasy about the Chinese ever since they surprised General MacArthur in November 1950 and almost pushed us off the peninsula. I have had the feeling that they might pull off another surprise and this time it would be against Task Force 77. If that were to happen, you and a few other radarmen would be the most important people in this entire fleet'… The topic of a surprise attack by the Chinese was always discussed in the ready room. The one factor in our favour was that the Chinese were mostly equipped with World War II vintage aircraft.

The detachments from VC-3 were involved in flying the night heckler and defensive missions at night on just about all the carriers in the war. They did most of their work in the F4U-5N Corsairs. With Naval air being limited on their chances of encountering enemy aircraft because of their CAS/interdiction role, there was very little chance for any of their pilots to score more than a couple of kills. It was the F-86 Sabre pilots that were racking up the big numbers. But, there was a flicker of hope for the Navy and it would fall on the shoulders of a VC-3 pilot that was assigned to Detachment D on the USS *Princeton*, and he would become the only Navy ace of the Korean War. This was Lieutenant Guy P. Bordelon Jr. His night kills came within a very short span of time (30 June 1953 and 16 July 1953). At that time, the enemy knew the war was over, but they continued to send mostly the bi-wing trainer type aircraft, with wooden construction, over into friendly territory to try and do some damage to the airfields at Suwon and Kimpo. They were well aware that these flight lines would be jammed with F-86 day fighters at night, so if they could come in under the radar and drop a few small bombs or grenades, they might cause some disruption.

   This problem became so regular that the USS *Princeton* sent a couple of their F4U-5Ns over to Kimpo for night alert. On the night of 29 /30 June, Lt Bordelon was vectored toward some incoming unidentified bogeys. Before the night was over, he had claimed two Yak-18s destroyed. These were single-engine trainer types similar to the American T-6 with two crew positions (normally an instructor and student). On 5 July, he was up north of Kimpo when he bagged two of the ancient Po-2 bi-wing aircraft. Finally, on 16 July, he got in behind another Po-2 at tree-top level and shot it down. This put a stop to all of the night heckler raids for the next eleven nights as the war ended on 27 July.

   On 20 July, Lt Bordelon was sent to Tokyo to receive the Navy Cross. It was presented by Lt General Samuel E. Anderson, Commanding General of 5th Air Force in Korea. The award had been quickly approved by Secretary of the Navy, Robert B. Anderson. From there, Lt Bordelon went back aboard the USS *Princeton* where he received a great welcome from all hands. There had been several Navy and Marine exchange pilots that did tours with the 4th and 51st Fighter Wings flying the F-86 Sabre. Many of them scored kills but only one became an ace (Major John F. Bolt USMC), while he was flying in Sabres with the USAF.

While the Korean War began just under five years after World War II ended, carrier operations for Korea had changed drastically since 1945. The heavier, more demanding jets were rapidly changing the face of naval aviation and bigger aircraft carriers with their angled decks were already in development by 1953. It was difficult to set up coordinated attacks when half of the strike force comprised prop types and the remainder comprised jets. With the advanced high-calibre anti-aircraft guns brought in by the Chinese, you had to have all of the planes arrive over the target at the same time, and the ones assigned to take out the Triple-A emplacements had to go in ahead of the bombers. The only full-scale operation conducted by the Navy in Korea that closely resembled the World War II strategy was the Inchon Landing in mid-September 1950, which was carried out to perfection. New aircraft types and more sophisticated weapons were being integrated into the standard tactical regimens and learning how best to use these new systems was ever changing. In some respects, the Korean War was beneficial for the American and British military because it better prepared them for the long Cold War that was just starting.

During World War II, there were no 'safe havens' allowed for the enemy, but with politics taking over the battlefield, that was not the case in Korea and Vietnam. You cannot keep casualties down and win a war if you have enemy strongholds that are off limits to attack. In Korea, the naval carrier operations did not have the mission where they hunted down and attacked enemy fleets, but, instead, they flew lengthy missions over land and deep into North Korea with the carriers sitting about 80–100 miles off shore waiting for the returning strike force.

If you are discussing the size of the force, then the Korean War could not be compared with World War II because it would be dwarfed in comparison. The number of aircraft lost by all three branches of the military in Korea was huge. In contrast, the number of sorties flown and ordnance delivered by the Navy and Marines was easily on a par with World War II. Bear in mind that there were never more than four big carriers on line at any one time with at least three of the small carriers (equipped with Marine Corsairs) on station at the same time. Some impressive figures were published by the Pentagon in 1954 and these statistics reflect a combination of Navy and Marine aircraft operations. In approximately 36 months of war in Korea, both services combined to fly 276,000 combat sorties, while dropping almost 177,000 tons of bombs and napalm. The number of 5-inch HVARs fired was an impressive 272,000. The total number of sorties flown in the Korean War by the Navy and Marines (combined) was within 7,000 sorties flown in World War II by both branches combined. Bear in mind that almost all of these two branches' operations were in the Pacific during World War II. The total tonnage delivered in Korea bettered that of World War II by 74,000 tons! During the 1942–5 period, Navy and Marine sorties equalled about 10 per cent of the total and this probably included the European Theatre. But, in Korea, both services combined to contribute more than 30 per cent of the total.

Each of the carrier air groups caused great levels of damage and destruction to the enemy on each of their combat cruises. All of the final figures posted by each group after a cruise were very similar with those during the better flying months (summer/autumn) having slightly better results. The following is the final tally from Air Group-5 on the USS *Essex*'s first cruise (August 1951 to March 1952). These figures were verified by post strike photos.*

USS *Essex* (CV 9)

Air Group-5

Destroyed

Enemy troops killed: 3,007	Wounded: 100
Ox carts: 341	Rail cuts: 3,139 places
Rails bent: 75 places	Tanks destroyed: 5
Trucks destroyed: 291	Rail cars destroyed: 485
Locomotives: 38	Highway bridges: 15
Supply dumps: 47	Ammunition dumps: 1
Factories: 3	Warehouses: 35
Buildings & barracks: 672	Gun emplacements: 103
Boats: 306	Power installations: 5
Bunkers: 33	Rail yards: 10
Railroad tunnel: 1	Rail bridges: 117
Railroad bypasses: 79	Highway bypasses: 8
Fuel dumps: 11	Dams: 3
Crane: 1	Observation posts: 2

Damaged

Tanks: 21	Trucks: 367
Autos: 17	Locomotives: 70
Ox carts: 121	Highway bridges: 47
Supply dumps: 52	Factories: 10
Warehouses: 45	Misc. buildings: 568
Gun emplacements: 95	Boats: 328
Bunkers: 3	Rail yards: 20
Railroad tunnels: 8	Rail cars: 933
Railroad bridges: 143	Rail bypasses: 44
Road bypasses: 11	Fuel dumps: 4
Observation posts: 3	Command posts: 2
Cranes: 3	

* Source: USS *Essex* newspaper *The Carrier Pigeon*, 3/25/52

The USS *Boxer* published its scores after its March 1951 to October 1951 combat cruise with Carrier Air Group-101. These dates provided much better flying weather than for Air Group-5's cruise on the *Essex*. This strike force was made up of Naval Air Reserve squadrons. During this cruise, they logged 8,567 sorties, which equated to 23,627 flight hours.

USS *Boxer*

Air Group-101

Destroyed

Rail bridges: 213

Rail cuts: 436

Rail cars: 493

RR maintenance buildings: 2

Roads cratered: 242

Trucks: 383

UN vehicles (abandoned): 107

Ammunition dumps: 22

Supply dumps: 57

Warehouses: 175

Misc. buildings: 1,996

Gun emplacements: 207

Casualties inflicted: 8,661

Railroad tunnels: 0

Locomotives: 22

Rail marshalling yards: 0

Highway bridges: 131

Tanks: 10

Vehicles (misc.): 33

Carts: 343

Fuel dumps: 40

Factories: 16

Barracks: 43

Pill boxes: 16

Boats: 50

Damaged

Railroad bridges: 80

Locomotives: 25

Marshalling yards: 73

Highway bridges: 80

Tanks: 16

Vehicles (misc.): 59

Fuel dumps: 10

Factories: 43

Barracks: 121

Pill boxes: 11

Boats: 49

Rail tunnels: 46

Rail cars: 741

Highway bridges: 80

Highway tunnels: 2

Trucks: 302

Carts: 98

Supply dumps: 80

Warehouses: 260

Buildings: 1,090

Gun emplacements: 65

CHAPTER FIVE

Naval Air's Top Aircraft in the Korean War

The Korean War proved to be a major milestone for naval aviation because the jet age hade made huge advances and all of the major aircraft manufacturers were concentrating on designing and building jet fighters and bombers in an effort to keep pace with the Russians.

The air war over North Korea was the greatest 'proving ground' for aerial combat in the fast lane. All of the major branches of the US military developed tactics and bombing techniques that would remain valid when the war in Vietnam was fought ten to fifteen years later. However, between 1950 and 1953, the Navy had a problem with its front-line jets: mainly the F9F Panther and the F2H-2 Banshee. The older *Essex*-class carriers had relatively short decks and for either of these aircraft types to carry a heavy ordnance load, the chances of getting airborne were at risk. Both of these fighters were designed for aerial supremacy, but when large numbers of the MiG-15 and F-86 were built up to be pitted against each other, the slower jets such as the F2H-2, F9F-2 and the USAF's F-80C were much more useful in the close air support and interdiction roles. The F-84 Thunderjet would also be classified in this group. It was the swept-wing faster jets that ruled the skies over north-west Korea.

Grumman F9F Panther

This tough little fighter was Grumman's first major foray into the jet world and it was the first mass-produced type to enter the fleet. Its first flight was on 24 November 1947 with outstanding test pilot Corwin 'Corky' Meyer at the controls. By the time the Korean War started, the Panther was a major factor in both the Navy and Marine inventory. After much testing, it was finally cleared for operations from the deck of a carrier in September 1949. The armament carried by the F9F was four 20-mm cannon, which was the preferred calibre of the Navy for the fighters that were coming into service.

There were six versions of the Panther that saw combat with the Navy in Korea: F9F-2, F9F-2B, F9F-2P, F9F-3 and F9F-5 and F9F-5P. The Dash-2 was the first production model and was available in the greatest numbers in the summer of 1950. The Dash-2B was fitted with underwing pylons that would allow the fighter to get involved in air-to-ground missions. All of the Dash-2s were soon fitted with the pylons and the 'B' was omitted from the description. The Dash-3 was powered by the Allison J33 engines and all other features from the Dash-2 were standard. The Dash-5 had the more powerful Pratt & Whitney J48 engine, which allowed it to get off the carrier deck with heavier loads of ordnance up to 2,000 pounds. Grumman built 616 of these for the Navy. The Dash-2P was a specialized photo-reconnaissance

F9F-2B Panthers from VF-721 are returning from a strike over North Korea during the last week of July 1951. They were part of Air Group-101 on the USS *Boxer*. All of the main strike aircraft in the group carried the 'A' on the vertical stabilizer. (*US Navy*)

model that traded in its cannon for cameras. It was used at low level over potential targets and was also used as a follow up for post-strike pictures.

Although the Grumman jet was not the fastest fighter around, it built up a solid reputation in combat for being rugged and effective in its close air support/ interdiction role. Its permanent tip tanks gave it added range and eliminated the need for external tanks attached to the underwing pylons, which gave it more room for rockets and bombs. The first squadron to use the F9F-3 in combat was VF-51, operating from the USS *Valley Forge* during the early days of the war. One of the greatest accomplishments of the Dash-3 was the fact that it made the Navy's first aerial kills of the war on the first strike flown on 3 July 1950. It bagged two Yak-9 prop-type North Korean fighters. Grumman built a total of approximately 1,385 F9Fs (all models included) before production halted.

The Navy's F9F jet fighter was heavy and they were all underpowered for taking off from a carrier deck without assistance. The hydraulic catapult was the standard device to get the heavier-loaded jets airborne, but it had limitations. There were numerous cold cat shots that could not get the jets airborne; they ended up in the water and many of the pilots drowned before the helicopters could get to them. Almost all of the *Essex*-class carriers used this system and according to a few of the air bosses, it required 33 knots over the deck to get a fully loaded Panther airborne and this was with a full load of 20-mm ammunition and six 5-inch HVARS. For every knot under the 33 figure, two HVARS had to be removed from the plane. This put several red shirt ordnance men standing by each catapult to remove the rockets

F9F Panther pilots walk to their fighters and prepare to launch after a mission briefing. This photograph was taken on the deck of the USS *Princeton* during its final cruise in 1953. These were pilots from both VF-153 and VF-154 serving with Air Group-15. (*US Navy*)

if the wind wasn't measured up to the required speed. This was a constant problem with all carrier ops during the Korean War.

The Panther's maximum speed was about 575 mph/925 km/h with a range of 1,300 miles. With the carriers roaming up and down both coasts of North Korea, any land target was easily reachable. At that time, there was no aerial refuelling. Its four 20-mm cannon each carried 190 rounds, which allowed for excellent strafing, but if it had got into a running gun battle with enemy aircraft, the Panther would have run out of ammunition quickly. Its hard points under the wings were well suited to carry six 5-inch HVARs. The loss records of F9Fs in the war are listed in this book.

Douglas AD Skyraider

The Navy's workhorse in the Korean War was the AD Skyraider. It inflicted more damage on the tougher targets than any other aircraft. The Marines had one squadron of ADs in Korea and they also destroyed a lot of bunkers, ammo dumps, dams and bridges just like the Navy ADs did. All of the major Aircraft carriers (*Essex* class) operating in the Korean War had one full squadron of the bomber version in each air group on board, along with numerous other detachments of specialized Skyraiders that were equipped for anti-submarine and night missions. Carrier-borne Skyraiders were limited to Navy operations, while the Marine version was land based.

These aircraft were produced too late to be operational in World War II, so their claim to fame would be centred on the Korean War and also the Vietnam War. The

VC-11 was the specialized composite squadron that had detachments on every major carrier cruise in the war with the exception of two. They flew the AD-4W that was equipped with the ventral radome and extended cockpit to accommodate additional crew members. This model of the Skyraider was called the 'Guppy' and was the key anti-submarine aircraft on board with its electronic detection gear. Note that they had the stabilizing fins on the horizontal stabilizer. This photograph was taken on the USS *Princeton* during its 1953 cruise with Air Group-15. (*US Navy*)

AD's first flight was on 18 March 1945 and before productions halted, there were over 3,175 built. The USS *Valley Forge* was the first carrier to get into action in Korea and its air group had VA-55 on board. Their first combat missions were flown on 3 July 1950 with devastating results against airfields close to Pyongyang. The F9F Panthers were focused mostly on protecting the bomb-laden Skyraiders and Corsairs, but the lengthy loiter time for the AD put the Panthers at a disadvantage because they had to return to the carrier much sooner due to fuel consumption.

The Skyraiders also pulled off another first when they carried out the only torpedo attack of the war against the Hwacheon Dam on 2 May 1951. A month before the war ended in July 1953, a Skyraider was also credited with a Po-2 biplane kill. Although the aircraft was extremely rugged, it sustained numerous losses, especially after the Chinese continued to defend key assets with some of the most sophisticated anti-aircraft weapons of the war. In the Korwald Action Report (Losses in the Korean War), there were 175 Navy Skyraiders listed as lost in operational accidents and to enemy fire while on combat cruises. This includes all of the AD models. While this may sound excessive, it was few compared with the Corsair losses.

The aircraft's greatest assets were loiter time over a target and heavy bomb loads. It was the most requested aircraft by the forward air controllers that were working

One of VC-11's 'Guppy' Skyraiders unfolds its wings as it readies for take-off on a last light night mission from the USS *Boxer* (CV 21). This AD-4W was part of Detachment-A on the carrier's 1952 cruise. (*Al Wagner*)

VC-35 was a composite squadron that deployed detachments on the majority of carrier cruises in the Korean War. The squadron flew the AD-4N and AD-4NL versions of the Skyraider. There were 307 AD-4Ns built and both types specialized in the night attack mission. All four of these Skyraiders carried the tail codes associated with VC-35. (*Tail Hook Association*)

around the front lines. Its load could reach 8,000 pounds and it was armed with four 20-mm cannon. Its maximum speed was set at about 325 mph and its cruise speed was slightly less than 200 mph. For this reason, it was usually launched first on group strength strikes, which were timed to have all three types arrive over the target area at the same time, hence, the jets were launched last.

Lt (jg) Sam Catterlin, a VF-194 pilot on the 1953 USS *Boxer* cruise, comments on the Skyraider:

> We flew the AD-4, which had a thicker and wider windscreen, and as they had stripped down night attack AD-4NLs, without dive brakes, most of our attack runs were at 45–50 degrees depending on the ceiling. Because the Skyraider was such a stable bomb platform, we were allowed to fly extreme close air support, dropping ordnance within 100 yards of our own troops. The forward air controller did not allow the new F-86F fighter-bombers to get that close to friendly troops. The AD could absorb a lot of damage and still make it back to the carrier. I was the first AD driver in the air group to be hit on our cruise. It was a 20-mm shell that left a big hole in the left outboard wing. However, there was no adverse effect on my aircraft and I returned to the carrier without further incident. There were many ADs, during the war that made it back safely with heavy damage.

The deck on the USS *Boxer* is jammed with Air Group-101's aircraft. The Corsair in the foreground was assigned to the NAS Memphis Reserve Squadron VF-791. The AD Skyraider was part of VA-702. This photograph was taken on 17 September 1951 during the *Boxer*'s second combat cruise. (*US Navy*)

Most of the carriers that served in the Korean War had two squadron detachments that flew specialized versions of the Skyraider. These units were VC-11, VC-35 and in four instances VC-33. VC-11 was flying either the AD-3W or AD-4W. The other detachment was flying a wide range of models, which included the AD-3N, Dash 4N, Dash 4NL or AD-2/3Qs. Each of these squadrons had a night-related special mission, which included anti-submarine capabilities. For instance, VC-35 on the USS *Essex* started out with AD-3Qs (countermeasures) that were replaced with AD-4NLs early on. The other detachment (VC-11) on the *Essex* was equipped with the AD-3 and AD-4W. These were the submarine hunters and the AD-4NLs were the 'killers' for any enemy submarine threats to the Task Force. Both of these squadrons were part of Air Group-5 on the *Essex*. VC-11 usually had three aircraft assigned to each carrier with at least five pilots.

The AD-3W and AD-4W were equipped with APS-20 radar with a 360-degree sweep that was housed in a large pod (radome) directly below the fuselage on the centreline. These Skyraiders were aptly called 'Guppies'. The AD-4NLs were equipped with a radar well outboard on the right wing that resembled a large tear drop. The early 3Q models accommodated one crewman who operated the sophisticated radar that was on board. This model specialized in countermeasure operations, anti-submarine warfare and was very good in the night heckler role, which became VC-35's primary mission. The AD-3W and Dash 4W were strictly

The Navy's early warning version of the Skyraider (AD-4W) was operated on almost all of the carriers by detachments of VC-11. This one was from Detachment-C on the USS *Philippine Sea*'s second cruise. The pilot was Lt Arthur Gripton. (*Arthur Gripton*)

An armament specialist with VF-54 works on one of the AD-4 Skyraider's 20-mm guns prior to a mission. This photograph was taken on the USS *Valley Forge*'s fourth and final combat cruise in late 1952. VF-54 was flying with Air Group-5 at the time. (*James Bray*)

anti-submarine scouts and, according to one of the crew members, 'very rarely encountered much more than a "rogue" Sampan!'

The AD-4NLs flown by VC-35 had two crew members stationed behind and below the pilot. They regularly flew combat over North Korea, at night, hunting down locomotives, which were their favourite target, as well as bridges, ox carts, railcars, troops and any targets of opportunity. During one of the carrier deployments, VC-35 destroyed eleven out of the twelve locomotives credited to that air group during their combat cruise. With the locomotives knocked out at night, the rail cars they were pulling were pounced on at first light by Navy fighter-bombers unless they could be moved to one of the tunnels beforehand.

The AD-4NLs had the advantage of being winterized with de-icer boots on the forward edge of their wings.

AT2 Jack Sauter served in VC-12 (Detachment 44) on the USS *Lake Champlain*. He was one of the more experienced aviation electronics technicians that flew in the AD-3W and AD-4W during the Korean War. He states:

We spent hour upon hour in very cramped quarters in our Skyraiders hunched over a small 5-inch screen, straining to pick out anything that shouldn't be there. Once we were airborne, there was no chance to stretch or move around as we were unable to shift position. This combined with the weight of a crash helmet, a .38 revolver, the cumbersome 'Mae West' and the loud roar of the

3,000 horsepower engine and the constant vibration made for some very long tiresome missions! The specialized radar-equipped AD-4Ws were the all-weather eyes of the fleet during the Korean War. There were no attacks against the carriers, but with our airborne early warning (AEW) radar, we were always in a position to warn the ships below if such as attack took place. These Skyraider Detachments only had 3 aircraft, at the most, but we filled a crucial role in keeping the fleet safe.

Vought F4U Corsair
For both the Navy and Marines, the Corsair was available in large numbers when the Korean War started. Navy carriers had two or more Corsair squadrons on most of their deployments, in addition to detachments of the F4U-5N for night operations and the F4U-4P and 5P for photo reconnaissance. The latter types were soon cut back in favour of the F9F and F2H photo ships. As far as losses are concerned, the Corsairs suffered a huge attrition rate just as the USAF's F-51D Mustangs did. This was attributed to the extremely low altitudes that they had to fly, which made them vulnerable to small arms fire in their primary role of close air support. The Korwald Loss Report shows that the Navy lost thirty-five Corsairs between 1 July and 31 December 1950 and their losses in 1951 amounted to 101 Corsairs. These losses

Every carrier had a detachment of night fighter types in their air groups. Most of these were equipped with the F4U-5N Corsair, which conducted nightly attacks on rail and road traffic in specific sectors of North Korea. Many of these missions were launched a couple of hours before first light. All of these detachments had the 'NP' tail codes. (*Tail Hook Association*)

were attributed to operational and combat activities. The Marine F4Us also suffered heavy losses during this period.

The F4U dated back to the early part of World War II with its first flight being recorded on 29 May 1940 and its operational status commencing in late December 1942. There were over 12,000 Corsairs (all variants combined) made during its long production run. Many of the Navy squadrons used the F4U-4 that was armed with six 50 calibre machine guns and other units were equipped with the F4U-4B that carried four 20-mm cannon.

Vought had built a sleek and very faster fighter that reigned supreme in World War II. With the arrival of jet warfare, the Corsair had to change its work description somewhat. The F4U-4 was capable of speeds in excess of 440 mph with a range of 1,000 miles. While its service ceiling exceeded 40,000 feet, it very seldom had a reason to fly that high in Korea. It could easily carry eight 5-inch HVARs or a 4,000-pound bomb load. Its specialty was delivering napalm and this weapon saved the lives of a lot of Marines during the Chosin Reservoir battles with the Chinese claiming the high ground. Its Pratt & Whitney R-2800-18W engine generated 2,450 horsepower, making it a formidable low-level bomber and strafer.

Production records from Vought show that there were 2,058 F4U-4s built with an additional 297 of the Dash-4B coming off the assembly line. These two models were the backbone of all Navy Corsair operations in the Korean War. There were only thirty of the photo reconnaissance version (F4U-5P) built and they were flown

VF-783 was equipped with F4U-4s during the USS *Bon Homme Richard*'s first combat cruise in 1951. One of the squadron's Corsairs is seen heading west into North Korea searching for targets of opportunity with a full load of 5-inch HVARS and .50 calibre ammunition. The squadron served in Air Group-102 during that cruise. (*Pete Colapietro*)

off the carriers by detachments of VC-61, while the specialized night hecklers fared a little better with a total of 315 being built, and many served with the VC-3 detachments during the Korean War. The usual profile for one of the detachments that served on the carriers with Task Force 77 was three aircraft and six pilots along with the necessary service personnel. The same was true for the photo detachments (VC-61) in that three aircraft were required with from four to six pilots.

Lieutenant William R. Clarke was the maintenance officer for VF-653 on the USS *Valley Forge*. He recalls that the squadron had to give up their particular model of the Corsair to the Marines once they arrived in theatre.

We departed San Diego with F4U-4Bs, which meant that our aircraft were equipped with 20-mm cannon rather than the .50 calibre guns. The standard belted load was as follows: 200 rounds per gun…ball, armour piercing, HEI and tracer. The 4B had a Pratt & Whitney R2800-42W engine that was capable of producing about 2,000 hp. It responded like a hot rod and flew like a Lincoln. Five days out of Japan, the squadron received orders that they were to transfer their 4Bs over to the Marines once we got to port. In exchange, we would pick up F4U-4s as replacements. This meant we would go back to the .50 calibre guns. During our cruise, we still had some 4B wings on board and on several occasions we replaced damaged Dash-4 wings with Dash 4Bs. It wasn't the way it was supposed to be, but it worked!

VF-63 was an F4U-4 squadron that carried out four combat cruises in the Korean War. They served twice on the USS *Boxer*, once on the USS *Valley Forge* and once on the USS *Philippine Sea*. All four tours were with Air Group-2 and each time they were identified with the 'M' on the vertical stabilizer. This photograph was taken on one of their missions along the east coast of North Korea. (*Jack Bucknum*)

During the early part of the war, the F4U-4P and Dash-5Ps carried out the photo reconnaissance, but were soon moved out because of their lack of speed when taking pictures deep in North Korea. The MiG-15 and the influx of more sophisticated anti-aircraft weapons were factors. Its cameras (one vertical and two oblique) were mounted in the lower ventral part of the fuselage. The newer and faster photo reconnaissance jets such as the F9F-2P and the F2H-2P moved into those slots and all of these photo reconnaissance planes were flown by detachments of the VC-61 squadron.

McDonnell F2H-2 Banshee

The fourth main line fighter type that the Navy used in the Korean War was the F2H-2 Banshee. Its first carrier deployment was with VF-172 on the USS *Essex* in the summer of 1951. The aircraft first flew on 11 January 1947 and it made its way into the fleet in the summer of 1948. In total 895 were built (all versions included). The model most used by the Navy during the war was the Dash-2 with its underwing pylons added to allow it to carry a light bomb load (1,000 pounds), which was nowhere near what the Skyraider could carry and only half what the Panther was capable of handling. This translated to two 500-pound bombs or four 250-pound GPs. It also had detachable wing-tip fuel tanks and an increased fuel capacity, giving it a range of over 1,700 miles. Its maximum speed was listed as over 570

The F2H Banshees began appearing on the carriers off the coast of Korea in the early summer of 1951. The photo version (F2H-2P) started flying combat missions in late December 1951. This photo Banshee is shown on the deck of the USS *Oriskany* (CVA 34) while serving under Air Group 102 in the early spring of 1953 with VC-61's Detachment G. (*Dan Keough*)

The USS *Boxer* prepares to launch a pair of F9F-2s from VF-24 to escort a photo-reconnaissance Panther from VC-61. This was standard procedure when sending an unarmed photo ship to take pictures of a potential target that was located within range of the MiG-15. The photo ship (F9F-2P) has the 'PP' on its vertical stabilizer. This picture was taken during the carrier's 1952 cruise. (*Guy Lyons*)

The key to keeping the carriers on station and their strike aircraft in-service was replenishment at sea. With daily operations for Air Group -2 consuming a tremendous amount of fuel, ammunition and ordnance, it was almost an ongoing operation. This supply ship is transferring bombs over to the USS *Boxer* during its 1952 cruise. (*Guy Lyons*)

The USS *Lake Champlain* (CVA 39) performed one combat cruise between April and December 1952 with Air Group-4. This was a unique cruise in that two of the main four attack squadrons on board were equipped with F2H-2 Banshees (VF-22 and VF-62). The Corsair seen here on the right was assigned to VF-44, which was on board only from 25 April until 30 June. (*National Archives*)

The USS *Philippine Sea* returns from a short stint at a naval base in Japan to the coast off North Korea. The two TBM Avengers on the left were the main shuttles between land bases in South Korea and the ship. The F4U-4 Corsairs in the background were assigned to VF-113 and VF-114. (*Ted Landrum*)

All of the strike aircraft from Air Group-11 have been loaded and moved to the aft section of the flight deck for launching. The AD-4 moving into take-off position was assigned to VA-115 on the USS *Philippine Sea*. (*Ted Landrum*)

The Skyraider was the most effective bomber the Navy used in the Korean War because it could handle the heavy loads. The aircraft were responsible for most of the destruction of the big dams and major bridges in North Korea with their 2,000-lb GP bombs. These AD-4s were on the USS *Princeton* in 1952 with VA-195. (*John Sherly*)

One of VF-191's Panthers goes to full power for a launch off the USS *Princeton* sometime in 1952. It was the only F9F squadron in Air Group-19 on that cruise. On the group strength strikes, they were the last aircraft to take off as timing was critical in that all of the aircraft in the groups would meet up over the target at the same time. (*John Sherly*)

All of the aircraft carriers that performed combat cruises in the Korean were periodically pulled off the line for replenishment, repairs and R&R for their personnel. Here, the USS *Princeton* is docked at the big Yokosuka naval base in Japan during its 1952 cruise. The aircraft on its deck were assigned to Air Group-19. (*John Sherly*)

The photo planes on all of the carriers were tasked with going in before the strike force to take pictures and then going in last to get photos of the damage. They always had an escort. This F9F-2P (PP tail code) is moving up to the catapult right after its escorting Panther takes off. This photograph was taken on the USS *Princeton*. (*John Sherly*)

The F9F-2P quickly replaced the F4U-5P in the photo-reconnaissance mission because of its speed, which increased the safety factor. This picture was taken on the USS *Boxer* during its cruise in 1951 with Air Group-101. Later on the Dash-5P model came into service with Task Force 77. (*John Hotvedt*)

The AD Skyraiders worked on a three-hour cycle on the carriers, which gave them the ability to hit targets that were a greater distance away and also a longer loiter time over a target. This was due to the big 326-gallon internal fuel tank. These AD-4s from VA-195 are returning from a mission en route to their carrier, the USS *Princeton*, in 1952. (*John Sherly*)

Pilots from VA-195 relax during a mission briefing right before walking up to the flight deck to climb into the cockpit of their AD-4 Skyraiders. This shot was taken on the USS *Princeton* during its 1952 cruise off the coast of North Korea. The photograph was taken in late summer before the cold weather had set in. (*John Sherly*)

The USS *Essex* performed two cruises in the Korean War and on each of them its air groups only had one full squadron of F4Us on board. This VF- 871 Corsair has been manned and ready for 'start engines' sometime in 1952 during the *Essex*'s second cruise. It also had two squadrons of F9F-2 Panthers in CAG-2. (*Wes Ralston*)

The USS *Boxer* (CV 21) takes on fuel in rough seas off the coast of North Korea some time in 1951 during its second combat cruise. Constant replenishment was the key to sustaining daily flight operations close to enemy targets. (*Jack Schlosser*)

Each carrier had Landing Signal Officers (LSOs) that were critical when the carrier was retrieving its aircraft. This picture was taken on the USS *Boxer* during its 1951 cruise. The LSO is signalling for the pilot to cut power as he is on the correct path to touch down safely. (*John Hotvedt*)

VF-24 flew two tours in the Korean War on the USS *Boxer*. The first one was in the F4U-4 Corsair and the second was in the F9F-2 as seen here on the deck of the carrier in 1952. On both cruises, they were under the control of Air Group-2. (*Guy Lyons*)

The USS *Lake Champlain* (CVA 39) made one cruise in the Korean War. For the first time in combat, there were two full squadrons of F2H-2 Banshees in the air group: VF-22 and VF-62. One of the Banshees is on the catapult ready to launch. (*National Archives*)

Deck crews move the AD-4Bs from VA-45 to the forward section of the deck in preparation for receiving strike aircraft returning from a mission. This picture was taken on the USS *Lake Champlain* in June 1953. (*National Archives*)

'Paper Doll' was an F9F-5 assigned to VF-121 on the USS *Oriskany* in March 1953. The squadrons in this air group went through a number change in February 1953. This squadron had been VF-781. (*National Archives*)

F4U Corsairs from VF-653 have already been loaded and await their pilots to finish briefing. They were part of ATG-1 on the USS *Valley Forge* during its 1951–2 cruise. The squadron was a naval reserve unit. (*Ray Edinger*)

Almost all of the carrier deployments in the Korean War had two specialized Skyraider detachments on board. They flew the night heckler and anti-submarine missions. This AD-4W from VC-11 is seen ready for take-off on the USS *Valley Forge* during the early spring of 1952. These ADs usually had the 'ND' tail codes. (*Ray Edinger*)

F9F Panthers from VF-111 are jammed on the forward section of the USS *Valley Forge*'s deck. They were one of two Panther squadrons in ATG-1 during that cruise. The Executive Officer of Corsair squadron VF-653, Lt Ray Edinger, stands alongside the Panthers. (*Ray Edinger*)

In 1951, VF-194 transitioned to the AD Skyraiders. The squadron flew the AD-4s seen here in the deck of the *Valley Forge* in early 1952. They used the 'B' tail code on the vertical stabilizer. At the time, they had just moved into the attack designation from fighters when they took on the ADs, thus they still retained the VF-194 squadron identification. (*Ray Edinger*)

Pilots from ATG-1 grabbed a ride on one of the *Valley Forge*'s elevators from the hangar deck to the top side as they headed for their aircraft. The F9F-2P was the photo ship assigned to Detachment-H of VC-61. It had the standard 'PP' on the vertical stabilizer. (*Ray Edinger*)

The USS *Antietam* (CV 36) did one combat cruise in the war that lasted from 8 September 1951 to 2 May 1952. They had Air Group-15 on board during this stint. This photograph was taken from the USS *Boxer* when both carriers were conducting strikes off the coast of Japan. (*Henry Champion*)

Lt Henry Champion poses with his flight gear on and his mission maps right before climbing into the cockpit of his VF-791 Corsair. The squadron was operating from the USS *Boxer* in 1951 under the command of Air Group-101. (*Henry Champion*)

The old World War II era Navy PBY Catalinas were involved in the war and were ready to help with any downed pilots at sea. This photograph was taken in early 1951 at Itazuke AB, Japan. The F-80Cs in the background were assigned to the 80th FBS 'Headhunters' that were originally based here before they moved up to Suwon AB. (*Richard Hellwege*)

Another F6F-5 Hellcat drone is prepared for take-off from the USS *Boxer* on 2 September 1952. (*National Archives*)

F4U-4s from VF-871 attack Chinese troop concentrations in North Korea during their 1952–3 cruise on the USS *Essex*. These targets were photographed earlier by the carrier's F2H-2Ps, which initiated the strike. On this cruise Air Group-2 only had one squadron of Corsairs on board. (*Bruce Bagwell*)

One of VC-33's Skyraiders recovers on the USS *Lake Champlain* (CVA 39) after a mission in May 1953. The carrier had Air Group-4 on board for the cruise with one squadron of F9F-5s, one squadron of F4U-4s and two squadrons of F2H-2s. This was the only carrier to use two squadrons of Banshee fighter-bombers in the Korean War. (*Bill Travolte*)

Once the Chinese entered the war, the intensity of ground fire increased dramatically. They brought in much higher calibre weapons that had greater accuracy. This F9F-2, from an unidentified Navy squadron, was hit by 20-mm fire in its vertical stabilizer and had to limp back to a land base sometime in 1951. (*Charles Parker*)

VF-51 was the first Navy squadron to receive the F9F-3s, which was in May 1949. The squadron was on the USS *Valley Forge*, which was the first carrier to respond to the North Korean invasion of South Korea. They flew their first combat missions on 3 July 1950. These two Panthers were returning from a mission over North Korea during their 1952/3 cruise on the *Valley Forge*. (*Bill Kelly*)

mph and it had a cruise speed of 460 mph. It was armed with four 20-mm cannon, which made it an effective strafer.

An early evaluation of the Banshee with VF-172 on the USS *Essex* produced the following comments.

The F2H-2 has proven satisfactory for operations from the bigger carriers, but highly skilled airmanship must be used in landing with a pitching deck. There were two instances on the *Essex* cruise where the landing gear struts were pushed up through the wing sections. The Banshee proved that it can absorb flak damage with the best of the fleet's aircraft and it is equipped with two extremely tough engines. There were at least two examples, on that initial cruise, where particles passed through the engines doing considerable damage to the blades but not causing undue vibration or engine stoppage. However, there were some failures of the fuselage supports of the catapult hook under stress of the catapult launches with high loading. Also, the F2H-2 tail hook has a tendency to hang on to the arresting gear when retracted.

There were two models of the Banshee that were widely used by Navy carriers in the war, but neither could compare with the total number of F9Fs, F4Us and ADs that were deployed. Records show that during the war the F2H-2 fighter-bomber

Pilots from the first F2H-2 Banshee squadron to fly combat go over the plans for their upcoming mission on the USS *Essex* in late October 1951. They were members of VF-172. Right to left are: pilots Lt (jg) Wayne Spence, Lt (jg) Paul Harlin, Lt Guy Warren and Ensign Bill Frith. (*Wayne Spence*)

was involved with only four squadrons; in addition to VF-172, the USS *Kearsarge* had VF-11 on one cruise and the USS *Lake Champlain* had two squadrons, VF-22 and VF-62, on its cruise. However, the photo-reconnaissance version (F2H-2P) was used in various detachments of VC-61 on seven carrier deployments with great success. This version had its nose extended by almost 2.5 feet in order to house all the camera equipment. This allowed space for six cameras. It was also widely used by the land-based Marine Corps on the same mission in the VMJ-1 Squadron.

While the Banshee might have been able to hold its own with the MiG-15 in certain circumstances, it never had the chance and scored no aerial kills. However, it did suffer some losses, both operational and combat related. VF-172 lost eight Banshees, VF-11 lost two, and VF-22 lost two as did VF-62. There were also two F2H-2Ps lost. The Navy retired its last F2H-2 in 1959 and, a year later, the last of the Dash-2Ps were retired.

APPENDIX I

US Navy Carrier Deployments in the Korean War

USS *Valley Forge* (CV 45)*
* (First US carrier to respond to the North Korean invasion)

Cruise dates: 1 May 1950 – 1 December 1950

Air Group (CVG-5)

Squadron	Aircraft	Tail code
VF-51	F9F-3	S
VF-52	F9F-3	S
VF-53	F4U-4B	S
VF-54	F4U-4B	S
VA-55	AD-4/Q	S
VC-3 (Det-C)	F4U-5N	NP
VC-3	AD-3N	NP
VC-11 (Det)	AD-3W	ND
HedRon 1 (Det)	F4U-5P	AZ
HU-1 (Det)	HO3S-1	UP

Lt Commander Joe Murphy, Executive Officer of VF-53, is loaded and inbound to the Inchon area to support the Marine landing there on 15 September 1950. All strike aircraft from the *Valley Forge* supported the landings that were successful and led to the breakdown of the North Korean Army around the Pusan Perimeter. (*Edward Laney*)

Taken from Ensign Laney's VF-53 Corsair, this photograph shows the landing craft loaded with Marines getting into position for the amphibious assault at Inchon in the early morning of 15 September 1950. This was taken one hour before they hit the beach. (*Ed Laney*)

USS *Philippine Sea* (CV 47)*
*Second US carrier to respond

Cruise dates: 5 July 1950 – 26 March 1951**

Air Group (CVG-11)

Squadron	Aircraft	Tail code
VF-111	F9F-2	V
VF-112	F9F-2	V
VF-113	F4U-4B	V
VF-114	F4U-4B	V
VA-115	AD-4/Q	V
VC-3 (Det-3)	F4U-5N	NP
VC-3 (Det-3)	AD-4N	NP
VC-11 (Det)	AD-4W	ND
VC-61 (Det-3)	F4U-4P	PP
HU-1 (Det-3)	HO3S-1	UP

** CVG-11 cross-decked with CVG-2 from the *Valley Forge*.

The USS *Philippine Sea* returned to San Diego on 26 March 1951.

USS *Boxer* (CV 21)
Cruise dates: 24 August 1950 – 11 November 1950

Air Group (CVG-2)

Squadron	Aircraft	Tail code
VF-23	F4U-4	M
VF-63	F4U-4	M
VF-64	F4U-4	M
VF-24	F4U-4	M
VA-65	AD-2	M
VC-3 (Det)	F4U-5N	NP
VC-11 (Det-A)	AD-3W	ND
VC-33 (Det)	AD-4N	SS
VC-61 (Det)	F4U-4P	PP
HU-1 (Det)	HO3S	UP

The USS *Boxer* (CV 21) was one of the first big carriers to enter the Korean War when it began its cruise in late August 1950. This heavily loaded AD-2, preparing to launch, was flown by VA-65 while assigned to Air Group-2. The aircraft carried the letter 'M' on their vertical stabilizers. (*James Williams*)

USS *Leyte* (CV 32)
Cruise dates: 6 September 1950 – 3 February 1951

Air Group (CVG-3)

Squadron	Aircraft	Tail code
VF-31	F9F-2	K
VF-32	F4U-4	K
VF-33	F4U-4	K
VA-35	AD-3	K
VC-4 (Det-3)	F4U-5N	NA
VC-33 (Det-3)	AD-4N	SS
VC-12 (Det-3)	AD-3W	NE
VC-62 (Det-3)	F4U-5P	PL
HU-2 (Det-3)	HO3S-1	UR

USS *Princeton* (CV 37)
Cruise dates: 9 November 1950 – 29 May 1951

Air Group (CVG-19)

Squadron	Aircraft	Tail code
VF-191	F9F-2	B
VF-192	F4U-4	B
VF-193	F4U-4	B
VA-195	AD-4	B
VC-3 (Det-F)	F4U-5N	NP
VC-11 (Det)	AD-4W	ND
VC-35 (Det-3)	AD-4N	NR
VC-61 (Det)	F9F-2P	PP
HU-1 (Det)	HO3S-1	UP

One of VF-191's Panthers returns to the USS *Princeton* with battle damage, which requires the barrier to keep it from ploughing into the air group's aircraft parked forward on the deck. The squadron was assigned to Air Group-19 during the *Princeton*'s 1952 cruise in the war. (*Wayne Russell*)

USS *Valley Forge* (CV 45)
Cruise dates: 6 December 1950 – 7 April 1951*

*CVG-2 cross decked with CVG-11 from the USS *Philippine Sea* on 29 March 1951 while the Valley Forge returned to San Diego on 7 April with CVG-11

Air Group (CVG-2)

Squadron	Aircraft	Tail code
VF-64	F4U-4	M
VF-63	F4U-4	M
VF-24	F4U-4	M
VF-65	F4U-4	M
VC-3 (Det)	F4U-5N	NP
VC-11 (Det)	AD-4W	ND
VC-35 (Det-4)	AD-4N	NR
VC-61 (Det-F)	F4U-4P	PP
HU-1 (Det)	HO3S	UP

Ensign Edward Laney poses by his loaded F4U-4B on the deck of the USS *Valley Forge* during its cruise in the early stages of the Korean War. Laney shot down what was identified as a Russian Il-4 that was within the twenty-five-mile safety zone of the Task Force. Years later, the kill was identified as an American-made A-20 Havoc that had been given to the Russians toward the end of World War II. The kill occurred on 4 September 1950. (*Ed Laney*)

USS *Boxer* (CV 21)
Cruise dates: 2 March 1951 – 24 October 1951

Air Group (CVG-101)

Squadron	Aircraft	Tail code
VF-721	F9F-2B	A
VF-791	F4U-4	A
VF-884	F4U-4	A
VA-702	AD-2/4Q	A
VC-3 (Det-F)	F4U-5NL	NP
VC-11 (Det-F)	AD-4W	ND
VC-35 (Det-F)	AD-4N	NR
VC-61 (Det-F)	F9F-2P	PP
HU-1 (Det)	HO3S-1	UP

One of VF-791's Corsairs veers off and is about to go over the side of the deck on the USS *Boxer*. This could have been the '791 Corsair, which had its tail hook snap when it caught the wire, causing it to veer off and almost leave the deck. It was secured before it could go into the water and the pilot was unhurt. (*John White*)

A rocket laden F4U-4 from VF-791 prepares to launch off the USS *Boxer* (CV 21) during its 1951 combat cruise. This was a reserve squadron out of NAS Memphis, Tennessee, that was assigned to Air Group-101. They participated in numerous spotter missions for the heavy cruisers and battleships like the USS *Missouri*. During their tour, each pilot in the squadron averaged about sixty sorties. (*John White*)

This small blast deflector was all the carriers had in 1950 to protect the deck hands when an F9F was running up prior to taking the catapult. This VF-721 Panther is preparing to launch from the USS *Boxer* for a mission in the summer of 1951. The rescue HO3S-1 helicopter is preparing to get airborne in case one of the aircraft has to ditch after taking off. (*John Hotvedt*)

USS *Philippine Sea* (CV 47)
Cruise dates: 28 March 1951 – 9 June 1951

Air Group (CVG-2)

Squadron	Aircraft	Tail code
VF-63	F4U-4	M
VF-64	F4U-4	M
VF-24	F4U-4	M
VA-65	AD-2/Q	M
VC-3 (Det)	F4U-5N	NP
VC-11 (Det)	AD-4W	ND
VC-35 (Det-4)	AD-4N	NR
VC-61 (Det)	F4U-4P	PP
HU-1 (Det)	HO3S-1	UP

USS *Bon Homme Richard* (CV 31)
Cruise dates: 10 May 1951 – 17 December 1951

Air Group (CVG-102)

Squadron	Aircraft	Tail code
VF-781	F9F-2B	D
VF-783	F4U-4	D
VF-874	F4U-4	D
VA-923	AD-3/4Q	D
VC-3 (Det-G)	F4U-5NL	NP
VC-11 (Det-G)	AD-4W	ND
VC-35 (Det-G)	AD-4N	NR
VC-61 (Det-G)	F9F-2P	PP
HU-1 (Det)	HO3S-1	UP

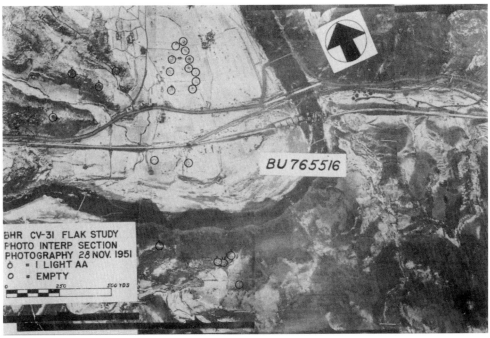

The air groups on all the carriers relied heavily on photographs taken by their VC-61 photo birds before they planned the missions against priority targets. This photograph was taken by an F9F-2P off the USS *Bon Homme Richard* in late November 1951. Note the anti-aircraft gun emplacements that were positioned around the target. (*Hal Schwann*)

The USS *Bon Homme Richard* (CV 31) sails out of Japan for combat duty off the coast of North Korea sometime in 1951. All of its aircraft were assigned to Air Group-102, which consisted of two squadrons of F4U-4s, one squadron of F9F-2Bs and one squadron of Skyraiders. They also had the usual detachments of speciality squadrons. All of its regular attack squadrons carried the 'D' on the vertical stabilizer. (*Pete Colapietro*)

USS *Princeton* **(CV 37)**
Cruise dates: 31 May 1951 – 29 August 1951

Air Group (CVG-19X)

Squadron	Aircraft	Tail code
VF-23	F9F-2	B
VF-821	F4U-4	B
VF-871	F4U-4	B
VA-55	AD-4	B
VC-3 (Det)	F4U-5N	NP
VC-11 (Det)	AD-4W	ND
VC-35 (Det-7)	AD-4N	NR
VC-61 (Det)	F9F-2P	PP
HU-1 (Det)	HO3S-1	UP

USS *Essex* **(CV 9)**
Cruise dates: 26 June 1951 – 25 March 1952

Air Group (CVG-5)

Squadron	Aircraft	Tail code
VF-51	F9F-2	S
VF-172	F2H-2	R
VF-53	F4U-4B	S
VA-54	AD-2/4/L/Q	S
VC-3 (Det-B)	F4U-5NL	NP
VC-11 (Det-B)	AD-4W	ND
VC-35 (Det-B)	AD-4NL	NR
VC-61 (Det-B)	F9F-2P	PP
HU-1 (Det)	HO3S-1	UP

USS *Antietam* (CV 36)
Cruise dates: 8 September 1951 – 2 May 1952

Air Group (CVG-15)

Squadron	Aircraft	Tail code
VF-713	F4U-4	H
VF-831	F9F-2B	H
VF-837	F9F-2B	H
VA-728	AD-4L/Q	H
VC-3 (Det-D)	F4U-5N	NP
VC-11 (Det-D)	AD-4W	ND
VC-35 (Det-D)	AD-4NL	NR
VC-61 (Det-D)	F9F-2P	PP
HU-1 (Det)	HP3S-1	UP

USS *Valley Forge* (CV 45)
Cruise dates: 15 October 1951 – 3 July 1952

Air Group (ATG-1)

Squadron	Aircraft	Tail code
VF-111	F9F-2B	V
VF-52	F9F-2B	S
VF-653	F4U-4B	H
VF-194	AD-2s & 4s	B
VC-3 (Det-H)	F4U-5N/NL	NP
VC-11 (Det-H)	AD-4W/2Q	ND
VC-35 (Det-H)	AD-4NL	NR
VC-61 (Det-H)	F9F-2P / F2H-2P	PP
HU-1 (Det)	HO3S-1	UP

USS *Philippine Sea* (CV 47)
Cruise dates: 31 December 1951 – 8 August 1952

Air Group (CVG-11)

Squadron	Aircraft	Tail code
VF-112	F9F-2	V
VF-113	F4U-4	V
VF-114	F4U-4	V
VA-115	AD-4	V
VC-3 (Det-C)	F4U-5N/NL	NP
VC-11 (Det-C)	AD-4W	ND
VC-35 (Det-C)	AD-4NL/2Q	NR
VC-61 (Det-C)	F2H-2P/F9F-2P	PP
HU-1 (Det)	HO3S-1	UP

USS *Boxer* (CVA 21)
Cruise dates: 8 February 1952 – 26 September 1952

Air Group (CVG-2)

Squadron	Aircraft	Tail code
VF-64	F4U-4	M
VF-63	F4U-4	M
VF-24	F9F-2	M
VA-65	AD-4	M
VC-3 (Det-A)	F4U-5N	NP
VC-11 (Det-A)	AD-4W	ND
VC-35 (Det-A)	AD-3N/4N/2Q	NR
VC-61 (Det-A)	F9F-2P	PP
HU-1 (Det)	HO3S-1	UP
GMU-90	AD-2Q /F6F-5K	V

USS *Princeton* (CVA 37)
Cruise dates: 21 March 1952 – 3 November 1952

Air Group (CVG-19)

Squadron	Aircraft	Tail code
VF-191	F9F-2	B
VF-192	F4U-4	B
VF-193	F4U-4	B
VA-195	AD-4	B
VC-3 (Det-E)	F4U-5N	NP
VC-11 (Det-E)	AD-4W	ND
VC-35 (Det-E)	AD-4NL	NR
VC-61 (Det-E)	F9F-2P	PP
HU-1 (Det)	HO3S-1	UP

There were several catapult failures during the war that resulted in aircraft going into the water ahead of the carrier. This F9F-5 flown by Ensign B.T. Sutherlin (VF-154) went in after the catapult did not provide enough airspeed to lift off. This photograph was taken on the deck of the USS *Princeton* (CVA 37) during its final cruise of the war in 1953. (*John Owen*)

The USS *Princeton* used Air Group-19 on three of its four cruises in the Korean War. The F9F-2s jammed in closely on its deck were from VF-191, which was the only Panther squadron on board during the third cruise. They also had a detachment of F9F-2Ps during that cruise, which was assigned to VC-61. (*Wayne Russell*)

USS *Bon Homme Richard* (CVA 31)
Cruise dates: 20 May 1952 – 8 January 1953

Air Group (CVG-7)

Squadron	Aircraft	Tail code
VF-71	F9F-2	L
VF-72	F9F-2	L
VF-74	F4U-4	L
VA-75	AD-4	L
VC-4 (Det-41)	F4U-4NL	NA
VC-33 (Det-41)	AD-4NL	SS
VC-12 (Det-41)	AD-4W	NE
VC-61 (Det-N)	F2H-2P / F9F-2P	PP
HU-1 (Det)	HO3S-1	UP

USS *Essex* (CV 9)
Cruise dates: 16 June 1952 – 6 February 1953

Air Group (ATG-2)

Squadron	Aircraft	Tail code
VF-23	F9F-2	M
VF-821	F9F-2	A
VF-871	F4U-4	D
VA-55	AD-4	S
VC-3 (Det-1)	F4U-5N	NP
VC-11 (Det-1)	AD-4W	ND
VC-35 (Det-1)	AD-4N	NR
VC-61 (Det-1)	F2H-2P	PP
HU-1 (Det)	HO3S-1	UP

This F4U-4B has just returned from a mission and is preparing to taxi into the parking area away from the arresting wires. This photograph was taken on the USS *Essex* (CV 9) during its first cruise and VF-53 was the only Corsair squadron on board with Air Group-5. (*Hal Schwan*)

USS *Kearsarge* (CVA 33)
Cruise dates: 11 August 1952 – 17 March 1953

Air Group (CVG-101)*

Squadron	Aircraft	Tail code
VF-11	F2H-2	T
VF-721	F9F-2	A
VF-884	F4U-4	A
VA-702	AD-4/L	A
VC-3 (Det-F)	F4U-5N	NP
VC-11 (Det-F)	AD-4W	ND
VC-35 (Det-F)	AD-4N	NR
VC-61 (Det-F)	F2H-2P	PP
HU-1 (Det-15)	HO3-1	UP

* CVG-101 redesignated CVG-14 on 4 February 1953

At one time in the early stages of the Korean War, this was a major rail / road junction that fed vital supplies and equipment from Manchuria to the front lines. A major carrier strike off the USS *Kearsarge* (CVA 33) in September 1952 destroyed just about everything of value to the enemy. This was carried out by Air Group-101. (*US Navy*)

USS *Oriskany* (CVA 34)
Cruise dates: 15 September 1952 – 18 May 1953

*Air Group (CVG-102)**

Squadron	Aircraft	Tail code
VF-781	F9F-5	D
VF-783	F9F-5	D
VF-874	F4U-4	D
VA-923	AD-3	D
VC-3 (Det-G)	F4U-5N	NP
VC-11 (Det-G)	AD-3W	ND
VC-35 (Det-G)	AD-4N	NR
VC-61 (Det-G)	F2H-2P	PP
HU-1 (Det)	HO3S-1	UP

CVG-102 redesignated CVG-12 on 4 February 1953
*VF-781, VF-783, VF-784 and VA-923 became VF-121,
VF-122, VF-124 and VA-125

Panthers from Air Group-5 are lined up along the edge of the deck on board the USS *Valley Forge* (CVA 45) during their 1952 cruise. The Panther with the light paint scheme was an F9F-2P photo ship assigned to VC-61. The F9F-5 (#113) was either flown by VF-51 or VF-53. (*Hal Schwan*)

USS *Valley Forge* (CVA 45)
Cruise dates: 20 November 1952 – 25 June 1953

Air Group (CVG-5)

Squadron	Aircraft	Tail code
VF-51	F9F-5	S
VF-92	F4U-4	N
VF-53	F9F-5	S
VF-54	AD-4	S
VC-3 (Det-B)	F4U-5N	NP
VC-11 (Det-B)	AD-4W	ND
VC-35 (Det-B)	AD-4N	NR
VC-61 (Det-B)	F9F-5P	PP
HU-1 (Det-6)	HO3S-1	UP

USS *Philippine Sea* (CVA 47)
Cruise dates: 15 December 1952 – 14 August 1953

Air Group (CVG-9)

Squadron	Aircraft	Tail code
VF-91	F9F-2	N
VF-93	F9F-2	N
VF-94	F4U-4	N
VA-95	AD-4/NA/NL	N
VC-3 (Det-M)	F4U-5N	NP
VC-11 (Det-M)	AD-4W	ND
VC-35 (Det-M)	AD-4N	NR
VC-61 (Det-M)	F9F-5P	PP
HU-1 (Det)	HO3S-1	UP

USS *Princeton* (CVA 37)
Cruise dates: 24 January 1953 – 21 September 1953

Air Group (CVG-15)

Squadron	Aircraft	Tail code
VF-152	F4U-4	H
VF-153	F9F-5	H
VF-154	F9F-5	H
VA-155	AD-4	H
VC-3 (Det-D)	F4U-5N	NP
VC-11 (Det-D)	AD-4W	ND
VC-35 (Det-D)	AD-4N	NR
VC-61 (Det-D)	F9F-5P	PP
HU-1 (Det)	HO3S-1	UP

Two F9F-5s from the USS *Princeton* return to the carrier after a strike in North Korea. This photograph was taken during the carrier's final combat cruise in 1953. The Panther at the top was flown by VF-154 and the other is from VF-153. They were both from Air Group-15. (*John Owen*)

The USS *Princeton* and her air groups contributed tremendously to the UN effort in the Korean War. Its final cruise ended in September 1953 after the Korean War had ended. This photograph was taken as the carrier arrived at its home port at the end of that cruise. The sailors were decked out in their white uniforms to form up the letters right before they docked and were reunited with their waiting families. (*George Smitman*)

Navy night fighter pilot Lt Guy P. Bordelon Jr was assigned to VC-3 on the USS *Princeton*. He served at Kimpo AB in an effort to stop the night hecklers (Po-2s). He shot down five aircraft during his night patrols to become the only Navy ace of the war. Here, he gets a royal reception on the deck of the *Princeton* upon his return to the carrier. (*Ben Sutherlin*)

The photo aircraft on the carriers had to fly some of the most dangerous missions because of their low-altitude runs and the fact they were unarmed. This F9F-5P was assigned to the USS *Princeton*'s Air Group-15 in 1953. These technicians are making sure the cameras are set properly before the mission. These aircraft had to fly the pre-mission and post-mission photo runs. (*US Navy*)

USS *Boxer* (CVA 21)
Cruise dates: 30 March 1953 – 28 November 1953

Air Group (ATG-1)

Squadron	Aircraft	Tail code
VF-111*	F9F-5	V
VF-52	F9F-2	S
VF-151	F9F-2	H
VF-44**	F4U-4	F
VF-194	AD-4NA/Q	B
VC-3 (Det-H)	F4U-5N	NP
VC-11 (Det-H)	AD-4W	ND
VC-35 (Det-H)	AD-4N	NR
VC-61	F2H-2P	PP
HU-1 (Det)	HO3S-1	UP

* VF-111 cross-decked (transferred) from CVA 21 to CVA 39 on
30 June 1953 and returned to the US in October 1953.
** VF-44 cross-decked from CVA 39 to CVA 21 on 30 June 1953.

One of VF-63's Corsairs moves into position to take off on the USS *Boxer* during its 1952 cruise.
Both squadrons of F4U-4s in the air group used the 'M' tail code during that period. The Corsairs
from VF-63 were identified by the white trim on the tip of the vertical stabilizer. (*Al Wagner*)

Air Group-2's aircraft cram the deck of the USS *Boxer* en route to their station off the coast of North Korea. The Skyraider with the 'NR' tail code was part of VC-35's detachment. (*Al Wagner*)

Suited out and ready, these VF-194 Skyraider pilots are ready to fly the next mission in their AD-4s. The squadron was part of ATG-1 on the USS *Boxer* on its final combat cruise in 1953. (*Howard Bentzinger*)

USS *Lake Champlain* **(CVA 39)**
Cruise dates: 26 April 1953 – 4 December 1953

Air Group (CVG-4)

Squadron	Aircraft	Tail code
VF-22	F2H-2	F
VF-62	F2H-2	F
VF-44*	F4U-4	F
VF-111**	F9F-5	V
VA-45	AD-4B	F
VC-4 (Det-44)	F2H-2B/F3D-2	NA
VC-12 (Det-44)	AD-4W	NE
VC-33 (Det-44)	AD-4N	SS
VC-62 (Det-44)	F2H-2P	PL
HU-2 (Det)	HO3S-1	UR

*VF-44 to 30 June
**VF-111 from 30 June

Bomb loaders on the USS *Lake Champlain* (CVA 39) move one of the blockbuster bombs down the deck for loading on an AD-4B Skyraider from VA-45 on 20 June 1953. The end of the war was about one month away and the carriers were hitting the enemy with everything they had in an effort to force an end to the fighting. (*National Archives*)

Deck crews move a loaded AD-4B forward into position for take-off. These Skyraiders carried the heaviest bomb loads of any single engine aircraft in the Korean War. This photograph was taken on the deck of the USS *Lake Champlain* in June 1953 with Air Group-4 aircraft flying the missions. The Skyraider was flown by VA-45. At this late date in the war, CVA 39 had two full squadrons of F2H-2 Banshees on board. (*National Archives*)

There were at least six of the smaller aircraft carriers (CVEs) that carried out crucial combat cruises during the Korean War. Although they were manned by US Navy personnel, their decks carried US Marine squadrons flying various models of the F4U Corsair. Even though this book covers only US Navy carrier ops, these CVEs should at least be mentioned, along with the dates that they served off the coast of Korean. These smaller carriers were known as a 'Commencement Bay-class escort carriers'.

USS *Sicily* (CVE 118)
1st cruise dates: 4 July 1950 – 5 February 1951
Marine squadron VMF-214 flying the F4U-4B

2nd cruise dates: 12 May 1951 – 12 October 1951
Marine squadron VMF-323 flying the F4U-4

3rd cruise dates: 8, May 1952 – 4 December 1952
Marine squadron VMA-312 flying the F4U-4B

USS *Badoeing Strait* (CVE 116)
1st cruise dates: 14 July 1950 – 7 February 1951
Marine squadron VMF-323 flying the F4U-4B

2nd cruise dates: 15 September 1951 – 1 March 1952
Marine squadron VMF-212 flying the F4U-4

3rd cruise dates: 19 July 1952 – 27 February 1953
Marine squadron VMA-312 flying the F4U-4/B
USS *Bairoko* (CVE 115)
1st cruise dates: 14 November 1950 – 15 August 1951
No Marine squadrons on board: only Navy TBM-3S/Ws

2nd Cruise Dates: 1 December 1951 – 9 June 1952
No Marine squadrons on board

3rd cruise dates: 12 January 1953– 24 August 1953
Marine squadron VMA-312 flying the F4U-4/B

USS *Bataan* (CVL-29)
1st cruise dates: 16 November 1950 – 25 June 1951
Marine squadron VMF-212 flying the F4U-4

2nd cruise dates: 27 January 1952 – 26 August 1952
Marine squadron VMA-312 flying the F4U-4/B

3rd cruise dates: 28 October 1952 – 26 May 1953
Marine squadron VMA-312 flying the F4U-4/B

USS *Rendova* (CVE 114)
1st cruise dates: 8 July 1951–22 December 1951
Marine squadron VMF-212 flying the F4U-4

USS *Point Cruz* (CVE 119)
1st cruise dates: 11 April 1953 – 18 December 1953
Marine squadron VMF-332 flying the F4U-4B

Navy Patrol Squadrons Involved in the Korean War

Land Based

Squadron	Date deployed	Date ending	Tail code	Aircraft type
VP-1	7 August 1950	27 July 1953	CD	P2V-3/5
VP-2	1 September 1951	1 December 1951	SB	P2V-4
VP-4	Unknown	Unknown	SC	P2V-4
VP-6	28 June 1950	15 January 1952	BE	P2V-3/3W
VP-7	30 June 1953	January 1954	HE	P2V-5
VP-9	29 June 1952	16 November 1952	CB	P4Y-2
VP-22	14 November 1950	30 May 1953	CE	P2V-3/4/5
VP-28	14 July 1950	30 November 1952	CF	P4Y-2S
VP-40	1 June 1951	24 February 1953	CA	PBM-5/5S
VP-42	21 August 1950	2 June 1952	SA	PBM-5/5S/5S2
VP-46	15 July 1950	15 March 1952	BD	PBM-5/5S/5S2
VP-47	25 June 1950	1 June 1953	BA	PBM-5
VP-48	29 May 1952	15 March 1953	SF	PBM-5//5S2
VP-50	5 July 1953	27 July 1953	SE	PBM-5
VP-57	29 March 1953	October 1953	BI	P2V-5/3W/5
VP-772	1 January 1951	3 August 1951	–	P4Y-2/2S
VP-731	29 May 1952	8 December 1952	–	PBM-5
VP-871	October 1951	March 1952	CH	P4Y-2/2S
VP-892	Nov. 23, 1950	Sept. 1, 1953	–	PBM-5

The Ready Room for VF-783 was a busy place prior to a mission. These Corsair pilots are going over the details for a squadron strength close air support mission close to the front lines during their 1951 cruise on the USS *Bon Homme Richard*. (*Pete Colapietro*)

US Navy Aircraft Lost in the Korean War

June 1950
No losses

July 1950

Date	Aircraft	Squadron	Carrier
3 July	F4U	VF-53	USS *Valley Forge*
4 July	AD-3W	VC-11	USS *Valley Forge*
4 July	AD-4	VA-55	USS *Valley Forge*
4 July	AD-4	VA-55	USS *Valley Forge*
4 July	HO3S-1	HU-1	USS *Valley Forge*
16 July	F9F-3	VF-52	USS *Valley Forge*
19 July	F4U	VF-54	USS *Valley Forge*
22 July	AD-4	VA-55	USS *Valley Forge*
25 July	AD-4	VA-55	USS *Valley Forge*
25 July	F4U-4B	VF-53	USS *Valley Forge*

August 1950

Date	Aircraft	Squadron	Carrier
5 August	F4U-4B	VF-113	USS *Philippine Sea*
5 August	F4U-4B	VF-113	USS *Philippine Sea*
7 August	F4U-4B	VF-53	USS *Essex*
7 August	F9F-2B	VF-112	USS *Philippine Sea*
10 August	F4U-4B	VF-54	USS *Valley Forge*
12 August	F9F-3	VF-52	USS *Valley Forge*
16 August	P2V-3	VP-6	Land based
19 August	F9F-2	VF-111	USS *Philippine Sea*
20 August	F9F-2	VF-112	USS *Philippine Sea*
27 August	F4U-4B	VF-54	USS *Valley Forge*
29 August	AD-4	VA-55	USS *Valley Forge*
30 August	F4U-4B	VF-114	USS *Philippine Sea*

September 1950

Date	Aircraft	Squadron	Carrier
11 September	HO3S-1	HU-1 (Det-3)	USS *Philippine Sea*
14 September	F4U-5N	VC-3	USS *Philippine Sea*
15 September	F4U-4	VF-24	USS *Boxer*
15 September	F4U-4B	VF-54	USS *Valley Forge*
16 September	F4U-4	VF-63	USS *Boxer*
16 September	F4U-4	VF-23	USS *Boxer*
17 September	AD-4	VA-65	USS *Boxer*
17 September	F4U-4	VF-23	USS *Boxer*
18 September	F4U-5N	VC-3	Unknown
18 September	F9F-2	VF-111	USS *Philippine Sea*
19 September	F4U-4	VF-63	USS *Boxer*
19 September	F9F-3	VF-51	USS *Valley Forge*
20 September	AD-4	VA-65	USS *Boxer*
22 September	F4U-4B	VF-53	USS *Valley Forge*
23 September	AD-4	VA-115	USS *Philippine Sea*
24 September	F9F	VF-111	USS *Philippine Sea*
25 September	F4U-4B	VF-54	USS *Valley Forge*
26 September	HO3S-1	HU-1	Unknown
26 September	F4U-4	VF-63	USS *Boxer*
26 September	P2V	Unknown	Land based
29 September	F4U-4	VF-24	USS *Boxer*
29 September	F4U-4B	VF-113	USS *Philippine Sea*
29 September	F9F-2	VF-111	USS *Philippine Sea*

October 1950

Date	Aircraft	Squadron	Carrier
1 October	F4U-4	VF-23	USS *Boxer*
7 October	F4U-5P	VC-62	USS *Leyte*
14 October	F4U-4	VF-33	USS *Leyte*
16 October	F4U-4	VF-64	USS *Boxer*
19 October	F9F-2B	VF-31	USS *Leyte*
22 October	AD-4	VA-55	USS *Valley Forge*
25 October	AD-4	VA-55	USS *Valley Forge*

November 1950

Date	Aircraft	Squadron	Carrier
11 November	AD-3	VA-35	USS *Leyte*
20 November	AD-3W	VC-11	Unknown
23 November	PBM-5A	VR-21	Land based
27 November	AD-4	VA-115	USS *Philippine Sea*
27 November	9F-2F	VF-112	USS *Philippine Sea*
28 November	F4U-5P	VC-62	USS *Leyte*

December 1950

Date	Aircraft	Squadron	Carrier
3 December	F4U-4B	VF-114	USS *Philippine Sea*
4 December	F4U-4	VF-32	USS *Leyte*
4 December	F4U-4	VF-32	USS *Leyte*
5 December	F4U-4	VF-193	USS *Princeton*
9 December	AD-4	VA-115	USS *Philippine Sea*
9 December	AD-4	VA-115	USS *Philippine Sea*
9 December	AD-4N	VC-35	USS *Princeton*
9 December	AD-4Q	VA-115	USS *Philippine Sea*
9 December	AD-4Q	VA-195	USS *Princeton*
9 December	F9F-2B	VF-31	USS *Leyte*
12 December	AD-4	VA-35	USS *Leyte*
15 December	F4U-4	VF-193	USS *Princeton*
16 December	AD-4	VA-115	USS *Philippine Sea*
19 December	AD-4	VA-115	USS *Philippine Sea*
19 December	F9F-2	VF-112	USS *Philippines Sea*
20 December	F9F-2B	VF-31	USS *Leyte*
23 December	F4U-4	VF-53	USS *Valley Forge*
23 December	F4U-4B	VF-114	USS *Philippine Sea*
24 December	F4U-4	VF-193	USS *Princeton*

January 1951

Date	Aircraft	Squadron	Carrier
9 January	HO3S-1	HU-1	USS *Philippine Sea*
13 January	AD-4W	VC-11	USS *Philippine Sea*
14 January	AD-3	VA-35	USS *Leyte*
15 January	F4U-4	VF-64	USS *Valley Forge*
21 January	P2V-4	VP-22	Land based
27 January	F4U-5N	VC-3	USS *Philippine Sea*
28 January	AD-4	VA-195	USS *Princeton*
28 January	F4U-4	VF-192	USS *Princeton*
31 January	F4U-4B	VF-113	USS *Philippine Sea*

February 1951

Date	Aircraft	Squadron	Carrier
7 February	F4U-4	VF-24	USS *Valley Forge*
7 February	F4U-4	VF-63	USS *Valley Forge*
10 February	AD-4	VA-195	USS *Princeton*
10 February	F4U-4	VF-193	USS *Princeton*
11 February	AD-4	VA-195	USS *Princeton*
13 February	AD-4N	VC-11	USS *Philippine Sea*
13 February	F4U-5N	VC-3	USS *Valley Forge*
18 February	F4U-4	VF-63	USS *Valley Forge*
20 February	AD-4	VA-115	USS *Philippine Sea*
20 February	F4U-4P	VC-61	USS *Valley Forge*

March 1951

Date	Aircraft	Squadron	Carrier
3 March	AD-4	VA-195	USS *Princeton*
7 March	AD-4W	VC-11	USS *Princeton*
8 March	F9F-2	VF-191	USS *Princeton*
9 March	F4U-5N	VC-3	USS *Princeton*
10 March	F4U-4	VF-192	USS *Princeton*
11 March	F4U-4B	VF-113	USS *Philippine Sea*
19 March	F4U-4	VF-24	USS *Valley Forge*
21 March	AD-4Q	VC-11	USS *Valley Forge*
31 March	AD-4	VA-195	USS *Princeton*

April 1951

Date	Aircraft	Squadron	Carrier
1 April	AD-4Q	VA-702	USS *Boxer*
2 April	F4U-4	VF-884	USS *Boxer*
5 April	F4U-4	VF-63	USS *Philippine Sea*
5 April	F9F-2B	VF-721	USS *Boxer*
7 April	F4U-4	VF-884	USS *Boxer*
16 April	AD-2	VA-65	USS *Philippine Sea*
17 April	F4U-4	VF-791	USS *Boxer*
18 April	F4U-4	VF-884	USS *Boxer*
18 April	F4U-4	VF-63	USS *Philippine Sea*
20 April	F4U-4	VF-24	USS *Philippine Sea*
21 April	F4U-4	VF-192	USS *Princeton*
22 April	F4U-5N	VC-3	USS *Princeton*
24 April	F4U-4	VF-63	USS *Philippine Sea*
25 April	AD-2	VA-65	USS *Valley Forge*
29 April	F4U-4	VF-193	USS *Princeton*

May 1951

Date	Aircraft	Squadron	Carrier
2 May	F4U-4	VF-192	USS *Princeton*
6 May	F9F-2B	VF-191	USS *Princeton*
7 May	AD-4	VA-702	USS *Boxer*
7 May	F9F-2B	VF-191	USS *Princeton*
11 May	AD-2	VA-702	USS *Boxer*
11 May	AD-4N	VC-35	USS *Princeton*
11 May	F4U-4	VF-791	USS *Boxer*
12 May	F4U-4	VF-192	USS *Princeton*
18 May	AD-4	VA-195	USS *Princeton*
18 May	F4U-4	VF-871	USS *Princeton*
18 May	F4U-4	VF-884	USS *Boxer*
18 May	F4U-4	VF-193	USS *Princeton*
18 May	F4U-4	VF-24	USS *Philippine Sea*
18 May	F4U-4	VF-884	USS *Boxer*
19 May	F4U-4	VF-64	USS *Philippine Sea*
19 May	F4U-4	VF-63	USS *Philippine Sea*
23 May	F4U-4	VF-63	USS *Philippine Sea*
24 May	F4U-4	VF-884	USS *Boxer*
24 May	HO3S-1	HU-2	USS *New Jersey*
29 May	F4U-4	VF-64	USS *Philippine Sea*
29 May	F4U-4	VF-64	USS *Philippine Sea*
30 May	F9F-2B	VF-721	USS *Boxer*
31 May	F9F-2B	VF-781	USS *Bon Homme Richard*

June 1951

Date	Aircraft	Squadron	Carrier
3 June	F4U-4	VF-783	USS *Bon Homme Richard*
5 June	F9F-2B	VF-23	USS *Princeton*
6 June	AD-4	VA-55	USS *Princeton*
10 June	AD-4Q	VC-35	USS *Princeton*
10 June	F4U-5NL	VC-3	USS *Princeton*
20 June	F4U-4	VF-884	USS *Boxer*
20 June	F4U-4	VF-871	USS *Princeton*
20 June	F4U-4	VF-821	USS *Princeton*
21 June	AD-2	VC-35	USS *Boxer*
21 June	AD-4	VA-55	USS *Princeton*
22 June	F4U-5NL	VC-3	USS *Boxer*
25 June	AD-4	VA-55	USS *Princeton*
28 June	AD-4	VA-55	USS *Princeton*
28 June	F4U-4	VF-884	USS *Boxer*
30 June	F4U-4	VF-871	USS *Princeton*

The prop aircraft had their share of problems when they lost power just as they lifted off the deck. The engine of this Air Group-102 Corsair's cut out at the wrong time and it went into the water right in front of the carrier, which was at full speed into the wind for the launch. This photograph was taken on the USS *Bon Homme Richard* in 1951. (*Pete Colapietro*)

July 1951

Date	Aircraft	Squadron	Carrier
2 July	AD-2	VA-702	USS *Boxer*
3 July	F9F-2B	VF-781	USS *Bon Homme Richard*
4 July	F4U-4	VF-783	USS *Bon Homme Richard*
6 July	AD-3	VA-923	USS *Bon Homme Richard*
7 July	AD-3	VC-35	USS *Bon Homme Richard*
7 July	F4U-4	VF-791	USS *Boxer*
11 July	AD-4N	VC-35	USS *Bon Homme Richard*
11 July	F4U-4	VF-874	USS *Bon Homme Richard*
11 July	F4U-4	VF-884	USS *Boxer*
15 July	F4U-4	VF-821	USS *Princeton*
18 July	AD-3	VA-923	USS *Bon Homme Richard*
18 July	F4U-4	VF-871	USS *Princeton*
22 July	F4U-4	VF-871	USS *Princeton*
22 July	F9F-3	VF-52	USS *Valley Forge*
27 July	AD-4	VA-55	USS *Princeton*
27 July	F4U-4	VF-871	USS *Princeton*

27 July	F4U-4	VF-884	USS *Boxer*
27 July	F9F-2B	VF-781	USS *Bon Homme Richard*
28 July	F4U-5NL	VC-3	USS *Boxer*
28 July	F9F-2B	VF-23	USS *Princeton*
30 July	F4U-4	VF-821	USS *Princeton*

August 1951

Date	Aircraft	Squadron	Carrier
4 August	F4U-4	VF-884	USS *Boxer*
7 August	AD	Unknown	USS *Princeton*
7 August	AD-2	VA-702	USS *Boxer*
9 August	F4U-4	VF-871	USS *Princeton*
11 August	F4U-4	VF-874	USS *Bon Homme Richard*
11 August	F4U-4	VF-874	USS *Bon Homme Richard*
14 August	F9F-2	VF-721	USS *Boxer*
23 August	F4U-4B	VF-53	USS *Essex*
24 August	AD-4L	VA-54	USS *Essex*
24 August	F4U-4	VF-874	USS *Bon Homme Richard*
24 August	F9F-2B	VF-781	USS *Bon Homme Richard*
26 August	AD-4Q	VC-35	USS *Essex*
26 August	F4U-4	VF-783	USS *Bon Homme Richard*
29 August	AD-3	VA-923	USS *Bon Homme Richard*
30 August	F4U-4	VF-874	USS *Bon Homme Richard*
30 August	F4U-5NL	VC-3	USS *Essex*

September 1951

Date	Aircraft	Squadron	Carrier
2 September	AD-3	VA-923	USS *Bon Homme Richard*
2 September	F4U-4	VF-874	USS *Bon Homme Richard*
2 September	F4U-4B	VF-53	USS *Essex*
3 September	AD-4L	VF-54	USS *Essex*
3 September	F9F-2	VF-51	USS *Essex*
4 September	F4U-4	VF-783	USS *Bon Homme Richard*
4 September	F4U-4	VF-874	USS *Bon Homme Richard*
4 September	F9F-2	VF-51	USS *Essex*
4 September	F9F-2	VF-51	USS *Essex*
7 September	AD-4L	VF-54	USS *Essex*
8 September	AD-4L	VF-54	USS *Essex*
8 September	F4U-4B	VF-53	USS *Essex*
11 September	F2H-2	VF-172	USS *Essex*
14 September	AD-4W	VF-54	USS *Essex*
16 September	F2H-2	VF-172	USS *Essex*
16 September	F2H-2	VF-172	USS *Essex*

16 September	F2H-2	VF-172	USS *Essex*
16 September	F2H-2	VF-172	USS *Essex*
16 September	F9F-2	VF-51	USS *Essex*
16 September	F9F-2	VF-51	USS *Essex*
18 September	F4U-4	VF-791	USS *Boxer*
18 September	F4U-4	VF-884	USS *Boxer*
19 September	AD-2	VA-702	USS *Boxer*
19 September	AD-4L	VF-54	USS *Essex*
20 September	AD-2	VA-702	USS *Boxer*
20 September	F4U-5NL	VC-3	USS *Bon Homme Richard*
21 September	F4U-5NL	VC-3	USS *Bon Homme Richard*
24 September	F4U-4	VF-874	USS *Bon Homme Richard*
27 September	AD-3	VA-923	USS *Bon Homme Richard*
27 September	F4U-4	VF-783	USS *Bon Homme Richard*

October 1951

Date	Aircraft	Squadron	Carrier
3 October	AD-3	VA-923	USS *Bon Homme Richard*
3 October	F4U-4	VF-783	USS *Bon Homme Richard*
3 October	F4U-4	VF-884	USS *Boxer*
3 October	F4U-4	VF-783	USS *Bon Homme Richard*
5 October	F4U-4	VF-874	USS *Bon Homme Richard*
6 October	AD-3	VA-923	USS *Bon Homme Richard*
6 October	AD-4	VF-54	USS *Essex*
6 October	F4U-4	VF-874	USS *Bon Homme Richard*
6 October	PBM-5	VP-46	Land based
8 October	F4U-4	VF-884	USS *Boxer*
16 October	AD-4L	VA-728	USS *Antietam*
16 October	F2H-2	VF-172	USS *Essex*
21 October	F9F-2P	VC-61	USS *Antietam*
22 October	AD-4W	VC-11	USS *Antietam*
25 October	F2H-2	VF-172	USS *Essex*
25 October	F4U-4	VF-713	USS *Antietam*
26 October	AD-4	VF-54	USS *Essex*
28 October	F4U-4B	VF-53	USS *Essex*
30 October	F4U-5NL	VC-3	USS *Antietam*

November 1951

Date	Aircraft	Squadron	Carrier
4 November	AD-2	VC-35	USS *Bon Homme Richard*
4 November	AD-4NL	VC-35	USS *Antietam*
4 November	F9F-2	VF-831	USS *Antietam*
4 November	F9F-2	VF-831	USS *Antietam*
8 November	F4U-4	VF-713	USS *Antietam*
12 November	F4U-5NL	VC-3	USS *Antietam*
13 November	F9F-2B	VF-781	USS *Bon Homme Richard*
17 November	AD-4	VF-54	USS *Essex*
17 November	F9F-2B	VF-781	USS *Bon Homme Richard*
18 November	F4U-4	VF-783	USS *Bon Homme Richard*
21 November	AD-3	VA-923	USS *Bon Homme Richard*
21 November	F4U-4	VF-874	USS *Bon Homme Richard*
21 November	F4U-4B	VF-53	USS *Essex*
21 November	F9F-2B	VF-781	USS *Bon Homme Richard*
25 November	PBM-5	VP-46	Land based
27 November	AD-4L	VF-54	USS *Essex*

December 1951

Date	Aircraft	Squadron	Carrier
1 December	F4U-4B	VF-53	USS *Essex*
1 December	F4U-4B	VF-53	USS *Essex*
2 December	F4U-5NL	VC-3	USS *Essex*
5 December	AD-4L	VF-54	USS *Essex*
6 December	AD-4L	VA-728	USS *Antietam*
6 December	AD-4L	VA-728	USS *Antietam*
9 December	AD-4	VF-54	USS *Essex*
9 December	AD-4	VF-54	USS *Essex*
9 December	F4U-4B	VF-653	USS *Valley Forge*
9 December	F4U-4B	VF-653	USS *Valley Forge*
13 December	AD-4NL	VC-35	USS *Valley Forge*
13 December	F4U-5NL	VC-3	USS *Antietam*
14 December	AD-4	VA-728	USS *Antietam*
14 December	HO3S-1	HU-1	Unknown
18 December	AD-3	VF-194	USS *Valley Forge*
18 December	F4U-4	VF-713	USS *Antietam*
19 December	F4U-4	VF-713	USS *Antietam*
22 December	AD-4	VA-728	USS *Antietam*
22 December	F4U-4	VF-653	USS *Valley Forge*
24 December	F9F-2	VF-52	USS *Valley Forge*
26 December	P2V-3	VP-6	Land based
28 December	F9F-2	VF-52	USS *Valley Forge*

January 1952

Date	Aircraft	Squadron	Carrier
3 January	F9F-2	VF-111	USS *Valley Forge*
6 January	F9F-2	VF-51	USS *Essex*
8 January	AD-3	VF-194	USS *Valley Forge*
8 January	F4U-4B	VF-653	USS *Valley Forge*
8 January	F9F-2	VF-52	USS *Valley Forge*
9 January	AD-3	VF-54	USS *Essex*
9 January	F4U-4B	VF-653	USS *Valley Forge*
11 January	AD-2	VF-54	USS *Essex*
13 January	F4U-4B	VF-53	USS *Essex*
13 January	F4U-4B	VF-653	USS *Valley Forge*
15 January	AD-3	VF-54	USS *Essex*
17 January	F9F-2	VF-837	USS *Antietam*
18 January	F4U-5NL	VC-3	USS *Antietam*
19 January	F2H-2	VF-172	USS *Essex*
21 January	AD-2	VA-728	USS *Antietam*
22 January	AD-3	VF-54	USS *Essex*
22 January	F4U-4B	VF-53	USS *Essex*
22 January	F4U-4B	VF-53	USS *Essex*
26 January	F9F-2	VF-51	USS *Essex*
28 January	F4U-4	VF-113	USS *Philippine Sea*
29 January	F4U-4	VF-713	USS *Antietam*
29 January	F4U-5NL	VC-3	USS *Antietam*
29 January	F4U-5NL	VC-3	USS *Antietam*
29 January	F9F-2P	VC-61	USS *Antietam*
30 January	AD-2	VF-54	USS *Essex*

February 1952

Date	Aircraft	Squadron	Carrier
2 February	F4U-4	VF-653	USS *Valley Forge*
2 February	F4U-4	VF-653	USS *Valley Forge*
2 February	HO3S-1	HU-1	Unknown
3 February	AD-3	VF-194	USS *Valley Forge*
3 February	F4U-4	VF-653	USS *Valley Forge*
4 February	AD-2	VF-194	USS *Valley Forge*
4 February	F4U-4	VF-713	USS *Antietam*
4 February	F9F-2	VF-837	USS *Antietam*
7 February	AD-4	VA-115	USS *Philippine Sea*
8 February	AD-3	VF-194	USS *Valley Forge*
8 February	F4U-5N	VC-3	USS *Valley Forge*
8 February	HO3S-1	HU-1	USS *Rochester*
11 February	F4U-4	VF-653	USS *Valley Forge*

19 February	F4U-5N	VC-3	USS *Philippine Sea*
19 February	F9F-2	VF-52	USS *Valley Forge*
19 February	F9F-2	VF-52	USS *Valley Forge*
21 February	AD-4	VF-54	USS *Essex*
21 February	F4U-4B	VF-53	USS *Essex*
22 February	AD-4	VF-54	USS *Essex*

March 1952

Date	Aircraft	Squadron	Carrier
2 March	AD-3	VA-728	USS *Antietam*
9 March	AD-4	VA-115	USS *Philippine Sea*
11 March	F4U-4	VF-653	USS *Valley Forge*
11 March	F9F-2P	VC-61	USS *Valley Forge*
17 March	F9F-2	VF-52	USS *Valley Forge*
21 March	F4U-4	VF-114	USS *Philippine Sea*
21 March	F9F-2	VF-52	USS *Valley Forge*
22 March	AD-3	VF-194	USS *Valley Forge*
27 March	F4U-5N	VC-3	USS *Philippine Sea*
27 March	F4U-5N	VC-3	USS *Philippine Sea*
30 March	F4U-4	VF-653	USS *Valley Forge*
30 March	F4U-5N	VC-3	USS *Philippine Sea*

April 1952

Date	Aircraft	Squadron	Carrier
3 April	AD-4L	VA-115	USS *Philippine Sea*
10 April	AD-4	VA-115	USS *Philippine Sea*
10 April	F4U-4	VF-114	USS *Philippine Sea*
17 April	AD-3	ATG-1	USS *Valley Forge*
18 April	AD-4	VA-65	USS *Boxer*
20 April	AD-3	VF-194	USS *Valley Forge*
22 April	F4U-4	VF-63	USS *Boxer*
26 April	F4U-4	VF-653	USS *Valley Forge*
27 April	AD-4NL	VC-35	USS *Valley Forge*
29 April	F4U-4	VF-63	USS *Boxer*
30 April	HO3S-1	HU-1	USS *Princeton*

May 1952

Date	Aircraft	Squadron	Carrier
2 May	F9F-2	VF-111	USS *Valley Forge*
2 May	F9F-2	VF-52	USS *Valley Forge*
2 May	F9F-2	VF-111	USS *Valley Forge*
5 May	F4U-4	VF-192	USS *Princeton*
7 May	F4U-5NL	VC-3	USS *Philippine Sea*
8 May	F4U-5N	VC-3	USS *Valley Forge*
8 May	F4U-5N	VC-3	USS *Valley Forge*
12 May	F4U-4	VF-192	USS *Princeton*
13 May	F4U-4	VF-653	USS *Valley Forge*
16 May	AD-4L	VA-115	USS *Philippine Sea*
16 May	F4U-4	VF-64	USS *Boxer*
19 May	AD-4L	VF-115	USS *Philippine Sea*
22 May	F4U-4	VF-63	USS *Boxer*
23 May	F4U-4	VF-64	USS *Boxer*
23 May	F4U-4	VF-63	USS *Boxer*
25 May	F9F-2	VF-24	USS *Boxer*
26 May	F4U-4	VF-653	USS *Valley Forge*
27 May	F4U-4	VF-653	USS *Valley Forge*
29 May	AD-4	VA-115	USS *Philippine Sea*
29 May	F4U-4	VF-113	USS *Philippine Sea*
29 May	F4U-4	VF-653	USS *Valley Forge*
30 May	F4U-4	VF-653	USS *Valley Forge*

June 1952

Date	Aircraft	Squadron	Carrier
1 June	F4U-4	VF-113	USS *Philippine Sea*
2 June	F4U-4	VF-113	USS *Philippine Sea*
4 June	AD-4	VA-195	USS *Princeton*
6 June	AD-4	VA-195	USS *Princeton*
8 June	AD-4NL	AD-4NL	USS *Princeton*
8 June	F4U-4	VF-192	USS *Princeton*
8 June	F4U-4	VF-193	USS *Princeton*
9 June	AD-4	VA-195	USS *Princeton*
9 June	F4U-4	VF-192	USS *Princeton*
10 June	F4U-4	VF-192	USS *Princeton*
10 June	F4U-4	VF-653	USS *Valley Forge*
12 June	AD-4	VA-195	USS *Princeton*
13 June	F4U-4	VF-63	USS *Boxer*
13 June	F4U-4	VF-193	USS *Princeton*
13 June	F4U-4	VF-193	USS *Princeton*
13 June	F4U-5N	VC-3	USS *Valley Forge*

13 June	F4U-5NL	VC-3	USS *Princeton*
14 June	F9F-2	VF-191	USS *Princeton*
16 June	AD-4	VA-195	USS *Princeton*
16 June	F4U-4	VF-114	USS *Philippine Sea*
17 June	AD-4	VA-65	USS *Boxer*
17 June	AD-4	VA-65	USS *Boxer*
17 June	F4U-4	VF-64	USS *Boxer*
18 June	F4U-4	VF-63	USS *Boxer*
20 June	F9F-2	VF-191	USS *Princeton*
23 June	F4U-4	VF-63	USS *Boxer*
24 June	F4U-4	VF-192	USS *Princeton*
25 June	F4U-4	VF-74	USS *Bon Homme Richard*

July 1952

Date	Aircraft	Squadron	Carrier
4 July	AD-4	VA-115	USS *Philippine Sea*
4 July	F4U-4	VF-113	USS *Philippine Sea*
4 July	F9F-2	VF-24	USS *Boxer*
5 July	F4U-4	VF-114	USS *Philippine Sea*
7 July	F4U-4	VF-193	USS *Princeton*
9 July	AD-4	VA-75	USS *Bon Homme Richard*
11 July	AD-3Q	VC-33	USS *Bon Homme Richard*
11 July	AD-4	VA-195	USS *Princeton*
11 July	F9F-2	VF-72	USS *Bon Homme Richard*
13 July	F4U-4	VF-74	USS *Bon Homme Richard*
15 July	F4U-4	VF-193	USS *Princeton*
22 July	F9F-2	VF-72	USS *Bon Homme Richard*
27 July	F9F-2	VF-191	USS *Princeton*
28 July	F4U-4	VF-193	USS *Princeton*
31 July	F4U-4	VF-193	USS *Princeton*
31 July	F9F-2	VF-71	USS *Bon Homme Richard*
31 July	PBM-5S2	VP-731	Land based

August 1952

Date	Aircraft	Squadron	Carrier
1 August	AD-4	VA-195	USS *Princeton*
2 August	AD-4	VA-55	USS *Essex*
2 August	F4U-4	VF-871	USS *Essex*
3 August	F4U-4	VF-193	USS *Princeton*
8 August	AD-4N	VC-35	USS *Essex*
14 August	F4U-4	VF-74	USS *Bon Homme Richard*

September 1952

Date	Aircraft	Squadron	Carrier
9 September	F4U-5N	VC-3	USS *Princeton*
12 September	F4U-4	VF-192	USS *Princeton*
13 September	F4U-4	VF-193	USS *Princeton*
17 September	F4U-4	VF-193	USS *Princeton*
30 September	F4U-4	VF-884	USS *Kearsarge*

October 1952

Date	Aircraft	Squadron	Carrier
4 October	F4U-4	VF-884	USS *Kearsarge*
5 October	AD-4N	VC-35	USS *Kearsarge*
5 October	F4U-4	VF-871	USS *Essex*
7 October	AD-4L	VA-702	USS *Kearsarge*
7 October	F4U-4	VF-193	USS *Princeton*
7 October	F4U-4	VF-192	USS *Princeton*
15 October	AD-4	VA-75	USS *Bon Homme Richard*
16 October	AD-4L	VA-702	USS *Kearsarge*
16 October	F9F-2	VF-72	USS *Bon Homme Richard*
17 October	AD-4	VA-55	USS *Essex*
17 October	F9F-2	VF-23	USS *Essex*
18 October	F4U-4	VF-871	USS *Essex*
20 October	AD-4	VA-55	USS *Essex*
29 October	AD-4	VA-55	USS *Essex*

November 1952

Date	Aircraft	Squadron	Carrier
1 November	F4U-4	VF-884	USS *Kearsarge*
1 November	F9F-2	VF-721	USS *Kearsarge*
4 November	AD-3	VA-923	USS *Oriskany*
8 November	F4U-4	VF-884	USS *Kearsarge*
15 November	AD-3	VA-923	USS *Oriskany*
15 November	F2H-2P	VC-61	USS *Oriskany*
21 November	F9F-2	VF-721	USS Kearsarge
21 November	F9F-2	VF-23	USS *Essex*
22 November	F9F-2	VF-23	USS *Essex*
23 November	AD-4	VA-55	USS *Essex*
23 November	F9F-2	VF-721	USS *Kearsarge*

December 1952

Date	Aircraft	Squadron	Carrier
4 December	AD-4	VA-923	USS *Oriskany*
5 December	AD-4	VA-75	USS *Bon Homme Richard*
6 December	F4U-4	VF-874	USS *Oriskany*
9 December	AD-4NA	VA-55	USS *Essex*
12 December	F4U-4	VF-871	USS *Essex*
13 December	AD-4NL	VC-35	USS *Antietam*
22 December	AD-3	VA-923	USS *Oriskany*
27 December	F4U-4	VF-884	USS *Kearsarge*
28 December	F9F-2	VF-23	USS *Valley Forge*
28 December	F9F-2	VF-721	USS *Kearsarge*
30 December	F2H-2	VF-11	USS *Kearsarge*

January 1953

Date	Aircraft	Squadron	Carrier
3 January	F4U-4	VF-92	USS *Valley Forge*
3 January	F9F-2	VF-51	USS *Valley Forge*
9 January	F4U-4	VF-92	USS *Valley Forge*
18 January	AD-4	VF-54	USS *Valley Forge*
22 January	F9F-5	VF-53	USS *Valley Forge*
23 January	F2H-2	VF-11	USS *Kearsarge*
26 January	F4U-4	VF-874	USS *Oriskany*
28 January	AD-4N	VC-35	USS *Kearsarge*

February 1953

Date	Aircraft	Squadron	Carrier
1 February	AD-3	VA-923	USS *Oriskany*
2 February	F9F-5	VF-781	USS *Oriskany*
8 February	AD-4	VA-145	USS *Kearsarge*
10 February	AD-4	VF-54	USS *Valley Forge*
12 February	AD-4	VA-95	USS *Philippine Sea*
16 February	F9F-2	VF-93	USS *Philippine Sea*
18 February	F9F-2	VF-93	USS *Philippine Sea*
24 February	AD-4	VF-54	USS *Valley Forge*
24 February	F9F-5	VF-51	USS *Valley Forge*
26 February	AD-4NA	VA-95	USS *Philippine Sea*

March 1953

Date	Aircraft	Squadron	Carrier
1 March	AD-4L	VA-95	USS *Philippine Sea*
1 March	F9F-2	VF-91	USS *Philippine Sea*
4 March	AD-4	VF-54	USS *Valley Forge*
4 March	F4U-5N	VC-3	USS *Valley Forge*
9 March	F9F-5	VF-51	USS *Valley Forge*
13 March	AD-4	VA-125	USS *Oriskany*
17 March	F9F-5	VF-153	USS *Princeton*
20 March	F9F-5	VF-122	USS *Oriskany*
21 March	AD-4	VA-95	USS *Philippine Sea*
22 March	F9F-5	VF-122	USS *Oriskany*
23 March	AD-4	VA-95	USS *Philippine Sea*
27 March	F4U-4	VF-94	USS *Philippine Sea*
27 March	F9F-2	VF-91	USS *Philippine Sea*
31 March	F4U-4	VF-92	USS *Valley Forge*

April 1953

Date	Aircraft	Squadron	Carrier
1 April	F4U-4	VF-94	USS *Philippine Sea*
1 April	F9F-5	VF-51	USS *Valley Forge*
4 April	AD-4	VA-95	USS *Philippine Sea*
7 April	F4U-4	VF-92	USS *Valley Forge*
13 April	F9F-5	VF-122	USS *Oriskany*
19 April	F9F-5	VF-153	USS *Princeton*
20 April	F9F-5	VF-121	USS *Oriskany*
21 April	F9F-5	VF-153	USS *Princeton*
23 April	F9F-5	VF-154	USS *Princeton*
25 April	F9F-5	VF-153	USS *Princeton*
27 April	F4U-4	VF-92	USS *Valley Forge*
28 April	F9F-5	VF-154	USS *Princeton*

May 1953

Date	Aircraft	Squadron	Carrier
1 May	AD-4N	VC-35	USS *Princeton*
2 May	AD-4	VA-155	USS *Princeton*
3 May	F4U-4	VF-152	USS *Princeton*
5 May	F4U-4	VF-152	USS *Princeton*
6 May	F4U-4	VF-152	USS *Princeton*
6 May	F9F-5	VF-153	USS *Princeton*
13 May	F9F-5	VF-153	USS *Princeton*

17 May	AD-4	VA-95	USS *Philippine Sea*
17 May	AD-4NA	VF-194	USS *Boxer*
20 May	AD-4NA	VF-194	USS *Boxer*
23 May	AD-4NA	VF-194	USS *Boxer*
24 May	F4U-5N	VC-3	USS *Boxer*

June 1953

Date	Aircraft	Squadron	Carrier
2 June	F9F-2	VF-52	USS *Boxer*
3 June	AD-4	VF-54	USS *Valley Forge*
7 June	AD-4 VA-95		USS *Philippine Sea*
7 June	AD-4W	VC-11	USS *Philippine Sea*
8 June	F4U-4	VF-94	USS *Philippine Sea*
11 June	AD-4NA	VF-194	USS *Boxer*
11 June	F4U-4	VF-94	USS *Philippine Sea*
13 June	F4U-4	VF-94	USS *Philippine Sea*
13 June	F9F-5	VF-153	USS *Princeton*
15 June	AD-4NA	VF-194	USS *Boxer*
16 June	F4U-5N	VC-3	USS *Philippine Sea*
19 June	AD-4	VA-45	USS *Lake Champlain*
19 June	F9F-2	VF-91	USS *Philippine Sea*
19 June	F9F-5	VF-111	USS *Boxer*
25 June	AD-4	VA-45	USS *Lake Champlain*
25 June	F9F-2	VF-91	USS *Philippine Sea*
26 June	F9F-2	VF-91	USS *Philippine Sea*
26 June	F9F-2	VF-91	USS *Philippine Sea*
29 June	F4U-4	VF-94	USS *Philippine Sea*

July 1953

Date	Aircraft	Squadron	Carrier
1 July	F4U-4	VF-152	USS *Princeton*
1 July	F9F-2	VF-91	USS *Philippine Sea*
2 July	F3D-2	VC-4	USS *Lake Champlain*
5 July	AD-4N	VC-35	USS *Boxer*
5 July	AD-4Q	VF-194	USS *Boxer*
8 July	F9F-2	VF-151	USS *Boxer*
9 July	F9F-5	VF-153	USS *Princeton*
12 July	AD-4N	VA-155	USS *Princeton*
13 July	F4U-5N	VC-3	USS *Boxer*
14 July	AD-4N	VC-35	USS *Boxer*
16 July	AD-4	VA-155	USS *Princeton*
17 July	F4U-4	VF-94	USS *Philippine Sea*
19 July	F4U-4	VF-152	USS *Princeton*

20 July	F9F-2	VF-93	USS *Philippine Sea*
20 July	F9F-5	VF-153	USS *Princeton*
22 July	F2H-2	VF-62	USS *Lake Champlain*
23 July	F2H-2	VF-22	USS *Lake Champlain*
23 July	F2H-2P	VC-61	USS *Boxer*
23 July	F4U-4	VF-94	USS *Philippine Sea*
24 July	F4U-4	VF-94	USS *Philippine Sea*
24 July	F9F-2	VF-52	USS *Boxer*
24 July	HO3S-1	HU-2	USS *Lake Champlain*
25 July	AD-4	VA-155	USS *Princeton*
25 July	F4U-4	VF-94	USS *Philippine Sea*
25 July	F9F-2	VF-151	USS *Boxer*
26 July	AD-4	VA-45	USS *Lake Champlain*
26 July	F2H-2	VF-22	USS *Lake Champlain*
26 July	F4U-4	VF-152	USS *Princeton*
26 July	F9F-2	VF-91	USS *Philippine Sea*
26 July	F9F-2	VF-151	USS *Boxer*

Navy Aircraft Losses by month*

	1950	1951	1952	1953
January	–	9	25	8
February	–	10	19	10
March	–	9	12	14
April	–	15	11	12
May	–	23	22	12
June	–	15	28	19
July	–	21	17	30
August	12	16	6	–
September	23	30	5	–
October	7	19	14	–
November	6	16	11	–
December	19	22	11	–

* From the Korwald Aircraft Loss Report

APPENDIX III

Aircraft Shot Down by Navy Pilots in the Korean War

3 July 1950: Lt (jg) Leonard H. Plog (F9F-3) with VF-51. Operating from the USS *Valley Forge*, he shot down a Yak-9.

3 July 1950: Ensign Eldon W. Brown (F9F-3) with VF-51. Operating from the USS *Valley Forge*, he shot down a Yak-9.

4 September 1950: Ensign Edward V. Laney Jr (F4U-4B) with VF-53. Operating from the USS *Valley Forge*, he shot down an American-made Douglas A-20 Havoc with Russian markings (one that was given to the Russians in World War II). It was originally mistaken for an Il-4.

9 November 1950: Lt Commander William T. Amen (F9F-2B) with VF-111. Operating from the USS *Philippine Sea*, he shot down a MiG-15.

18 November 1950: Lt Commander William E. Lamb (F9F-3) with VF-52. Operating from the USS *Valley Forge*, he shot down a MiG-15.

18 November 1950: Ensign Frederick C. Weber (F9F-2) with VF-31. Weber shot down a MiG-15 while operating from the USS *Leyte*.

22 December 1950: Lt Commander Paul E. Pugh destroyed a MiG-15 while attached to the USAF's 4th Fighter Wing flying F-86As.

1 June 1951 Lieutenant Simpson Evans Jr destroyed a MiG-15 while attached to the USAF's 4th Fighter Wing flying the F-86 Sabre.

23 October 1951: Lieutenant Walter Schirra destroyed a MiG-15 while attached to the USAF flying an F-84E.

18 November 1952: Lieutenant E. Royce Williams shot down a MiG-15 while flying in an F9F-5 with VF-781. (He was credited with only one kill, but probably shot down at least three as some of the MiGs did not make it back to their base.)

30 June 1953:   Lieutenant Guy P. Bordelon Jr shot down two Yak-18s while flying an F4U-5N with VC-3 (Detachment D) out of Kimpo Air Base.

5 July 1953:   Lieutenant Guy P. Bordelon Jr shot down two Po-2s. He was assigned to VC-3 from the aircraft carrier USS *Princeton* while standing alert at Kimpo Air Base in his F4U-5N.

16 July 1953:   Lieutenant Guy P. Bordelon shot down a Po-2 while operating out of Kimpo Air Base in his F4U-5N.

Combat operations in the Korean War officially ended on 27 July 1953.